This book is dedicated to the journey, and all the people who are walking with me on it . . . past, present, and future. You have all helped me to become more myself and I am deeply grateful.

# CONTENTS

# MORE MYSELF

# FIRST WORD

The moment in between what you once were, and who you are now becoming, is where the dance of life really takes place.

—Barbara De Angelis, spiritual teacher

I am seven. My mom and I are side by side in the back seat of a yellow taxi, making our way up Eleventh Avenue in Manhattan on a dead-cold day in December. We hardly ever take cabs. They're a luxury for a single parent and part-time actress. But on this afternoon, maybe because Mom has just finished an audition near my school, PS 116 on East Thirty-third Street, or maybe because it's so freezing we can see our breath, she picks me up. The cab inches crosstown before finally turning north onto a stretch of Eleventh Avenue dotted with peep shows, massage parlors, and crumbling tenements. We pull up to Forty-second Street, around the corner from our building. Something catches my eye.

"Mommy?" I ask, pointing. I've climbed onto my knees on the seat and pressed my face, crowned with its usual frizz and my hair swept into box braids, right against the glass. "Why are they dressed like that when it's so cold?"

Mom clasps my hand and pulls me back toward her while glancing out the window. There on the corner stand three women, each rubbing her hands together to stay warm. All are in brightly colored knit dresses with hemlines that end miles above their knees. One is wearing fishnet stockings that reveal flashes of her bare skin. Another has on black boots that extend up the full length of her thighs. None are wearing coats. As locals bundled up in puffy jackets scurry around them on the sidewalk, seeming oblivious to their presence but probably not, the women's eyes dart back and forth to the other side of the wide boulevard. They look like they're waiting for someone.

"Mommy," I ask again, "how come they're out there?"

My mother sweeps her long auburn hair to one side, draws in a breath, and looks over at me. "When people go through hard times, Ali," she says slowly, "they often have to do things they don't want to do. Those women are just trying to survive."

I stare at my mother for a long moment, attempting to wrap my little-girl brain around what she has just told me. She doesn't explain what a sex worker is or exactly how one earns money. I'm too young for that. She doesn't tell me that the women are controlled by pimps, street hustlers who force them to turn tricks in exchange for drugs or cash. I wouldn't have understood. What she does somehow convey is a truth I still carry with me: the women I've spotted aren't on that corner by choice, but by circumstance. Without another word, I slide down into the cracked leather seat and make a silent agreement with myself. I will never be in a situation like that. Half-clothed. Vulnerable. Powerless. Exposed.

———

I am eleven. I already know I'll one day be a singer. I've known that in my gut since I was four. Even still, my agent has been rounding up all kinds of little jobs for me. One is to model bras and underwear for a department store catalog. I show up at the shoot, flat-chested and a little anxious, even with my mom at my side. Behind a dressing room curtain, I pull on the white padded bra and cotton panties. I then peer at myself, head to toe, in the full-length mirror, not sure how I feel about what I've signed up for. Moments later, I smile awkwardly into the camera, glancing over at my mom on the side. *I don't know why I was nervous*, I think in an attempt to calm myself. *This isn't that bad.*

And then, a few weeks later, the catalog arrives. "Here it is!" Mom calls out, holding it open to the page I'm on. I reach for the magazine and flop down with it on our couch. My heartbeat quickens as I study the photo. Until that moment, I haven't quite realized that what happened in the privacy of a studio is now on full display for the whole world—*my* world.

"So, you mean, my friends are gonna see me like this?!" I say. Mom, probably surprised at my reaction, doesn't respond. The picture is not at all racy, especially since my boobs are more like tangerines than grapefruits. Yet I still feel judged. Naked. Embarrassed. Exposed.

———

I am nineteen. In a few months, my first album will drop and my life will suddenly be divided into two distinct halves: all that came before *Songs in A Minor*, and all the miracles and challenges that followed. But I don't know that yet. As 2000 draws to a close, all I know is that I've been booked to appear on a magazine cover, one of my first. In my business, publicity just comes with the job, particularly for a new artist who's excited to break in. *This is my shot,* I tell myself, *a chance for my music to get noticed.* The stylists, my manager, the team at the record label—everyone is eager for this opportunity.

The photographer greets me with a firm handshake, and I immediately feel his vibe—strong and a bit pushy. A stylist has chosen my outfits, among them a pair of jeans, a jacket, and a white button-up shirt. As I dress, the photographer somehow convinces my team that he'll need to shoot me alone. When I emerge from the dressing room, there's just the two of us on set. "Open up your shirt a little," he directs while firing off a flurry of camera snaps. My spirit is screaming that something is wrong, that this feels sleazy. But my protests, lodged in the back of my throat, can't make their way out. "Pull the top of your jeans down a bit in the front," he urges. *If I say no, what doors will be closed to me?* I swallow my misgivings, tuck my thumb between the denim and my skin, and obey.

That night at home, I cry harder than I ever have. This isn't about me showing some skin, which I'll do on my own terms, for my own purposes, in the coming years. It's about feeling manipulated. It's about being objectified. It's about a crop of streetwalkers on a corner in Hell's Kitchen and a girl who once made a pact with herself.

"What the hell is this?" my manager, Jeff, asks me one afternoon a few months later. He's holding up the magazine cover. I stare at the image and do not recognize the woman staring back at me: midriff bare, nipples covered by her arm extended across her chest, the slightest hint of pubic hair spilling over the top of her jeans. Everything about the photo is wrong, from the pose itself to the lighting that makes me look washed-out. I am beyond embarrassed, ashamed that I've sold part of myself.

I now understand why the photographer wanted my team out of that room. A nineteen-year-old girl is more pliable than a set of her grown-ass managers. Had Jeff been in there, he would've voiced what I couldn't at the time: Hell no. Close that shirt. Take your hand off your tit. And you're not going to yank down your jeans. In fact, Jeff would've been over there pulling my shirt closed. The photographer clearly wanted a provocative image, but rather than disclosing that vision from the start, he led me into it.

On the day of the cover's debut, I pass a newsstand where the magazine is on display. I almost throw up. I want to buy every copy on every stand around the world, just so no one will see me in a photo that does not represent who I am. I swear that I'll never again let someone rob me of my power. It's a promise I still work to keep.

———

I am here—in the present, standing on the shoulders of all who've paved my way, in awe of where my life has led me. My path to this place began in a city jungle, wove its way through the peaks and canyons of the music business, surpassed all of my wildest dreams, and carried me back, time and again, to a pair of questions: Who am I, really? And as I discover my true essence, am I bold enough to live in that truth?

Those questions live at the heart of my story. Gathering the raw pieces of my experience and holding them up to the light has, for me, been a transformational exercise in truth telling. I've spent so many years withholding parts of myself, sacrificing my spirit to make others feel comfortable. But now, I'm done with pretending, with living in a prison of my own creation. I'm done with dimming my light. Writing this book has been about meeting myself, with all my wounds and vulnerabilities, exactly as I am—and then, at last, having the courage to reveal my full face. It has been about realizing that in order for the truth to set me free, I must first be brave enough to birth it.

I'm a person in process, from the me I once was to the me I am now. I'm also a breathing set of contradictions: a child who has known the greatest love there is, and one who longed for an affirmation that eluded me. I've been a builder of inner walls and a burier of feelings. I've been both someone in denial and a free spirit, an artist in hiding and a 'hood hippie. And all of those spaces and faces have led me to who I am now: Uncensored. Fearless. Awake.

On this part of my journey, I'm at last quieting the noise of our world—removing all the external distractions and opinions and judgments and tuning in to my own voice. I'm recognizing my own power and owning it. I'm finally trusting myself, believing I already have inside me the answers I most crave. And above all, I'm discovering who I am at my core—and becoming, day by day, more myself.

# PART ONE

# DREAMING

---

*Keep dreaming in color*
*And drawing your dreams*
*On cement floors*
*Until they are realized.*

—Alicia Keys

# 1

## UNMASKED

*Fall 2006, New York City*

I'm in my dressing room, if you can call it that. It's really a tiny gray space, one that feels as small and colorless as I do on this day. I'm seated in a barber's chair, facing a mirror encircled with bulbs. In moments, I'll begin my second photo shoot of the day—my fourth this week—on the three hours of sleep I live on. My head pounds with exhaustion and my lips surrender to a slight tremble as I clutch the edge of the stool. In a voice that sounds at once distant and familiar, I hear my name: "Ali?"

Three years earlier, I'd released my second album. The album everyone calls an artist's jinx. The one that's *supposed* to fail. But beyond my greatest expectations, *The Diary of Alicia Keys* exploded. With adrenaline in my veins and gratitude at my back, I'd hit the road on my second tour, glimpsing as little of the country as I had the first time around. "Even the circus stays in one place longer than we do," I'd joke with my crew. We'd do a show one night and then, boom, we were on to the next city. The next hotel room. The next stage. The next blur of buildings flashing past my car window. Half the time, I wasn't sure where we were. "What's the city again?" I'd ask my manager backstage, fearing I'd go out and yell, "Houston!" to a crowd in

Oakland or Atlanta or Detroit. My team was filling every available space in my days while I, overly obligated and out of breath, sprinted hard on a treadmill I knew might suddenly halt. With a lioness's focus and a hustler's determination, I charged ahead.

By then, my armor was securely in place. If I woke up feeling down or lethargic or cranky or pissed off, I'd taught myself never to show it. Instead, when any hint of my humanity broke the surface, I shoved it down and plastered on a grin. "Alicia, can I take a picture?" *Sure.* "Hey, Alicia, can you do another photo shoot?" *Absolutely.* "Alicia, can I have your autograph?" *Of course.* I no longer belonged to myself; I'd become captive to every request, every demand, every surge of fear that came with even the thought of saying no. And amid the constant moving, the constant packing and unpacking, the constant pleasing and pretending, I'd delivered my grandest performance yet: convincing the world that, behind my smile, all was as perfect as it appeared.

In my dressing room on this damp autumn day, the show ends. I study my reflection in the mirror. My face is covered in the layers of makeup used to create another character, another pretense, another retouched version of someone I am not. And all at once, my iron mask turns to thread, unraveling to reveal the face—and the emptiness—I've kept so carefully hidden away. I do not speak. I do not move. For a moment, I stop breathing. A single tear escapes.

"Ali?" I hear again. I look up to see Erika, my day-to-day manager and my best friend since we were four. She walks toward me. "What's going on?"

The compassion in her tone sends me into a full-fledged Ugly Cry. My tears tumble out and splash onto my white shirt as I cup my palm over my mouth and attempt to squelch my sobs. Through gulps and stutters, I try to tell her what words feel inadequate to convey. That I'm beyond burned out. That I've never felt more alone or disconnected from myself. That after years of running, rarely slowing down to breathe and reflect, my body and spirit have come unhinged—disassembled, scattered, lost.

"You know, you don't have to do this," Erika says, gently resting her hand on the small of my back. "We'll cancel this thing today. Forget it. You can take a break."

*A break.* On this miraculous path I've walked, this dream that so many stretch toward but seldom grasp, the idea of stepping away has never occurred to me. For my place in the limelight, my role at center stage, relentlessness is the price of being cast. It's the cost of sharing my music, my soul, with a world I feel most connected to through song. And in such a magical story line, you don't take a break. You don't dare imply you're unhappy. You don't tell your truth and risk appearing ungrateful. Instead, you strap on your boots, you keep your gaze fixed on the road ahead, and you work. You put away your feelings and you pull on your daily armor. Until the afternoon, beneath a merry-go-round of unforgiving hot lights, when a quarter century of tears and suppression collapses onto your shirt.

I don't just want a break, I tell Erika. I want to bolt. I want to run as far away as I can from this cage I've lived in, this land of fake-believe. I stare at my friend but don't speak the questions reeling through my head. *If I take a break, what would happen to all of this—the appearances, the photo shoots, the concerts, all of it? And where would I go?*

And then, from someplace underneath my soul and beyond my comprehension, an overwhelming response arises.

*Egypt.*

# 2

## BEGINNINGS

### TERRI AUGELLO, ALICIA'S MOM

When I got pregnant with Alicia, I was almost thirty and thinking about moving from New York to LA to see what acting opportunities I could get out there. It was 1980. I'd never had a pregnancy, and I called my mother. She said, "Well, you don't do anything easy." There were a couple of candidates who could've been the father. . . . In those days, we were in "free love" mode. I used the calendar and figured out who it was. I'd known Alicia's father for a long time. We'd been going out but weren't serious. On our third date, I got pregnant—*with* protection. People want to come through, don't they? And if you're the vessel, you'd better accept it. I made an appointment for an abortion, and when I got there, I was told, "Go away and think about it." I talked to my mom. I talked to my girlfriend. I made a list of pros and cons. Can I do it? I had a good job. I wasn't a teenager. I had a place to live. By the time I told Alicia's father I was expecting, I'd made a decision: I was keeping my baby.

Mommy's body is covered in freckles. The two of us stand close, at the intersection of Forty-third and Ninth, her warm, spotted hand wrapped fully around my tiny one. It's just her and I, both on this corner and in this life. I stare at our fingers intertwined, a swirl of beige and brown. "Mommy," I announce, "you're still white."

My mother glances at me, and then back up at the streetlight as it turns green. "Yes, Ali," she says, a smile spreading across her face. "I'm still white. Now let's go."

At four, I don't understand why my mom's skin doesn't look like my own. I've been waiting for the day when, all at once, her hundreds of small dots will march toward one another, link arms, and magically blend to make her brown like me. I know nothing about race, about how it can be used to separate and conquer and shame. And in the collage of faces filling our Hell's Kitchen neighborhood, I have no judgment about why we don't resemble each other. Few here do. All I know is that my beloved mother, this woman who braids my bushel of curls on weekends and sweeps me close at bedtime, is my family. My rock. And in my view, in my innocence, our skin shades should match as closely as our hearts do.

My story begins on that corner, in the moment when my curiosity opens its lids. There, hand-in-hand with the woman who gave me life, I am noticing. I am wondering. For the first time I can recall, I am trying to make sense of the world. And I am questioning how, in the triad I was born into, Mommy and I fit together.

———

My mother is the blackest white woman I know. On Sunday afternoons in our apartment, she'd put on one of her favorite jazz or R & B albums and just let the spirit carry her away. With Miles or Ella or Stevie or Thelonious crooning over long-lost love and heartache, Mommy would close her eyes and sway her hips to each soulful note as I, her wide-eyed audience of one, giggled and sang along from my spot on our couch. She was as easily moved by music as she was likely to throw shade at anyone who crossed her. It is from her that I get my silliness. My spontaneity. My passion for the arts. And it was her own parents who once passed those gifts on to her.

Mom is a daughter of Detroit—birthplace of Motown and the city where, in 1950, she entered the world as the fourth child in what would grow into a tribe of nine. Mom's parents, Donna Jean and Joseph "Little Joe" Augello (pronounced Ah-GEL-o), had met years earlier at Wayne State University. Joe was sitting in a grassy courtyard on campus one afternoon when he heard the voice of an angel, a woman practicing her music in a nearby chorus room. "I'm going to marry that girl," he joked to his friends even before he'd seen Donna Jean. My grandmother turned out to be as gorgeous as she was musically brilliant, and their courtship began. Joe, the son of Italian Catholic immigrants, and Donna, English and Scottish and two years younger than her admirer, wed not long after.

My grandparents began their lives together in Detroit but didn't stay there. When my mother was six, her father, a radio disc jockey, moved the family to Toledo, Ohio, so he could take a job at WOHO radio. With equal measures of charisma and talent, my grandfather soon won over his listeners as skillfully as he'd once sweet-talked my grandmother. He served not just as the DJ with the silky voice, but also as news director and actor for two radio series, *The Lone Ranger* and *The Green Hornet*. When Joe wasn't at the station, he was usually rolling around Toledo in his 1955 Thunderbird convertible, preparing to lend his charm to store openings and dance hops. Joe might've stood only five feet, six inches tall, but as my mother recalls, his hundred-foot-tall presence filled every room he entered.

At home, Donna, an accomplished pianist and vocalist, set aside her musical aspirations to become a homemaker. She was every bit as talented and gregarious as my grandfather but—around the edges— more emotionally delicate. Even before they married, she'd begun to cope with the seesaw of chemical imbalances brought on by manic depression. Joe, though he worked a lot, was his wife's anchor; and to their children, he was both a joyous spirit and a strong disciplinarian. On Sundays after the family returned home from eleven o'clock Mass, he'd sometimes roughhouse with the boys or tease the girls, a thunderous laugh rising from deep in his belly. But if anyone got out of line, or if one of my mother's constant pranks went too far, he could shut it down with a single stare.

One night in 1963, life in their house forever shifted. My mother, then twelve, shared an upstairs bedroom with three of her sisters.

Annoyed by a strange noise one of her sisters made while sleeping, Mommy escaped to a pallet on the floor. Through the wooden planks that evening, she heard a scream. She stumbled to her feet, dashed to the top of the staircase, and looked down to see her mother wailing into the receiver.

"Please send an ambulance now!" her mother begged the operator. Mommy raced downstairs to witness a horror that still lives in her memory: There lay her father, slumped over in his TV chair, holding his chest and gasping for breath while descending into full-blown cardiac arrest. Moments later, the squeal of sirens filled the living room, and a rescue squad wheeled Joe away on a stretcher. He never returned.

For weeks after her father's passing, my mother placed his picture on her desk at school. It was her way of keeping him close. And yet even as she and the family grieved the devastation, they did what the Augellos do best: They soldiered forward. My grandmother looked for work, but because of her fragile mental state, any job she took didn't last. When on her meds, she was steady. But when she'd stop taking them, she'd find herself in the grip of a depressive episode. Her doctors resorted to a treatment that was the go-to remedy at the time—shock therapy. During the electroconvulsive procedure, small electrical currents are sent through a patient's brain, and these shocks are meant to trigger a brief seizure that alters the brain chemistry and temporarily reverses symptoms. I can't imagine the pain my grandmother must've felt as she endured years of this.

Donna received some financial help from her own family, but not nearly enough to support nine children. So everyone who could work did. Mommy had always taken on odd jobs around town, but now she and her siblings worked as a matter of survival. Throughout junior high and high school, my mother weeded yards, worked at the National Biscuit Company, even painted backstops at the baseball field. At school, she kept up with a slew of activities—glee club, dance, cheerleading—with a pace that would later be the blueprint for my own whirlwind childhood. And in her quiet moments, scarce as they were, Mommy dreamed of taking the path her father had once chosen: a career in the arts.

She'd caught the acting bug early. A few years before Joe's passing, my mother, while out looking for a babysitting job, connected with Lillian Hanham Dixon, a dance teacher who lived across the street. Mom—the kind of child who'd belt out "Somewhere Over the Rainbow" while making her bed, a girl with creativity coursing through her veins—spent a lot of time in Ms. Dixon's world. She took jazz dance classes down at the Jewish Community Center where Ms. Dixon taught. She got involved in theater. And the summer before my mother graduated from Central Catholic High School, Ms. Dixon took her to New York City to experience the magic of a Broadway show.

"Your father never would've wanted any of his children in the arts," my grandmother would often tell my mother. "It's a nasty business." But Mommy's desire had already taken root.

"You know how to dance," Ms. Dixon told her after she'd finished high school. "Now go to New York and learn how to act." In 1969, she auditioned for and was accepted into New York University's Tisch School of the Arts. With only the waitressing tips she'd saved up, she set out for the world's most fiercely competitive city.

Mommy hustled. Between coursework and auditions, she worked for the telephone company and took on temp jobs. She landed a handful of roles in off- and off-off-Broadway productions, but even after she'd completed her degree, she couldn't fully support herself with stage work. She was still living from one temp gig to the next when she got her miracle on Forty-second Street: Manhattan Plaza, a sprawling residential complex spanning West Forty-second and Forty-third Streets between Ninth and Tenth Avenues in Hell's Kitchen, flung open its doors to artists. More than two-thirds of the federally subsidized units were set aside for those who made their living in dance, theater, music, and television; rent, thankfully, was a percentage of residents' feast-or-famine incomes. Mommy applied and got a forty-sixth-floor studio—the first place she could comfortably afford.

Those towers would end up being the backdrop for my childhood, the set on which my own dreams took shape and took flight. In that complex, in the shadows of Mommy's apartment on a spring evening in 1980, I was conceived. And what began as an act of passion grew into an uncertainty—a question mark over whether I'd ever make it into the world.

———

My father wasn't there when I was born. On that January evening in 1981, as the city's temperatures flirted with the freezing mark, Mommy arrived at the hospital already in labor. Her own doctor didn't make it in time for the delivery so she was placed in the care of a resident, one who didn't give her the episiotomy she needed. Mommy, ripped and swollen and stitched back together, lay in bed wondering how she'd come up with the money for the hospital bill. The next day—before Mommy and I left the hospital, but well after the delivery drama was over—my father, Craig Cook, strode into the newborn ward with his newest girlfriend at his side. The whole scene can be summed up in three words: awkward as hell.

The story of that day is, in many ways, the story of my relationship with Craig. He wasn't there, and then, once the difficult moments had come and gone, he'd suddenly show up, only to vanish again. There were occasions, of course, when he spent time with me, memories now scattered and dim. Like the time when he and his first wife took me, then about four, to St. Thomas on a beach vacation. Or those afternoons, starting when I was around ten, when he'd occasionally pick me up from school and call me "Skittles," the nickname he gave me in tribute to one of my favorite candies. But for a young girl like me, one who clung to my mother's hand as closely as I did to her side, my father's easy grin and handful of annual visits were not enough. And when he did come see me I felt uneasy around him, the way you feel uncomfortable in a new pair of shoes. Technically, they fit. But the leather hasn't lived on your feet long enough to learn their grooves and tendencies.

I'm sure Craig loved me in the ways in which he was then capable; like all parents, he did what he knew how to do. I'm also sure there were circumstances involved that I couldn't have grasped, grown-folk issues that somehow blocked the doorway of our connection. Yet at five and eight and eleven, I only knew the world through the eyes of a child. I only understood what it felt like, in the early hours of the morning as I lay staring at the ceiling from my futon, to wonder why I had seemingly been set aside. And in that world, in that reality, I grasped only what I was missing—the irrefutable affirmation that I, my father's child, mattered more to him than anything.

When Craig showed up at the hospital after my birth, he stepped into our shared story and out of his personal one. My father, who is about two years younger than my mom, came of age in the '70s, a time when America itself was at a pivot point. In Harlem, Craig was reared under the gracious palm of his mother, Vergeil, who'd moved from Annapolis, Maryland, to New York City to study nursing in the early 1950s. She was a pioneer in her day: A black woman from the South was expected to marry young and become a maid or house-wife, not venture north hundreds of miles to attend college. While a student, she got pregnant with my father and began raising him on her own, even as she completed her studies and eventually graduated as a nurse. She and Craig's father never married.

My paternal grandmother—in a display of interracial free-spiritedness rarely witnessed during her times—then met and fell in love with Miguel "Michael" Giuseppe DiSalvatore, an Italian Amer-ican who worked with his brothers-in-law at a fruit stand in Harlem. They'd already been together for years when my nana and fafa, as I call them, traded vows.

"I'm going to buy you a house," Fafa announced to Nana after they'd tied the knot. Nana already had an enormous, beautifully decorated apartment in Harlem. But wanting to let Fafa step into his role as the man of the family, she allowed him to move her to a rancher that was two-thirds the size of her former place. In their new Long Island home, they adopted and raised two more children. By then, Fafa had already set aside his work at the fruit stand to become a cop. Craig, who was sixteen when Nana and Fafa married, was only a couple of years away from leaving home to attend Morehouse College in Atlanta.

College, it turned out, wasn't for him. After a year of studies, he returned to New York to work briefly as a clerk in the district attorney's office and then for a year as an NYPD officer in Harlem's Twenty-eighth Precinct. He eventually landed a job as a salesman at a high-end clothing store on the Upper East Side. Tall, dapper, and charismatic, Craig was already a hit with the ladies when a mutual friend introduced him to my mother. Their friendship grew into a mild flirtation that later blossomed into the night I was conceived. By then, Craig had traded his sales job for a career as a flight attendant—based first in Queens, and later in Missouri and Colorado. For most of my childhood he was constantly on the road, flying in and out of town with the same unpredictability with which he seemed to show up in my world.

Craig never knew his own biological father. His birth certificate listed only his dad's name and occupation: policeman.

"Do you want to meet him?" his mother had asked a few times when he was a boy. Craig had no interest. Between his mom and his stepfather, Michael, he had all the love and nurturing he needed, he'd tell me years later. Yet I've often thought about how the absence of Craig's father must have impacted his relationship with me, perhaps in ways he was not conscious of. I can only imagine how Craig, fatherless himself, must have felt on that summer afternoon when my mother sat across from him and said she was expecting me, and that, yes, he was the father. He was just twenty-seven then and, as he recalls it, still trying to find himself. As far as he was concerned, things had turned out well enough for him even without his dad around. The child my mother was carrying was undoubtedly his, but as he told her on that day, he wasn't prepared to put on the heavy mantle of fatherhood. Only now, as a parent myself, can I understand what may have been true: Craig was living out of the template he'd inherited.

In the empty space left by Craig, my nana and fafa stepped in. When Craig first told his mother that he had a baby on the way, she said to him, "Until that child crosses my threshold, I don't know anything about it." Upon my arrival, my mother wrote a letter to Craig's mom, telling her everything sweet about her new grandbaby. Not long after, Craig showed up at his mother's doorstep, cradling me in the crease of his elbow.

"Here's your grandchild," he announced proudly, handing me to Nana. She took me in her arms and never let me go.

In Nana and Fafa's unfailing embrace, I thrived. A couple of weekends a month, my grandfather would make the drive from Long Island to pick me up for a visit at his and Nana's house. They rarely missed one of my piano recitals or pageants. My mother's mom, Grandma Donna, did watch me when she flew in from Toledo, but Nana and Fafa, my only local extended family, served as my mother's primary safety net. They kept me whenever Mommy traveled for the job she'd taken by then as a paralegal at a law firm in Rockefeller Center. Each time Mom walked me down to meet Fafa in front of our building, he'd already be there waiting: gray fedora, trench coat, leaning back against his car, gun holstered on his hip, old-school Italian style. "That's my girl!" he'd call out as soon as I emerged from our building's revolving door. Moments later, I was buckled in and on my way to the only other home, outside of our apartment, where I felt seen. My nana and fafa—and later my brother, Cole, who is a decade younger than I am—would be Craig's greatest gifts to me.

Yet even with such committed grandparents, I had a deep sense early on of the truth: In this world, it was my mother and me. That was all. She was my person and I was hers. Never was that said aloud, but the feeling permeated our every exchange. In one of my favorite photos, now bent and faded, my mother stares down at me, her hair cascading over her plaid shirt, her eyes soft. I, then three, sit quietly at her side. In my mother's gaze, I see grace. I see her profound love for her only child, a baby she once bravely chose to keep. I see a woman whose father was gone too soon and a mother determined to protect her own little girl from life's sharpest edges. I see someone who, on a prayer and a paralegal's meager paycheck, called on heaven to help her firmly ground me.

———

A defining experience of my childhood began with a simple question: "Got room for a piano?"

It was spring of 1987, and my mother and I were visiting our neighbors in the Ninth Avenue building of Manhattan Plaza. While I was playing with my friend, our mothers caught up. My friend's mom mentioned that her family would be moving soon. Her husband, a musician and piano tuner, had an extra piano. That's when she asked my mother the question that would alter my path: Did we have space for an upright? "I'd love to take it," Mommy said without hesitation.

"Well, if you can move it," the woman said, "you can have it."

One week and fifty bucks later, two men from Beethoven Pianos showed up and loaded the upright onto a dolly as I watched from the terrace window in our living room. The piano teetered on its platform as the workers wheeled it across the center courtyard, toward our tower on Tenth Avenue, up the service elevator, and, at last, into the doorway of our apartment. Since the afternoon that piano was scooted into the center of our living room, little has been the same.

The first time I'd seen a piano, I was mesmerized. My kindergarten teacher, Ms. Hazel—a former dancer intent on opening up the world of artistic expression to her students—would put together shows like *Cats* and *Dreamgirls* and have us audition for roles. I was once chosen to play Dorothy in *The Wizard of Oz*, which is how I discovered I had a voice and loved to use it.

But it was the piano that called to me. Ms. Hazel would often invite musicians to perform for us in our school's auditorium, and there, one afternoon, sat a woman at an upright, her long, slender fingers dancing gracefully over the charcoal and ivory keys. For me, the initial attraction was entirely visual: I loved the way the splintered piano stood, proud and unapologetic, and how the beauty of its sleek, shiny keys contrasted with the roughness of its wooden frame. When the performance ended that day, I lingered in the auditorium just so I could run my little fingers across the keys, marveling as much at its sound as I did at its beauty.

Mommy never had to push me toward the piano; as a first grader, before we received the upright, I asked her if I could take lessons, and she agreed, probably while calculating the overtime she'd have to work in order to pay for them. Upon hearing I'd requested training, my fafa bought me an electric keyboard, one small enough to tuck into the far corner of our living room. Margaret Pine, a pianist who came highly recommended to my mother, would be my only piano teacher—from when I was six until I graduated from high school. From the first C-major chord I struck, I was smitten.

By then, my mother—determined to help me discover my muse and keep me out of trouble in a neighborhood known for it—was already filling my days with one activity after another; my schedule would eventually include Alvin Ailey dance classes, gymnastics, and ballet. A friend of my mom, Lecke Brown, even helped me land my first TV gig: at age four, I played Maria, a playmate of Rudy Huxtable on *The Cosby Show*. I enjoyed acting, but time and again as I grew older, I'd always return to the art form that still draws me in most powerfully—piano. As much of a miracle as Fafa's keyboard was for me, it didn't have the same feel and sound as a real piano. I secretly longed for an upright like the one I'd seen at school. Which is why, on that afternoon when our secondhand piano bumped across our threshold, I felt like I was inheriting a Steinway grand.

The upright was dented and scratched and badly out of tune. Mommy said it appeared to be one of those player pianos that could operate itself, a relic of the 1920s and '30s. The self-playing mechanism had been removed, but the space for it remained. The yellowed keys were badly chipped in a few places. The bench, with its crooked legs and cracked seat, hadn't come with the piano; its wood was an entirely different shade. And yet its very imperfection—the way the bench and piano didn't resemble each other any more than my skin matched my mother's—is what made it so perfect.

The piano instantly became our living room divider, replacing the Chinese folding screen we'd been using up to then. By this time, my mother had traded her studio for a one bedroom. She'd tried for a two bedroom so we could each have our own space, but the building management wouldn't allow it. If I'd been a boy, she was told, we could've had two rooms; I guess they figured a girl could sleep with her mother. Over the years, that little apartment got rearranged a lot. Sometimes my mother carved out her own space in the living room and gave me the bedroom. Other times, our tall bookcase served as the divider while the piano rested flush against a wall. But for most of my childhood, that upright compartmentalized my two worlds. My futon bed and dresser sat on one side of the living room. Our couch, entertainment center, and small dining table lived on the other.

With each passing year, Ms. Pine gently prodded me into new musical territory. In the beginning, I'd sit for hours on the hard bench, tediously plucking through my scales until the coral streaks of sunlight filling our apartment gave way to gray shadows; as I advanced, I trained in the Suzuki method, a rigorous Japanese approach to piano mastery. I took on Beethoven sonatas, Mozart concertos, and Satie preludes before eventually moving on to the jazz standards of Ellington, Waller, and McPartland. During my afternoon rehearsals, my rendition of Joplin's "The Entertainer" rose to mix with the musical gumbo of Hell's Kitchen: the thumpity-thump of hip-hop and salsa and Tupac and Salt-N-Pepa and Prince right alongside the flutes and banjos and script readings overheard in the halls. Over many decades, Manhattan Plaza served as home to a parade of artistic masters, from Samuel L. Jackson, who once worked as a building security guard, to Tennessee Williams, Larry David, Kenny Kramer,

Terrence Howard, and Patrick Dempsey. In such a haven, my daily rehearsals drew no death stares or neighbor complaints.

Chopin was my homie. His compositions were poetry for the piano: layered, measure by measure, with the dark passion and poignancy that still speak to me. Ms. Pine believed, as I do, that great music is not confined to one style. As she guided me in studying the greats in every genre, she also encouraged me to add my own flair, to play from my heart. If I heard a song I loved on the radio, like Brian McKnight's "Never Felt This Way," she'd have me create and perform my own composition. Her approach wasn't traditional, but it was genius because it kept me tuned in, kept me coming back. Even when, at age eleven, I begged Mom to let me quit because A, I could see that we couldn't truly afford it, and B, I wanted to play outside with my friends when the weather was warm, my mother flatly refused. "Quit what you like," she told me, "but you're not quitting the piano." We eventually struck a compromise: As long as I practiced diligently during the school year, I could have summers off.

Mommy knew then what I know now: I was put on the planet to play. I'm not sure how much of identity comes threaded in our genes and how much of it is shaped by our environment, but as far back as I can recall, placing my fingertips on a keyboard felt like coming home to myself. There was no courtship phase, no period of becoming acquainted with the piano; rather, the connection was instantaneous, as comfortable and familiar for me as breathing. On those afternoons when I had the apartment to myself, I'd slide up to the keys and lean into the music, the world growing quieter as I gave myself over to the flow of the notes. Through my fingertips, through hour after hour of delicious solitude, I expressed what words felt inadequate to convey.

———

"Who is this?" my mother snapped. On our house phone, I'd been flirting with some boy from school when Mom picked up the second receiver. "Alicia has to go," she cut in before either of us could speak. "It's past her bedtime." *Click.*

My mother was no joke. By day, she prepared legal briefs and draft pleadings; by night, she served as Chief Justice Augello, the enforcer whose sole mission was to keep me in check. When your mother sits on the high court, you've gotta learn to be slick. You've gotta live on your tiptoes. You must stay ready to present your evidence when she launches into one of her rapid-fire cross-examinations: "What were you thinking? What do you mean when you say that? And why the hell is there a used condom underneath the couch?" Most of the time when she tore into me, I stood there looking as stupid as I felt on the evening when she hung up on my crush.

"He's just a friend," I pleaded as she reminded me of the rules: No calls after nine p.m. And no boys in our apartment between the time I arrived home from school and when she came in from work. I frequently got busted on both fronts.

Mommy was intense. She still is. If my father's absence is part of what formed me, Mommy's fire and fervor completed the job. With her, there was seldom an emotional middle ground. If she was angry, she was one thousand percent furious, and I, the only other person in our apartment, became skillful at peacemaking. If she was offering you her time or a listening ear, she was the most generous and beautiful giver known to womankind. And if Mom and her friends grooved to the sounds of Smokey or Curtis or Sly and the Family Stone, she was the first to tear up the dance floor and the very last to leave it. No one was more passionate, and I and everyone else knew exactly how she was feeling because she never pretended otherwise. What I didn't know, from one day to the next, was which side of her I'd encounter: Mom the Nurturer or Mom the Interrogator.

The year I turned thirteen, I asked my mother if I could go with my friends to see *The Mask,* a Jim Carrey flick. She agreed. The next day as she and I were taking the bus somewhere together, she quizzed me.

"How was the movie?" she asked.

"It was *soooo* funny!" I exclaimed, laughing a bit too hard. "Man, I can't believe how *crazy* that story was!"

Mommy stared at me without smiling or blinking. "And what happened that made it so crazy?" she asked.

"There was the part where he, um . . . Jim Carrey got stuck," I said.

"Got stuck how?"

"I mean, he just got stuck," I told her. "I can't really remember."

I don't know why I even tried to lie to my mother. That woman can sniff out a pile of horse manure from the farthest corner of Queens. In less than a minute, she'd squeezed the truth from me: I'd never seen the Carrey film. Instead, I'd watched the movie she'd been forbidding me to see. My friends and I had sneaked our way into some theater that was playing *Basic Instinct*—complete with an interrogation scene in which Sharon Stone uncrosses her legs to reveal a panty-less crotch. I rightfully almost got a beatdown for that one.

Later that same year, I had the nerve to beg my mother for a beeper, the device that was all the rage before cell phones were hot. "What does a fourteen-year-old need with a pager?" she asked me. Case closed—until I got creative and teamed up with an ally. My friend Misha, who's several years older than me, had always been my big sis in our building. My mother trusted her. If I got a beeper, Misha persuaded my mother one evening, then she could track me down anytime; upon receiving a page from my mother, I could find a pay phone (remember *those*?) and immediately call her. Mom bought that argument but couldn't afford the beeper, so my god-mother, Titi Ali, paid for it. I won that round but lost plenty of others. Like my quest to get some doorknockers, those hoop earrings so enormous you can fit your fist through them. "Out of the question," said Mom.

My mother had to be strict as a matter of my survival. I grew up near Times Square before it became Disneyland, during a time when Hell's Kitchen lived up to its name. The kitchen, in most homes, is the place where the action goes down, where everyone passes through or congregates. It's hot. It attracts dirt. It's often loud and odorous—all accurate descriptions of my old stomping grounds.

During the early '90s, the "crossroads of the world" was still an X-rated cesspool of filth open for business around the clock. At any one of the shops on the street around the corner from our apartment, a kid could easily get anything and everything: a fake ID (like the one I used to sneak into a club called Tunnel), a fistful of blunts (I smoked my share), a pack of condoms (which led to the used one that somehow got lost under the couch on the afternoon I lost my virginity). Trouble lingered on every corner: pimps beating down sex workers who were short on their earnings, homeless people laying huddled in garbage bags to protect themselves from the blistering cold, addicts slumped forward in heroin stupors, gypsy cabs dropping off men in search of a good time. It was home to the city's have-nots, a hotbed of society's misfits.

Mom, who usually crawled in from work after grueling fourteen-hour days, taught me early how to handle myself on the streets. "Stay aware of your surroundings," she'd warn me. Honestly, she didn't have to teach me much because the city itself hands you its rulebook: Walk the other way. Never stare. Don't engage. And at all times, keep moving. By age eleven, I was already catching the train and city bus alone from school and back to our apartment—arriving just in time for a check-in call from a mother who was not to be effed with.

I always felt older than I was. For one thing, New York grows you up fast. And for another, I skipped two grades: first and eleventh. I entered kindergarten already able to read, probably because my paralegal mom had taught me to sound out big words like *affidavit* and *subpoena*. All through school, I was simultaneously ahead and behind: a smart and enthusiastic student striving for my gold star, and the youngest (though somehow still the tallest) of all of my classmates. But you couldn't have told me I wasn't grown. As my mother recalls, I showed up on Earth as a bit of an old spirit, one who savored my alone time. I was happy to play with other children but also content to see them leave—eager to reclaim my space, my silence, and my solo hours at the piano. I'm still that way.

I was a tomboy, mostly out of necessity and partly because I thought the wardrobe was fresh. Oversize sweaters, baggy pants, Timberland boots—that's all I wore from fifth grade on. I dressed so I could outrun any stranger who might try to test me; plus, wearing anything formfitting could get you mistaken for a hooker, or at least send the message that you might be interested. I pulled my thick hair back into the tightest bun, my frizz forced into submission by a single rubber band and gel. Occasionally, I'd wear some '70s-style Stevie Wonder braids with beads, but that was as girly as I got. I never (ever) got my nails done, and besides, I needed to keep them short for rocking the piano. I hated anything froufrou: floral prints, lace, pink, skirts. And to go along with my boyish attire, I had a mouth on me—a hard edge meant to scare off the crazies while guarding my sensitivities.

My self-protective instinct spilled over into my social relationships. Even as a small child, I seldom fully trusted anyone, nor did I reveal the real me. Too risky. To this day, I don't know exactly what led me to build mountains between myself and others. Maybe it began with the teasing. When I was four, one of my friends accidentally scissored off several of my long braids, and a barber then had to chop all of my hair short. "You look like a boy!" the other kids screamed when they saw my little crop of cotton. My 'fro eventually grew into a heap of wild, disobedient curls that Mom often swept into two giant poofs. The teasing grew louder. Having a name like Alicia Augello-Cook didn't quiet the insults.

"Alicia cooks JELL-O!" I'd hear constantly.

When I was around nine, I joined my school's track team. Those tiny shorts put on display my thick legs, which drew stares and whispers from my classmates. Or maybe I turned inward the year I was eleven. My ballet teacher, thin and lanky, ordered me to "tuck in" my thick behind after I'd already tried to do so. With her second request, I became acutely aware that my butt was never going to "tuck in" as tightly as those of my classmates with smaller backsides. I suddenly felt self-conscious about a curvaceous figure that I'd been mostly happy with up till then.

It's hard to pinpoint the precise moment when we internalize others' assessments; it's usually not just a single experience but rather a series of moments that bruise the spirit and lead us to distrust ourselves and those around us. And then we wake up at age seventeen or twenty-five or thirty-seven and realize we don't know the last time we've lived life only to please ourselves.

Thankfully, race was never a part of what made me feel guarded. Being mixed, for me, didn't come with a major identity crisis or the typical interracial angst. That's in part because New York City is one enormous United Nations, a stew pot of ethnicities and cultures and head wraps and accents representing more than 150 countries around the globe. No one even questioned my heritage in a city that cares most about your aspirations and less about where you've come from. Based on the chorus of daily "Hey, Mami!" catcalls I got from construction workers along Ninth Avenue, many assumed I was Puerto Rican or some other kind of Latinx.

"You're the best of both worlds," my mother would often remind me. And she was right. Yet since my mom understood that America would always compel me to choose, to mark one box versus another, she raised me with an awareness that's still intact: I am a black girl.

I had a tight crew from a young age, and while I felt at home with them, even they didn't glimpse the full me. I'd known Misha, my beepergate coconspirator, practically since birth; the same was true of two other girls: Kat, whose mother was both friend and neighbor to my mother before Kat and I were born; and Erika, Misha's younger cousin and the childhood friend who, years later, would work with me. It was Misha and two of her other cousins, Sasha and Julie, who invited me to join their musical girl group. Misha, whose father, Norman Hedman, was a renowned percussionist who at that time worked with New Kids on the Block, was probably eighteen then; her cousins might've been sixteen or seventeen. At nine, I was by far the youngest, and I had to be a little fast to keep up with their speed. We took ourselves super seriously, rehearsing our pop songs, coordinating our moves, and vibing out in the building's plaza for hours on end. I was convinced we'd be the next Jackson 5, which would've made me the new baby Michael. That was my secret dream.

At eleven, I moved on to entrepreneurial pursuits. I, along with a few friends, started a babysitters club, inspired by the book series. From my living room, I managed the entire operation: five bucks an hour for us to watch any school-age child in the towers. That gig lasted a couple of years before I joined another girl group during my first year in high school. Because of the grade skip, I enrolled in the Professional Performing Arts School when I was just thirteen. Being there felt like living on the set of *Glee*, but our one-building school was a much smaller version. There was algebra and English and chemistry and French to learn, of course. But seemingly right there with us, in our classrooms and roaming the halls, were the legends we studied—from Duke Ellington, Sarah Vaughn, and Billie Holiday to Scott Joplin, Led Zeppelin, and Carole King. My jazz instructor, Miss Aziza, is one of the greatest teachers on the planet—a badass pianist and vocal powerhouse who turned me on to composing, arranging, and the beauty of harmonizing. She was one of the first black women I knew who did it all as an artist, my real-life Nina Simone. My classmates, all of whom reveled in song and dance and theater as much as I did, became my people.

And yet through every age and stage, I kept my mask in position. The less others really knew about me, I reasoned, the less ammunition they'd have to make me look foolish. Only if I revealed my tender spots could they wound me. My true self, the one I kept so deeply concealed, only emerged in my diaries. There, I could unveil. If Mom got heated and I got tongue-tied, I could escape to sort out my thoughts and gather my words before the two of us spoke again. And alongside my musings and misgivings lived my poetry, my unfinished lyrics, my schoolgirl crushes, my feelings about Craig. On cotton pages scrawled with purple ink, I didn't have to be tough or brave or capable or strong. I could just be me.

# 3

## FLYING SOLO

**CRAIG COOK, ALICIA'S FATHER**

When Alicia was fourteen, she sent me a letter. She said she didn't want to have any part of me and that she wanted me to go away. I was living in Colorado with my second wife, Marsha, and our son, Cole, then three. I won't deny that I was hurt when I read her words. But I also looked at what she was saying, and the circumstances, and I understood where she was coming from. Did I try to rationalize why I wasn't around more? In some respects, yes. She was a teenager and already developing into who she was going to be, whereas Cole was still young. I also needed to tag team with his mother since we were both working for an airline. When one of us was leaving, the other was coming home, and getting to New York was a challenge. Yet I cannot negate what Alicia was feeling: when she needed me, I wasn't there for her. I didn't respond to the letter, but I did say to myself, *I'm not going anywhere.*

Three things happened the year I turned fourteen. I started a friendship that would frame my world for more than a decade. I ended my relationship with Craig. And I stumbled my way onto the front porch of the music business—all before I was old enough to drive.

The year was 1995, and New York City had become my concert hall. From Harlem to Bed-Stuy, Mount Vernon to Queens Village, my girl group and I took our harmonies directly to the streets, performing in parks and rec centers, schools and cafés, anyplace where we could draw an audience. During hip-hop's golden moment, music lived not just in us, but all around: wedged between the sidewalk cracks, reverberating through back alleys and brownstones, soaring up from neon-lit bodegas to mirrored high-rises. The city came most alive on summer weekends. Beatboxers laid down their freshest rhythms as onlookers whooped and wailed their approval. Show-boaters rolled past the Apollo on 125th Street, blasting Biggie's thunderous bass lines from their car stereos. The electricity of it all crackled in the air.

The Village was a major hot spot, a nightly playground for aspiring musicians and artists of every kind. There, late one evening when my young ass probably should've been at home and in bed, a friend and I found our way into a cipher, a musical gathering right along Sixth Avenue. Khulandi, my classmate and neighbor but not a member of my girl group, hung with me a lot. Once at the inner ring of the circle, we both immediately recognized the rapper, this tall, caramel-colored cat known around town by his MC name, Krucial; he and his partner, Laquantum Leap, a killer beatboxer who was unmissably tall with long dreads, performed frequently near Washington Square Park. The two, as usual, rocked their freestyle show, and then the crowd dispersed. As Khulandi and I headed toward the train, I looked back to spot Krucial catching up to us.

"I'm Kerry," he said, a little out of breath as he offered his real name. Khulandi and I exchanged a quick glance that said, *He's cute*.

"Nice rhymes," I said to him. He thanked me and then explained that he was on break from his job as a security guard at a parking lot a few blocks over, where he worked the graveyard shift.

"Can I call you?" he asked me as we parted. I suppressed the girlish smile threatening to spread across my face and gave him my beeper number. Khulandi and I walked over to the C train on Eighth Avenue and headed uptown. That was around ten thirty.

I got off first, at Forty-second Street; Khulandi, who lived a bit farther north, stayed on an extra stop. My mother wasn't home that evening, but she of course expected me to be there by my eleven p.m.

curfew. I made it in with only one minute to spare. That's when my beeper screen lit up with Khulandi's code: 52, which was her street number.

I froze. *Why is she calling me so soon after I just saw her? Did she make it home okay?* My hands trembled as I dialed her up, fearing what I'd hear on the other end of the receiver.

"Hello," said a baritone voice on the line. My heartbeat quickened. "Who's this?" I asked.

"It's Kerry," I heard. "Remember we met tonight?"

I stared at my beeper to be sure I'd seen the number right. I had. "What's your code?" I asked him.

"It's fifty-two," he told me. K (as in Kerry) was number 5 on the keypad, he explained, and B (as in Brothers, his last name) was 2. He and Khulandi, it turned out, had the same code, which seemed funny to me then, but perhaps was more providence than coincidence.

Over the next hour until I heard Mom's key turn in the lock, Kerry told me more of his story. Born in Brooklyn and raised between Harlem and Far Rockaway, he'd been dreaming of the emcee life since the day he first heard "Rapper's Delight" banging from his radio. When he was eighteen, word spread that the producers at B-Boy Records were in search of new artists. Kerry and a friend showed up at the label with their hastily created VHS demo, and not long after, they signed a contract. The deal ultimately went south, but Kerry's passion for rap remained. By day, he sharpened the lyrics that Village bystanders applauded; by night, he worked his security job as a way to keep the lights on until his next break came around. We found immediate common ground in our desire to one day share our creations with the world—me, a classically trained pianist steeped in soul and R & B, and him, a striver with as much of a deep love for hip-hop as I've always had.

No romance arose between us initially. From time to time over the next year, we'd catch up by phone and, as friends, we'd talk music and trade mixtapes; or when I was downtown, I'd occasionally swing by his security guard booth and chill.

"Sing me something," he said to me one evening after I'd told him about my latest performance with the girls. In the cold night air, I cleared my throat, drew in a breath, and belted out the opening notes of "Been So Long," the Anita Baker hit. Kerry stared at me so intently that I stopped singing after the first line. "Yo, if I was a record exec," he finally said, "I'd sign you right here on the spot." I blushed and did not finish the song.

The chemistry was thickening, but I contained it. For one thing, as grown as I thought I was, I knew Kerry was out of my age range. The first time we spoke, he mentioned he was twenty-four—five years older than he looked to me. He of course also asked my age, and I told him I was seventeen rather than the fourteen that I actually was. Given that I roamed around the Village so late, my proclamation must've rung true. Kerry had also told me he had a young son, a revelation that placed him squarely in a life season beyond my own. Though he and his ex had parted ways, he was determined to raise and provide for his child. He eventually squeezed in a third job as a UPS mail handler.

In ways that I'd come to understand only years later, Kerry's commitment to fatherhood is in large part what drew me so powerfully toward him. He represented the deep dependability that I yearned for in my relationship with Craig. It has been said that a girl grows up to choose a man who either bears a striking resemblance to her father, or one who is nothing like him. Both choices are, at their core, reactions. In my view then, Kerry was not only Craig's opposite, he also served as a salve for the wound created by my father's absence—a sore spot that, in those days, I was not aware I was nursing.

By the time I turned fifteen, our connection had evolved from friendship to relationship—and I worked up the nerve to ask my mother if Kerry and I could go out on a date.

"I need to meet him first so I can tell the police what he looks like in case you don't come home," she told me. When he stopped by our crib that evening to take me to dinner, my mother's breezy conversation and occasional smile told me she approved of his gentlemanly manners. She of course had no clue how old he was or that he had a son, and surprisingly, her inner attorney didn't think to ask him his age. Kerry could've passed for being anywhere from seventeen to twenty-five.

By spring of 1996, after months of dreaming and connecting with each other, I decided it was time for me to tell Kerry the truth. Sort of.

"You know how I said I was seventeen when we first met?" I casually brought up one afternoon. He nodded. "Well, I was really sixteen," I said. Before he could respond, I quickly added, "But I'm seventeen now"—also not true.

The Original Lie had slid so easily from my tongue that it couldn't have been the first time I told it. And every time I'd aged myself up, others seemed to believe me. I had the face of a teenager, yes, but my womanly curves whispered a different tale. I'd of course fooled around with boys my age, but in truth, most of them felt like exactly that to me: boys. I'd grown up having to hold my own in disagreements with one of the sharpest women on the planet. That gave me early entrée into the universe of adult reasoning, and it also made me bored with young men close to my age. And given my grade-skipping, I always felt older than I was.

From Kerry's viewpoint, my false claim seemed to square up with my life stage: he knew I was near the end of high school. What senior is not at least seventeen or almost eighteen? To be any younger, I would've had to have skipped two grades, which Kerry had no idea I'd done. I cared more about watering the roots of our connection than I cared about our age difference. So I kept on distorting the truth for months, until circumstances would later yank the wig right off my bald head.

———

The letter I sent to my father began not with "Dear Dad" or even "Dear Craig," but simply with the date in the upper left-hand corner: 7/10/94.

"It saddens me that most of my heart is bitter towards you," I wrote. "It's only that little part that feels sad that's not bitter . . . all I want is for you to mind your own business. I don't want the phone calls. I don't want the letters. I don't want the fake acts you pull to try and make me think you care. I don't want anything."

By the time those words rolled from the tip of my pen and onto my notebook paper, my longing for my father had hardened into resentment. My mother still recalls the many times when Craig said he'd fly in to see me but, for reasons unknown to me then, he did not show up. I'd sit beside the window in our living room, looking down over the terrace to see if I could glimpse him arriving. An hour or so after the appointed time, the phone would ring and I would overhear my mother, in hushed tones in her bedroom, saying, "Okay, I understand." Moments later she'd emerge into the living room with disappointment etched on her forehead as she announced, "He can't make it." That was it. Conversation over. Expectations once again dashed.

When I did see Craig, it was often at Nana's house. Just as he'd done after I was born, Craig stepped through my grandmother's doorframe cradling Cole before gently handing him to his mother so she could bond with her new grandbaby. In fact, it had been Cole's birth that drew me back toward Craig after our connection had grown strained. To his credit, my father seemed intent on ensuring that Cole and I would grow up knowing each other. So in the first two years of my brother's life, I saw Craig a little more frequently than I ever had.

"This is Cole," he'd said when he introduced me to the tiny, precious human being who immediately clasped his miniature pink fingers around my thumb. I wanted to be in my brother's life as much as I'd wanted Craig to be a more consistent participant in my own. If I pushed Cole away because of my difficult relationship with my father, I reasoned, that would've made me exactly like him.

Yet by my freshman year of high school, the gash I'd sustained was freshly sliced open. Mom was enduring a particularly stressful financial season, and even with the blessing of an affordable apartment, she often found herself short on rent. We regularly danced along the knife-edge of solvency while Craig, on the other side of the country, nurtured and provided for his wife and other child. Craig now explains that he, too, was then struggling in a paycheck-to-paycheck existence and couldn't help us as much as he wanted to. But it wasn't his money that I most desired; it was a sense of his concern and caring.

Mommy took on additional work that often kept her away from the apartment for long stretches. That left me, a latchkey kid, with plenty of time to contemplate Craig's whereabouts while seated at the piano, emptying my soul into bluesy jazz compositions. On the afternoon that I picked up my pen and paper and began my letter to him, I'd grown weary with the promises not kept. The last-minute cancellations. The long silences between the annual birthday cards. I sat at our small table and finally wrote out, in bubble cursive, exactly what I felt. I then carefully tore off the frayed edges along the perforations, folded the paper in half, shoved it in an envelope, and slid it into the slot of a blue mailbox.

Craig didn't answer my letter. My father, in those days, was more of a pacifist than a fighter. Confrontation was not in his nature, which may be one reason he and my mother, seldom one to back down from a brawl, were attracted to each other from opposite ends of the personality spectrum. But Craig says he had no intention of allowing me to push him off the ledge of our relationship. He says he attempted to stay connected from the back row of my life, often checking in with Nana to hear the latest on what was happening with me.

Even after I mailed those divorce papers to Craig, some part of me must have hoped he'd fight to stay in my life. But at fourteen, I felt sure I never wanted to hear from him again.

———

We called ourselves EmBishion—our cutesy teenage take on the idea of striving, of catapulting ourselves from New York's boulevards onto center stage in the music business. My friends, Taneisha and Natalia, were around sixteen when we formed our girl group. And just as in my first group, I was the young'un at fourteen. Our a cappella selections made us sound more like En Vogue (the fierce foursome that emerged in the '90s) than we did like my original blueprint, The Jackson 5. I now understand that trying to be the "next" anyone is as foolish as it sounds. The shoes you dream of filling have already been worn ragged through their soles. You've gotta step into your own kicks and just do you.

What I lacked in age I made up for with experience. In the years since I'd made my preschool debut as a brown-skinned Dorothy, I'd swiftly moved through my classical training and onto composition. I wrote my first song when I was twelve, after losing my dear fafa. I hadn't been there on the day he passed away. But when I later heard that an ambulance had to be called multiple times before help arrived, that news nearly broke me.

Not long after we lost him, I saw the movie *Philadelphia*. There's a moving scene in which Tom Hanks's character, Andrew Beckett, a lawyer suffering with AIDS, narrates a stirring aria, Maria Callas's "La Mamma Morta" from the opera *Andrea Chénier*. I seldom cry in movies, but during that ten p.m. show, both my mother and me bawled our eyes out. When I returned home from the theater after midnight, I sat down at my piano and wrote my first song, called "I'm All Alone." Though it was way past my bedtime, Mom allowed me to stay at the piano as long as I wanted. Creating, she understood, was my way of grieving.

My grandfather, in his death, left me with a treasure I've carried with me through life. His memory opened up in me an emotional vault I hadn't even known existed, and what poured out was a deluge of lyrics: "I sit here all alone / And I wonder what is wrong / Why are there so many deaths? / So many lost survivors?" My early compositions clearly weren't all that deep, but they came from a real place. My first experiences of longing, of heartache and anguish and love— they have a certain vibrancy to them, a passion and immediacy that pale in life's later rounds. The magic in any art is not only in its technique but in its authenticity. Truth in its rawest form is what resonates most powerfully.

Penning my first song became another step in my quest to find my musical footing, my own flow. I'd already graduated from mimicking other artists to attempting to create my own vibe. Even still, I drew inspiration from the musical geniuses in my mother's record collection, as well as the collection I'd started for myself. I studied every note of Marvin Gaye's *What's Going On,* the white cassette tape that I played until it fell apart. It blew me away each time I heard it. I admired how artists like Marvin and Nina Simone stayed in tune with their political times, how their music reflected and defined the spirit of change. I dreamed of one day doing the same with a sound I was only beginning to define.

By 1994, that sound had taken the form of the harmonies I'd composed for EmBishion. One day that summer, my girls and I rehearsed our show at Harlem's Police Athletic League (PAL); I rounded out the performance with my piano rendition of "Butterflyz," one of my earliest compositions and my first love song. Taneisha's uncle Greg had arranged our rehearsal; he and another friend of his had been helping us refine our show. On this afternoon at the PAL, Conrad Robinson, a vocal coach who oversaw a youth program in the Bronx, had been invited by Greg to hear us perform.

"Did you write these songs?" he asked me afterward. I nodded and smiled. "Listen," he said, "maybe we can start doing a little work together to polish up your set." Once outside the building, the girls and I high-fived and gushed. If Conrad was asking to work with us, maybe we really had something.

I didn't know it at the time—and it's probably best that I didn't, because I truly might've lost my teenage mind—but Conrad was the brother of R & B manager Jeff Robinson, whose connections ran deep and wide throughout the entertainment world. After weeks of Conrad and Greg helping us fine-tune our pitches, Conrad had called Jeff. "Man, you've gotta come see these girls," he told him.

Jeff, who'd heard that refrain one too many times, didn't exactly race to our next showcase. But Conrad persisted. Probably just to get his brother off his back, Jeff at last stopped in at the PAL and, unbeknownst to us, took a seat in the back of the room. We launched into our first song, Groove Theory's "Tell Me," complete with its large dose of swag, and then ended the way we always did—with me at the piano.

Afterward, Conrad and Jeff approached us.

"I want you to meet my brother," Conrad said, introducing Jeff. "He works in the music biz." We each shook his hand and I tried to play it cool, though my heart was hammering away in my chest.

"That was good" was all Jeff said; in fact, he was so understated that it immediately dampened my excitement. But then, as we were preparing to leave, Jeff pulled me aside.

"Come with me and we'll make millions," he whispered. It was a statement as effusive as it was unexpected. My eyes filled with light, but then quickly dimmed as a realization took root: He wasn't extending an invitation to all three of us. He was singling me out.

That was the start of Jeff's campaign for me to go solo.

"You need to be on your own," he told me later. "You can sing. You can play. You can compose. You're the whole package." I was stunned and flattered. What artist wouldn't be gratified by such an affirmation, one I'd longed to hear in the years since that tattered upright slid across our doorway? But I didn't feel ready to go out on my own. The group thing was all I'd known. It was comfortable. At fourteen, I hadn't yet developed the muscle required to push past my zone of familiarity and into new and frightening territory. I still had it in my head that I would break onto the scene as Little Ali; and only after me and the girls reached stardom might I moonwalk out, Michael style, and claim my own stage. Through my eyes at the time, the solo life looked lonely. No friends with me on the road. No fam around to have my back. No fun. "You're wrong," Jeff kept telling me. I repeated my hesitation, and he finally left me with a choice: "Call me when you're ready."

That sentence is what drove me to push our girl group to the next level. The truth is that our harmonies weren't as tight as they could've been. We were flat. We were sharp. We were, at times, totally off-key. We worked harder than ever under the guidance of Conrad and Greg, as well as a few musicians we brought in, and though that effort lifted our game by an inch or two, we were still miles away from where we needed to be. We were eager, yes, but we were complete amateurs in a business in which the seeds of potential mastery serve as the entrance requirement. So we doubled up on our rehearsals and doubled down on our chords. And then, when Greg helped us arrange an audition with a record exec (who I pray doesn't remember me), we didn't land on a single one of our chords.

I wanted so badly to make the group happen. We'd dreamed our dream in unison, and the thought of us disbanding made me wilt inside. But what's true in the music industry is also the case in life: Growth requires movement. And often, the only way forward is through an exit door.

Soon after our failed audition, I rang Jeff. "I'm ready" were the only words I spoke into the receiver. Within months of that declaration, I found myself near the top floor of a glistening skyscraper, an uncertain future stretched before me.

# 4

## COLUMBIA

**KERRY BROTHERS, A.K.A. KRUCIAL,
ALICIA'S WRITING PARTNER AND FIRST SERIOUS BOYFRIEND**

After Alicia moved out of her mother's place in Hell's Kitchen, we lived together in a one-bedroom walk-up in Harlem. I was hustling together jobs by day, and at night, Alicia and I had jam sessions. At first, I just had a keyboard and a drum machine. Then after she got a record deal, I was like, "Yo, we should buy some equipment." We went down to Sam Ash and got everything we needed. We turned the bedroom into our studio . . . the acoustics are better in a small, closed-off space. We used nails and tape to put blankets on the walls and comforters on the ceiling, for soundproofing. Until the early hours of the morning, we were in there jamming and vibing and listening to the greats, from Stevie Wonder and Nina Simone to Aretha Franklin and Curtis Mayfield. We were like, how come our music sounds so thin? We studied the credits on Stevie's records and were like, "Man, these guys are layering. They've got a Wurlitzer"—an electric piano. We'd bought this rolling rack mount with all these sounds you can trigger with a keyboard, and sure enough, when we turned it on, we were like, "Look, we got a Wurlitzer!" That's how we got into making our music sound fuller—by trial and error.

I'd just played out my soul on a marble-white baby grand, the most gorgeous piano I'd ever seen. To my right stood Jeff, my manager, and a row of Columbia Records' top brass—Tommy Mottola, Donnie Ienner, Michael Mauldin. To my left stood the city that raised me, sparkling anew through pristine floor-to-ceiling windows looking down over Madison Avenue.

"If we can close the deal," Donnie said to Jeff, "she can have the piano. I'll give you fifteen minutes to talk it over." Without another word, Donnie strode out of the room.

This wasn't my first audition. Just before my fifteenth birthday in January 1996, I'd at last teamed up with Jeff, who got to work on attempting to land me a solo deal with one of the top labels. Jeff immediately connected me with his longtime friend and colleague Peter Edge, then an artist development executive at Warner Bros. Records. Peter was excited about my prospects in the music business, but he was also in transition. Years later I'd learn that by the time he met me, he was already planning to leave Warner Bros. to work with Clive Davis at Arista. After watching me perform, he wanted to sign me—but *after* he'd fully transitioned into his new role at Arista.

Meanwhile, I forged ahead with work on a demo, one that could be distributed to various record labels. Even as we put together my sample and sent it around town, I was performing. Though I was mostly appearing in talent shows and events around my neighborhood, I also set out on the road. I played all around the tri-state area, sometimes even in venues where I would've otherwise been turned away at the entrance. I was too young to drink but apparently old enough to put on a show for the partiers who gathered nightly.

By spring of 1997, Jeff had lined up several showcases—private sessions where record label heads could see me perform live and on my own. No band. No backup singers. No soundtracks. Just me and my quivering hands on a piano, weaving together my best original songs alongside the elaborate compositions of Chopin and Bach. At every showcase, I played my music like it was the only chance I'd ever get to land a contract, because in my view, it was. Coming from a place where the sense of struggle lingers as strong as the smell of piss, I'd grown up seeing life through a single lens: survival. And from that vantage point, opportunity is never a promise. Rather, it is a hope and a powerful hustle, the kind I watched my mother keep up year after year. As I saw it, these showcases were my potential way out—my passport to a different existence.

My passion must have resonated. Within days of my series of performances, every label executive had expressed interest. I was a musical combination they'd seldom witnessed: a classically trained pianist with Stevie-inspired cornrows, a fresh face with an old spirit, and a neo-soul sound reminiscent of the '70s. Jeff, eager to maximize our payday, created a bidding war. Peter ultimately did not bid. After we'd pulled together my demo and began meeting with various labels, things had moved so quickly that Peter hadn't yet made the transition to Arista. And he didn't want to sign me to Warner Bros. only to abandon me shortly after. Many made offers, and Columbia made the most lucrative one. That's when Michael Mauldin invited me to Columbia's stunning, marble-floored offices for a final performance—and perhaps a chance to cement a deal.

Jeff, a savvy businessman from the Bronx, had his gaze fixed on the financial opportunity. So did I. Yet I also had one wandering eye on a prize that felt just as important to me as the overall contract terms: that luxurious baby grand, which had to be worth more than $25,000. In fact, the moment Donnie mentioned that it could be mine, I began visualizing my mother and me moving out my dinted upright and making space in our living room for this beauty. Jeff cut my daydream short.

"We can't make a deal for no freaking piano," he said after Donnie was out of earshot. Even before I had a chance to launch into my plea, he'd decoded what was written all over my face: I would've signed just about any contract in order to claim this gem right in front of me. Donnie might as well have been dangling the Winston Blue diamond in my face—that's just how enticing this piano was. In my state of deep salivation, I laid out for Jeff all the reasons I had to have this piano. "It's crazy, Ali," he kept telling me. "No way."

A week later, I signed the contract—not just for that piano, but I'll admit it did sway me. In addition to the baby grand, the label executives also offered us the highest advance, a fact that pleased Jeff as much as it did me and my mother. And Donnie ultimately kept his promise to give me a new piano, though not the one I'd played that day. A baby grand of the same brand was delivered long after my deal was done. By then, the music business had already begun teaching me its first pair of lessons: Always study the fine print in your contract. And after you've negotiated the best possible deal for yourself, buy your own damn piano.

————

In spring of 1997, I graduated as class valedictorian from the Professional Performing Arts School. I gave some cringeworthy speech about teachers trying to box you in and tell you who to be. In one hand, I held my diploma and a scholarship to Columbia University. In the other hand, I clutched a newly signed label contract that would change my course in ways I couldn't have anticipated. And among the crowd of proud parents, relatives, and friends gathered for the ceremony, there stood my steady boyfriend—a man who still had no idea I wasn't old enough to vote.

If I thought I was grown at fourteen, by sixteen, my mother couldn't tell me anything. Mom was as forthright and impassioned as she'd always been. What changed was me. As I grew out of my natural introversion and into my voice, I challenged her in every regard. At all hours, I ran around the city with Kerry. I ignored Mom's incessant messages on my beeper, along with her demands that I check in with her regularly. I was still technically a minor, but circumstances had prematurely edged me into purgatory—that transition away from the dependence of adolescence and toward the autonomy of adulthood.

The record deal had already given me financial liberation, and I longed for every other freedom that I thought went along with that. I wanted to roam the streets, from the Village to Harlem, whenever I felt like it. I wanted to spend my nights in the arms of Kerry, never pausing to wonder whether I'd blown past my curfew. And yet I also still wanted the comforts of my childhood: a stocked refrigerator, a mother whose very presence gave me a deep sense of stability, the solid grounding I felt each time I walked through our apartment door. In essence, I longed for two mutually exclusive realities: inextricable connection and full-fledged self-reliance.

Rather than reconciling those two existences, I leapt into a new one. A few weeks after I graduated, I moved into Kerry's rent-controlled apartment near 137th Street and Malcolm X Boulevard. My mother, of course, didn't approve. She had every legal ability to stop me. In fact, because I was still under eighteen, she'd had to cosign my record contract. And yet as much as Mom did not want me to go, she wisely anticipated what I see so vividly in retrospect: Forcing me to stay would have widened the chasm between us. In a sense, I'd purchased my freedom with a contract and a six-figure advance. She understood that and just let me go.

Soon after I moved, the truth about my age finally came spilling out. One afternoon, I was venting with Jeff about a conflict I'd had with my mom; though I was no longer under her roof, she still had plenty to say about how I should manage my life and career.

"You know that you can go to court and be emancipated as a minor," Jeff told me. Kerry, who was standing next to me, stared at Jeff.

"What do you mean, *emancipated as a minor?*" he asked. "Why would she need to do *that?*"

Later that evening at the apartment, I came clean.

"You know how I told you I was seventeen when we met, and then I later said I was sixteen?" He looked at me but didn't say anything. "I was really fourteen," I admitted. *Silence.*

Kerry was understandably upset that I'd misled him. For a few days, we even stopped speaking. But the truth hung thick in the air:

After two amazing years together, there was too much love between us to turn around.

———

I'd always felt capable as a student. Even when, during high school, I was balancing my performing arts curriculum with my academic one, the work was manageable. The As in English and French and trigonometry flowed as easily for me as my daily practice at the piano. That all changed when I enrolled at Columbia University.

Mom had always insisted that I go to college, just as she had; I'd grown up expecting that I'd one day apply. She was adamant about excellence in education. During our initial meetings with the team at Columbia Records, she'd often find a way to pipe in with, "And when Alicia finishes her studies . . ." Jeff and everyone else in the room would silently gaze at her like she'd just suggested I fly to Jupiter. No one wanted to cross my mother by stating the obvious: Working as a full-time musician while keeping up with a rigorous Ivy League curriculum is about as easy as giving birth while enduring a root canal. And yet I was up for the challenge. Like my mom, I saw the value in a traditional education, and given how good of a student I'd always been, I actually looked forward to my time on campus. I also knew I'd never hear the end of it if I chose not to enroll.

As a liberal arts major, I started with a full course load—and I felt overwhelmed practically from week one. Professors assigned an enormous amount of reading, sometimes hundreds of pages a week. My plan was to attend all of my classes during the day, and then stay on top of the reading while en route to my evening studio sessions. There I'd sit on the train, doing my best to concentrate on long passages of Homer's *Odyssey* while struggling to hold my book steady and keep my eyes open. The New York City subway has to rank as one of the worst places in the world to focus. It's noisy. It stinks. And seemingly at every stop, a street musician rolls in, attempting to earn a little applause and enough tips for a meal. I usually did more ogling or dozing than I did studying.

I'd then get to the studio at around six p.m. and stay until two or three a.m. Later that same morning in my eleven o'clock class, I'd be in the back row, half asleep with my hoodie over my forehead. *What are they even talking about?* I'd think as my classmates discussed the homework. *Please don't let this professor call on me.* I was a total wreck. I was too exhausted to recall the little I'd managed to read, and nothing was computing.

I also felt incredibly lonely. Kerry, as usual, was juggling multiple jobs, and our schedules didn't always align. I'd stop in at my mother's place, only to find she was out, probably working overtime or enjoying her new season as an empty nester. She'd been away from the apartment a lot when I was younger, and in those days, I'd relished my silence and alone time at the piano. But during this new chapter of my life, a time when I first felt truly on my own, the ground beneath me seemed shaky. It didn't help that I was facing the enormous responsibility of making a record, a task I had no idea how to even begin.

A few weeks into my courses, I reached for a lifeline. I made an appointment to talk with my dean in her office.

"So I have this record deal," I told her, "and I'm also trying to get through my program here."

"And how's that all working out?" she asked gently, as if she knew the answer.

"Well," I said, "not that great." Tears welled up in my eyes, but I managed to hold them back. "It's tough to get everything done."

She nodded sympathetically. "You know, Alicia," she said, "Columbia will always be here." I stared at her but didn't respond, mostly because I was surprised. I'd expected her to convince me to stay at Columbia. "And if you decide to invest your energy into music full-time," she continued, "you could always come back."

For a week after I left my dean's office, I wrestled with my decision. The thought of disappointing my mother broke my heart. I'd wanted to prove to her, and to myself, that I could balance college and a career on stage. And yet, in a sense, I'd already chosen my path years earlier, when I'd entered Ms. Hazel's magical world of song. From that moment on, music had grabbed hold of me and never put me down.

On the afternoon when I'd signed my record deal, I was so elated I almost could not speak. That evening, I lay awake staring up at the ceiling and thinking, *This is really happening for me.* After a childhood of dreaming and praying for some way, *any* way, into the music industry, that dream was now firmly in my grasp—and now that I had the opportunity, it scared me. *What if I fail?* Musicians often spend years toiling away at their craft, playing in small venues and hoping to get discovered and signed. Most never do. And here I was, at just sixteen, with a yellow brick road in front of me. Yes, the thought of telling my mother that I might leave Columbia scared me. But what frightened me more was squandering a chance I might never again get.

My conversation with the dean gave me the courage to do what I dreaded: appear before the bench of Chief Justice Augello. If I was going to leave Columbia, I knew I had to present a watertight case to my mother. I spent days thinking through my best arguments and writing down what I'd say. I then called my mother and asked her if she could do lunch; she happily agreed. I chose a restaurant in Hell's Kitchen, this Italian spot that was usually crowded. If Mom got upset, I reasoned, she'd likely restrain herself in such a public setting. When my mother arrived at the appointed time, I was already there waiting. We began with a general catchup before the conversation shifted into second gear. I pulled out my paper, carefully unfolded it, and laid it out on the table.

"So school is pretty hard," I began.

"Hard?" she said, wrinkling her brow. "What do you mean *hard*? You graduated at the top of your high school class."

I fidgeted with the paper. "With being in the studio at night," I explained, "and then trying to keep up with my classes, I'm just not coping that well. It's difficult to concentrate on both school and music. I spoke to the dean. . . ."

Mommy laid down her fork. "You spoke to the dean about *what?*"

"I mean, the dean, well . . . yes. And she said that maybe it's better for me to just do music and come back to school later."

Mom glared at me. "And why is that a good idea?" she asked, the volume of her voice rising with each syllable. A few people glanced over at us, and I looked back down at my paper in search of my next justification. "Don't you think you need a strong education in order to excel at what you're doing in the music business?"

"Well, yes," I whispered in an attempt to take down Mom's temperature. "But maybe I could get going with what I'm doing musically and then return to Columbia."

"And what makes you think you'll ever get back around to that?"

I didn't have a good answer to that question, nor did our conversation have a definitive conclusion. I'm sure my mother was as displeased about my choice to leave Columbia as she'd been about my move out of her apartment. But just as she'd done in the latter case, she set aside the reins and let me charge ahead. As a creative spirit herself, she'd tell me years later, she understood my predicament: I could not take on two major pursuits without significantly compromising at least one of them.

I don't believe in regret. So I never look back on my choice to leave Columbia and wish that things had turned out differently. Life's current was so obviously carrying me in the direction of music, and rather than trying to swim back upstream, I simply let the tide carry me forward. At the time, I wouldn't have described it that way, nor did I truly understand that there was a flow with my name on it. But from this side of life, I can see how every moment, every experience, every pivot, even my supposed missteps have been life's way of getting me where I have always been meant to go. Rather than resisting the current, I've learned to surrender.

————

"You need a different last name," Michael Mauldin said to me in his thick Southern accent. Michael, the father of artist and producer

Jermaine Dupri, and then president of Columbia Records Urban Division, had been the one to sign me. "Choose something memorable," he told me.

I had no idea what I'd call myself, but this I knew for sure: Alicia Augello-Cook doesn't exactly roll off the tongue. I spent a week brainstorming names but made little progress. So I reached for a dictionary and scrolled through every entry, from A to Z, in search of any word that might make a great last name. Alicia Anchovy? Nope. Alicia Monopoly? Try again. By the time I got to the last few letters of the alphabet, I was desperate.

"What about Alicia Wild?" I asked my mom one evening.

"It sounds like a stripper's name," she said bluntly. She was right.

A few days later, Michael checked in with me to find out what I'd come up with. *Nada.*

"I might have an idea for you," he told me. "Last night I had this dream, and I couldn't find the keys to my briefcase. I was looking everywhere for those keys, because I really needed to get into my case to get to some documents. This morning, I woke up with one word on my mind . . . *keys.* What do you think about Alicia Keys?"

I smiled.

"Keys," I said slowly. "Alicia Keys." Right away it felt natural to me, as if it had always been my name. It just fit. It of course also hinted at the piano, a defining feature of my performances. And keys open doors. "I love it," I told Michael. "Let's use it."

The new name slid right into position. The early months of producing the album, however, didn't go quite so smoothly. When I had signed my contract that spring, I was over the moon. By summer, I'd crashed back down to earth as I grappled with the reality that I was clueless about how to make a record. A contract with a label is an open doorway. And what no one tells you is that once you step through that door, you're mostly on your own. No grooming. No weekly team meetings. No general artistic direction. It's just you and a few producers, trying to pull off a feat that frightened me to my core. At sixteen, I had no idea how to create a commercially viable album.

I plunged right into writing with a couple of established producers. That collaboration quickly veered off the rails. During our studio sessions, I'd bring in some new lyrics and play them with a piano composition I'd been refining.

"It needs to be more upbeat, less piano driven," I'd hear after delivering a few measures. *Less piano driven? Did he know anything about me?* Other times, the producers would attempt to write lyrics for me. The material did not reflect my truth or perspective. There was a total disconnect between who I was as an artist and what I was bringing to the table musically.

When I pushed back, the label execs responded by sending in a revolving cast of producers. None of them was any better for me. The low point came when, one evening after a session, a producer approached me with a question on his lips and something hard poking through the crotch of his jeans.

"Yo, do you want to meet me at my house later?" he asked. I didn't even bother responding to that foolishness; I just brushed it off and kept moving. Meanwhile, I was hearing the same weekly refrain from Columbia: "Where's the music?" For months, I set out for the studio with dread in my chest, feeling disgusted with the process and unsure of myself. There was no way I could do my best work in that frame of mind, surrounded by producers who were so busy trying to push up on me that they couldn't effectively partner with me. I had to find my own path forward.

It's not that my efforts had produced nothing—just not nearly enough. I'd hammer out lyrics while in the studio with the producers, and then attempt to forge ahead on my own. I always made the most progress at home, in the makeshift studio Kerry and I had created. Using all that equipment I'd purchased with my advance, the two of us would often be up until sunrise, vibing and jamming and just enjoying the music. There was a freedom and playfulness in the air. That's because we were creating simply for the love of the process. Our partnership as musicians felt as magical and unexpected to me as our personal connection always had. So several months after I'd signed with Columbia, I asked Kerry to be my producing partner. He agreed and set aside his other work to collaborate with me.

That move was one of the smartest I've ever made. Because from then on, the music just flowed. Kerry, who'd already taught himself a lot about the intricacies of producing, invested his full passion into mastering the best techniques. Our occasional jam sessions blossomed into nightly improvisations that surely put us on thin ice with the neighbors. We were super serious. Once it was time to begin work at six p.m. sharp, all beepers and cell phones were turned off. Then for six hours straight, we'd lose ourselves in a shared intention: creating music powerful enough to move us, as well as all others who heard it.

Our home sessions were just stage one. Once we had a couple of great songs going, Jeff would book us time at an actual studio where we'd have the complete range of equipment. We'd sometimes bring in bass guitarists or drummers so we could record them and later weave in their creations alongside my piano and voice soundtracks. Thanks to a mother who taught me the twin *d*'s of success—discipline and diligence—I lived and breathed my work. I may not have known exactly how to complete an album, but I knew how to focus. I also knew how to write from my soul, my center. Every song we produced was an expression of some aspect of life through my eyes. Both Jeff and Michael Mauldin, who'd been in favor of my evolution toward working on my own, loved what they heard.

In the summer of 1998, my album was nearly complete. Or so I thought. Because by this time, Columbia had undergone a major staff shake-up. Michael Mauldin, my greatest advocate, was gone and the label was now headed by a new set of executives. "What's this?" one of the label heads asked Jeff after he'd heard my music. "I mean, it's kind of soulful. But where are the pop smashes, the radio hits? This sounds like a demo."

That shift in expectations began with my music and extended to my public image. They wanted my mass of curls blown straight and flowing down my back. They wanted me to lose weight. They wanted my hemlines shorter, my teeth whiter, my cleavage on full display. They wanted me, the tomboy from Hell's Kitchen, to become the next teen pop idol. In short, they wanted to alter my entire identity.

A record label is a marketing machine. Behind its doors, fledgling artists are crafted into whatever image the label's execs believe they can sell. And what was selling in the late '90s? Female pop stars like Whitney Houston, Mariah Carey, and Janet Jackson. Most label executives aren't all that interested in artistic innovation. It's not about carving out a niche; it's about shoving an artist into an existing one. Commercial success, not imagination, is the primary goal. There's nothing wrong with being a pop princess. It's just not who I am. Trouble was, no one quite knew what to do with a piano prodigy in cornrows, mixing classical music with hip-hop beats and bass lines alongside a dash of gospel.

"We can help you get a more radio-friendly sound," the new leaders of Columbia told me. But it was too late for that. The genie hadn't just escaped the bottle; she was already way down the street and around the corner. I'd gotten used to doing things my way, on my terms, during my private jam sessions with Kerry. No way was I going back into the studio with one of the label's recommended producers.

When I heard that my album had been referred to as a *demo*, it was soul crushing. I felt as if someone had just called my precious newborn ugly.

"This will work out," Kerry kept trying to reassure me as I spiraled into a depression so deep I couldn't pry myself out of bed for weeks. "Don't give up."

Meanwhile, Jeff and the attorneys we brought in tried to work out a compromise with Columbia. To Jeff's credit, he stood strongly in my corner at a moment when many other managers would have bolted or, worse, pressured me to get in line with the label's vision.

"If they don't get who you are," he told me, "then we'll just find someone who does." That began the battle for me to get back the master rights to my own work—rights I had relinquished back when I thought Columbia was my dream home.

"Just let us have our masters back and we'll go," Jeff and my lawyers argued to the executives. But they would not budge, even though they apparently hated what I'd produced.

I didn't want to walk away without my music. Doing so would've given Columbia a financial stake in any of my future profits. The label also would've been able to license my master recordings to third parties (for placement in television shows or films, for instance) without my consent. Most artists, and especially new ones, sign away their master rights because that's the price you pay for an on-ramp into the business. That's exactly what happened to a whole generation of Motown artists, many of whom sold millions of hit albums, yet ended up flat broke because they didn't own their creations. Labels are not in the business of selling rights, they're in the business of acquiring them and then holding on to them tightly.

Maybe I didn't yet own my music, but I would always be in control of my voice. My image. My actions and intentions. The person and artist I am at my core. And I am the girl who spent hours with my head bowed over the keys of a secondhand upright, praying I'd one day get to share my creations with the world. I am the girl who wore my tough exterior as proudly as I did my soft heart. I am the girl who sported hoodies in place of sequined dresses, Timbs in place of stilettoes. If I betrayed that girl—if I sold myself out by succumbing to the label's vision of who I should be—I might have been an extraordinary success. But I would've also been utterly miserable. I would've been up there on some stage, singing songs I didn't truly believe in. I would've been living someone else's dream instead of celebrating my own. For me, that sacrifice was unthinkable.

My fight to leave Columbia Records was my first major act of artistic defiance, and a deeply personal one. Late one evening while alone in the apartment, I turned down the world's volume and tuned in to the whisper of my spirit—that deep inner knowing, that quiet voice and inkling I believe we all have. I knew my answer. Each of us usually does, but the calls for us to conform are nearly overpowering. They come in the form of a ballet teacher who demands a tucked-in behind or a classmate who throws shade at thick thighs and a curly 'fro. We adjust ourselves to fit, to adapt to others' ideas of who we should be. We shift ourselves not in sweeping pivots, but in movements so tiny that they are hardly perceptible, even in our view. Years can pass before we finally discover that, after handing over our power piece by small piece, we no longer even look like ourselves.

Even if I couldn't retrieve my master copyrights, I told Jeff, I wanted to somehow break free from Columbia. I might have to start over and create an entirely new album in order to completely cut the ties, but so be it. At least my music and my image would be authentic to me. At least I would still recognize my own reflection in the mirror.

# 5

## TRANSITIONS

### ANN MINCIELI, ALICIA'S LONGTIME SOUND ENGINEER AND FOUNDER OF JUNGLE CITY STUDIOS

Alicia's approach to music is retro-futuristic. She captures the old ways of recording, and yet she does it in a modern setting. We might watch an Aretha Franklin video from the '70s, where all these artists were vibing together, and we'll go out and find the actual guitars or drums they played. Then we'll bring in musicians to play those instruments in our studio. With today's technology, many artists never even meet their drummers or guitarists or keyboardists. Those musicians might be thousands of miles away in some other city, just sending in files that are eventually pieced together, like a puzzle. That process creates a disconnect that can be felt in the sonic. It also dilutes the quality, because the music is missing the human element—the gathering of real instrumentalists making magic in one space. By bringing artists together, Alicia infuses her material with a depth, emotion, and authenticity that software can never duplicate.

I was late. Jeff, who was already in the Arista Records lobby when I came sprinting and huffing through the front door, had arranged for us to meet with Clive Davis—the renowned music man with the golden touch. The legend who'd launched the careers of greats like Janis Joplin, Whitney Houston, Carlos Santana, and Bruce

Springsteen. The label executive who, on this afternoon in 1998, had agreed to sit down with my tardy ass.

The gathering was scheduled for three p.m. When I came whirling in at three-fifteen, out of breath and full of excuses, Jeff stood there, arms folded, wearing a frown that shouted, "Do you know what the hell is at stake?" I did—which is exactly why I'd taken some extra time to pick out my best outfit. I don't recall what I wore that day, but I do know that, after a major subway delay and a cab stuck in traffic, I got lucky: Clive, it turned out, was also running behind schedule.

Peter Edge, by this time the head of Arista's artists and repertoire (A & R) division, had been the one to connect us with Clive. When my relationship with Columbia spiraled downhill, Jeff began exploring other possible partnerships for me around the industry. He gave a recording of some of my songs to Peter, who then handed it off to Clive, his boss. Clive was intrigued enough by what he heard to agree to a meeting and a short audition.

"Come right in," Clive said, extending his hand to both Jeff and me. Clive—or Mr. Davis, as I respectfully called him then—offered us a seat and launched right into a story, as if the three of us were longtime friends, sitting around at a barbecue in someone's backyard. Though impeccably dressed (that man is sharp: suit and tie, matching hankie poking out of his jacket pocket), Clive came off more like a favorite uncle than the stuffy mogul one might expect. I, with my jaw on the ground and my heart palpitating, heard little of what he initially said. All I could do was gawk.

Walking into Clive's office felt like stepping into a time capsule of music history. All over his walls, in row after row of perfectly positioned frames, hung photos of the scores of musical masters whose paths had intersected with his own. Patti Smith. Earth, Wind & Fire. The Grateful Dead. Simon & Garfunkel. Barry Manilow. Biggie and Puffy. On and on. Many of these artists Clive had personally discovered. All had in some way been touched by his leadership and brilliance. Just sitting across from Clive, in this space where so much magic had happened, filled me with awe.

"Peter showed me a video of one of your performances," Clive said, pulling my attention back to earth. "Your music is special." *Me? You're talking about* my *music?*

Moments later, right there on the piano in Clive's office, I put on my best show for an audience of one. I strung together most of the songs I'd written, pouring my soul into every refrain. You get only one chance to impress music's all-time most celebrated hit maker. This was my opportunity. Once the vibration of the last note had faded, Clive stood quietly for a long moment with his hands folded, as if he were soaking in what he'd just heard. He smiled and nodded approvingly.

"You know," he said, "I only go into the studio with artists who need my input. Aretha is one of the greatest, but she's not writing her own records, so of course I help her get those records. The same is true with Dionne and Whitney. But you're like a Patti Smith," he said. A shiver rose up through me. *Was he really comparing me, a seventeen-year-old newbie, to a songwriting genius?*

"With Patti," he continued, "I've never stepped foot in the studio once 'cause I don't have to. And that's how I see you. You write your own lyrics. You compose your own songs at the piano. You're the whole package. How do you see yourself?"

I stared at him. Before that moment, no one of Clive's stature had ever asked me how I viewed myself as an artist. The question itself served as confirmation that he understood me. He recognized I was a self-contained musician. He knew how important it was for me to define myself, to go into the studio and chart my own course through music's landscape. I'm sure I meandered my way through some long-winded answer to Clive's question, but by the end of our meeting, all was clear. I saw myself as an artist potentially on his team—a singer and songwriter with the full freedom to evolve.

"Look," he said. "I think you're absolutely phenomenal and I'd love to sign you to Arista. But Columbia would be crazy to let you out of your contract. There's no way in the world they're going to let you go." Jeff insisted otherwise.

"Leave that to me," he told Clive.

Near the start of 1999, Jeff somehow pulled off the miracle he had promised. Behind the scenes, he at last talked Columbia into both releasing me from my contract and selling my masters to Arista. It was one hell of a fight. But Clive believed so strongly in our future partnership that he was willing to buy me out of my deal for a hefty sum of about half a million dollars. Months later, when Clive's professional world was shaken from all sides, I'd have my chance to partially repay him for his faith in me.

———

When you've chosen the right path for yourself, you usually know it immediately. The choice just sits right in your spirit. You're not second-guessing your decision or thinking about turning back. You realize there are challenges ahead, but you're not looking over your shoulder, wishing you'd gone left instead of right at the last fork in the road. It was with this sweet assurance that I moved ahead with Clive. On the day I signed the contract, all my internal bells and whistles and dancing emojis shouted *yes*.

The transition to Arista provided me with a pause—an opportunity for the seasoning to settle on my creations before I presented them, robust with flavor, to the world. The tentative plan was to roll out the album in 2000. With input from Jeff and Peter about possible new sounds and collaborations I could include, I returned to the studio in a new headspace. Finally, I could exhale and focus solely on creating. It felt like freedom.

I'm often asked where my melodies and lyrics come from. I may never fully comprehend how a song sprouts from nothingness into existence, and truthfully, I'm not tempted to decode the mystery. I hope to be constantly surprised, in amazement of how the tiny seed of a possible chord or lyric miraculously springs to life. That unexplainable process, that alchemy, is part of what separates art from logic and reason. I don't create from a set of rules or formulas. I tap into my true feelings and experiences and allow them to guide me.

Creativity is inherently messy. It's chaotic and nonlinear. It comes to life in fits and starts, disjointed and seemingly random. That chaos, for me, often begins with a fleeting inspiration, a sudden burst of an idea or sound. The spark might come from a line I've read in a novel, a conversation I've overheard, or an abiding sense of calm I've felt during a Sunday stroll through Harlem's Mount Morris Park. In the case of the latter, I might return home, sit down at the piano, and play around with some chords that embody the feeling I've experienced. Or I might hear a beautiful chord in a song and think, *What key is that?* and later try to pick it out on my keyboard. That chord might lead me to a different set of chords, which might later become the foundation for a melody. Other times, I may have some lyrics scribbled down on a random piece of paper, with no idea how they may fit together with notes. I can never predict how the music will come to me. I only know that, once a song has fully revealed itself, its face is somehow a reflection of my experience. To create a great song, my friend, songwriter Van Hunt, has often said, "All you really need is three chords and the truth."

"Troubles" is that kind of truth. In the tunnel of anxiety I navigated in my early months at Columbia, I glimpsed little hope in the distance. The thought of creating a finished album, given the circumstances, completely unnerved me. I was alone a lot that winter. When I felt myself slipping into a dark place, I'd sometimes escape to my mother's place and channel my anxiety into songwriting. The next morning, back at the Harlem apartment, I'd wake up and remember just how lost and confused I was. I'd lay there watching the light stream through the window bars, casting its long and ominous shadows.

"Dear Lord, can you take it away," I wrote out one morning. "This pain in my heart that follows me day by day, and at night it stalks me like the shadows on my wall." Real pain. Real shadows.

Real sentiments that became the lyrics of a song, one I considered titling "A Conversation with God" because it so clearly expressed all of the anxieties and frustrations of that time. The verses were my doubts; the chorus was God speaking.

Once those words came to me, my fingers landed on a trio of chords that seemed to express my mood. I played those chords over and over, hypnotized by the progression. As the song developed, Kerry and I made our way through Harlem, with me clutching a DAT machine to record the sounds of the city—the squeal of sirens, the shouts of bystanders, the roar of traffic along Malcolm X Boulevard, the rumble of the 2 or 3 train underground—to use as background on the recording. "Yeah, I'm going to take it nice and slow!" some guy yelled out. Kerry and I traded a glance, and then a smile, as we both had the same thought: We knew exactly where we could slide that in, which we did.

My dear sister-friend Taneisha and I wrote "The Life" together, with me on piano and her on bass. I'm convinced that, in some other existence, I was a child of the '60s and '70s. The sounds and fashion trends of both eras have always resonated with me. The music is so sonically lush, so layered and interesting, so alive and funky. Artists like Curtis Mayfield and Nina Simone weren't focused on creating a pop hit; their intention was to reflect their surroundings, and that comes through in their songs. I've heard Mayfield's *Super Fly* album a million times, and when I listen to it even now, I'm still blown away by every horn, every guitar string, every roll of the piano keys, every story reverberating through the bass lines. Curtis brought together real musicians, each a master at his or her own instrument. There is no substitute for such a collaboration, no electronic enhancement that can replace the sound of multiple musicians gathered together in one room.

My team and I definitely use modern gear like Pro Tools and drum machines to create a foundation with keyboards and virtual sounds, but on top of that base, we layer in the human element, which gives the music its retro-futuristic feel. Digital equipment has so much to offer, and yet humanity can never be faked. A spirit flows through every drum and guitar, through every note of every chorus. "The Life" was my attempt at capturing that spirit. Kerry and I brought in instrumentalists to create a song that pays musical homage to the neighborhood that raised me.

Sometimes a song's concept is solidified in my mind long before the melody and lyrics come together. When I was still signed with Columbia, I once spent Thanksgiving in North Carolina with Michael Mauldin and his family. After a massive, delicious meal that made me very sleepy, I flopped down on the couch to watch some television. A L'Oréal hair color commercial came on. Toward the end of the ad, the model uttered the brand's trademark slogan: "Because you're worth it." I'd seen that commercial countless times, but for whatever reason in that particular moment, the message struck me—and it was exactly the idea I wanted to convey in a song. Later, in the studio, I put that sentiment to music for a song we called "A Woman's Worth."

During my first months with Columbia, I'd started "Fallin'." I'd wanted to create my own melody, but one with a similar energy to songs from the '60s, something like the Jackson 5 would sing. I can imagine little Michael, throwing back his head onstage, singing about crazy-deep experiences he surely knew nothing about at his age. I messed around with some ideas but nothing seemed to gel, so I set my efforts aside. Meanwhile, I may not have been actively working on the song, but it continued working on me. A piece of a lyric or a couple of notes or chords would come to me here and there while I moved around our makeshift Harlem studio. Fast-forward to my transition to Arista. Kerry and I, as well as Jeff and the label team, all felt the album was still missing something: that one song that would raise the hair on your arms and make people listen. So a few months before my album's release, I pulled out my early draft of "Fallin'."

My relationship with Kerry definitely prompted the lyrics of "Fallin'," and yet the song is more than a testimony to our connection.

What is true in most romances was true in ours: The journey is riddled with curves and U-turns, valleys and mountaintops. One of the many things that initially drew me to Kerry was how wholeheartedly he embraced his responsibilities as a dad. He cared for and provided for his biological son, and he'd also maintained a real fatherly connection with his ex's first son from a previous relationship. Though Kerry's boys didn't live with us, they were around the apartment a lot. As much as I loved having them there, both in the apartment and as a big part of my life, I also found it difficult to balance with everything else I had going on. I was still so young myself, and slipping into the role of stepmother was a lot for me to handle—especially against the backdrop of creating an album while establishing my own sense of independence for the first time.

I also wasn't the greatest communicator then, and neither was Kerry. Growing up in a house where my own voice was seldom the loudest one, I hadn't yet learned how to speak my truth. So if something bothered me, I struggled with articulating that to Kerry, and as I'd done during childhood, I'd escape to my piano or my journal. Then, after months of nursing resentment, my feelings would come crashing to the surface, and following an argument, I'd draw even further inward. I'd then flee to my mother's apartment and stay there for a few days so I could sort out my feelings.

At one point, Kerry and I even broke up for several months and I rented my own place. One minute, the energy and connection between us would be incredible, and the next, we'd be escaping to our own corners. It was hard. It was easy. It was difficult again. Then, just as I'd be on the verge of backing away once more, I'd remember all the things I loved about this man. His desire, always, to protect me. His kind and gracious manner. And especially his spiritual openness. Though I hadn't grown up in a church, my mother, whose parents raised her Catholic, instilled in me an understanding of myself as God's child. And I have always carried with me a deep feeling of connection to and respect for all living things. In a way, because

I wasn't brought up in any one particular tradition, I've had the freedom to explore the thread of truth that I believe runs through all of them.

Kerry, through his own spiritual exploration and our ongoing conversations, expanded my awareness. He exposed me to the universal law of cause and effect—of how the energy we put out always circles back to us. Of how our intentions, words, and actions create our reality. It was Kerry who first opened my eyes to the power of words. "With my luck," I'd often say, "this will never work out." "Why do you always say that?" he finally cut in. "It's just a phrase," I insisted, shrugging it off. Growing up, I'd heard my mother use that phrase repeatedly and I'd adopted it. "You should stop saying that," Kerry told me. It might've sounded like a joke, he explained, but it was actually a reflection of my belief: that things would always turn out badly for me. That I was doomed, no matter what. That my so-called luck would always be unfavorable. And by putting those words out there, I was attracting the energy of failure. What we repeat is who we ultimately become. I banned "with my luck" from my vocabulary.

Our shared interest in these ideas lived at the center of our relationship, but it wasn't the strongest glue. The real magnet was our love for music; that's what powerfully drew us back together over and over. We set aside all else, including any personal disagreements, when it came to our focus on the album. We carried on with making music, even during the most difficult days at Columbia. "Fallin'" is also about that tough chapter—that transition from one label to the next. As good as it felt to sign on with Clive's team, that whole period still brought a lot of uncertainty. When exactly would my album—this set of songs I'd already lived with for so many years—finally debut? What alterations did I still need to make? Would listeners love my baby, my personal work, as much as I'd come to cherish it? "Fallin'" captures the spirit of those questions, of the ups and downs and doubts and unpredictability.

Nothing but uncertainty is certain. Circumstances come together, only to fall apart moments or months later. And then, in a flash, we must rise up and regain our footing. In the rearview mirror, I now see so clearly what escaped me then: It's not that the ground underneath me was suddenly shifting; it's that it is never still. That's part of the work of my journey—getting comfortable with life's groundlessness.

———

The year 2000 ushered in another big change. There was a lot happening behind the scenes: the team at Bertelsmann Music Group (BMG), Arista's parent company, asked Clive to trade his top spot at the label for a position as chairman of worldwide A & R for BMG. If he made that move, however, he would no longer have equity participation in the company and would lose his share in the profits. Clive, blindsided by the request, refused to make that change without continuing in profit shares. To keep from losing him, BMG offered him a historic amount of funding, $150 million, to start his own label, J Records, and that label would be distributed through BMG. Clive was able to take with him ten artists in total—five platinum or multiplatinum artists, and five totally unknown—but there were, of course, some caveats. Those ten artists had to decide on their own whether they'd move, and Clive could not offer them better terms than those in place in their Arista contracts. Arista, however, could sweeten the deal as much as they wanted to entice artists to remain at the label.

At Arista, record executive L.A. Reid took the top spot. Initially, there was no question in my mind which direction I'd take: I'd of course follow Clive to his new label. Peter Edge, who'd supported me from the start of my career, had already followed Clive to J Records. Clive made it abundantly clear that he'd love to continue our partnership and would make me a priority at the new label. Done and done. But then L.A., who years earlier had expressed interest in one day working with me, put a killer financial offer on the table, and that suddenly made my choice feel less straightforward. Jeff, who knew that opportunities like this didn't come up very often, felt strongly about getting the best financial offer while it was in front of us. "Let's go with L.A.," he said to me.

Jeff and I debated for days. I can still feel the below-freezing wind gusts cutting through my jacket and into my bones as I stood out on Fifty-seventh Street, arguing with him about why I wanted to remain with Clive. "Come on," Jeff kept saying, "let's just do the deal with Arista. Clive is great. L.A. is great. Both understand who you are as an artist, so either way, you win professionally. You might as well go with the best deal." As much as I understood and appreciated that logic, and as eager as I was to carve out a Grand Canyon between me and an empty checking account, I didn't feel good about walking away from Clive. He clearly cared about my career; I'd sensed that from our very first meeting. He'd also invested mightily in helping me untangle myself from Columbia. I also felt loyal to Peter, who'd wanted to sign me from the beginning, long before the universe brought us together at Arista. "I'm staying with Clive," I finally told Jeff, who rolled his eyes and threw up his arms. My instincts had led me to sign with Clive, and now, that sixth sense urged me to remain loyal to our partnership. For one of the first times in my relationship with my manager, I refused to be swayed. In the coming years, he'd often say to me, "I will never doubt your instincts."

*Songs in A Minor* was finally given a release date: June 2001. At the new label, Jeff, Peter, Clive and the team immediately began laying the groundwork for a spectacular rollout. In the months leading up to the big debut, they found every opportunity they could to provide me with a stage. They were intent on creating a groundswell of interest by raising my visibility and letting others discover me, one performance at a time. In those days, radio promotion was critical to an album's success, so Clive assembled ten of the country's most influential promoters at his Park Avenue apartment and brought me in to play for them. If he was asked to speak at an industry event, he took me along and talked me up. "To understand who Alicia is as an artist," he'd often say, "you have to see her perform live." And there

I would be, a twenty-year-old with braids and beads, with a large helping of soul and a sprinkle of classical.

———

Ahead of the album's release, I had one last box to check—and the thought of it made the hairs on the back of my neck rise up in unison. One of my songs, "How Come You Don't Call Me," was a cover of a song written by an artist I'd spent my whole childhood idolizing— Prince. Before I could include the cover song on my album, I needed personal permission from a legend who, I'd heard, seldom granted others the okay to use his material. In spring of 2001, I set out to try.

You don't just dial up The Royal One. Jeff first had to connect me with someone on Prince's team, and I'm sure that person then sent us a secret phone number that would disintegrate five seconds after we'd read it. I gathered my courage and dialed the number—which, of course, wasn't Prince's direct line. The nice woman who answered put me on hold before transferring me to another line. Three additional transfers later, I finally heard that raspy, instantly recognizable voice: "Hello?"

"Hi!" I chirped a bit too enthusiastically in an attempt to disguise my shaky voice. *What the hell do I say to one of the most celebrated musicians on the planet?*

"I've been watching what you're doing," he told me.

My heart nearly fell out of my chest. "Really?" I said incredulously.

"Yeah, really," he said. "It's cool. So are you writing and producing your own music?" I told him I was. "That's great," he told me. "Keep that up."

I thanked him for his advice, cleared my throat, and then shifted into the purpose of my call. "So I'm doing a cover of your song, 'How Come U Don't Call Me Anymore,'" I explained. "It's one of my all-time favorite songs, like . . . ever. And, uh, I was wondering if I could use it on my album."

*Silence.*

"Why don't you come play at Paisley Park?" he said.

I paused. "You want *me* to come play at Paisley Park?"

"Sure," he said. "You should come down. I can show you the place, and then you can play the song for me."

Weeks later, I was standing at the outer gates of Prince's gray, concrete, sixty-five-thousand-square-foot fortress in Chanhassen, Minnesota, shivering in the too-thin leather jacket I'd been wearing all winter. A staff member graciously welcomed us at the front door, and moments later, Prince sashayed toward us down a long hall, his heels clicking with each one of his smooth diddy-bop steps. He greeted me with a handshake. "Thanks for coming," he said. "Let me show you around."

Visiting the mansion was like reliving some of the most iconic moments of Prince's illustrious career. The walls were covered with memorabilia, from his old guitars and framed platinum records and sheet music, to the costumes he wore in 1984's *Purple Rain*. In one room sat a grand piano, its top engraved with the lyrics of "How Come U Don't Call Me Anymore." In several other rooms sat even more pianos, all as stunningly unique as their owner. We passed a cage full of cooing white doves, a head nod to one of his most enduring musical creations. At nearly every turn were recording studios and exquisitely designed lounge spaces with overstuffed leather couches. And, as you might expect, there was purple all around. A lot of it.

We rounded the corner into the performance space, a sprawling yet somehow intimate room about the size of a school gymnasium. A couple hundred people—a group of superfans Prince often invited in for performances—were already gathered. Before my backup singers and I began setting up for our sound check, Prince pulled me aside. "I only have one request for you," he said. "No cursing allowed. That's my one ask." "I'll try," I said, nodding and blushing.

Prince sat in the corner, hidden from my view, as I, with my black fedora propped over one eye and my fingertips sweaty on the keyboard, lifted the rafters with my first note of "Fallin'." I played every song on my album, including the one that had brought me to Paisley Park. Afterward, Prince met us backstage in the dressing room. "Great show, great sound," he told us as we beamed. On our way out, he pulled me aside again. "You're going to have to put a dollar in my curse jar," he said, a grin spreading across his pale face. No, I hadn't dropped the f-bomb, but I had committed a couple of minor infractions. I laughed and thanked him, and he saw me out. Later, back at the hotel, I did not sleep a wink. *What just happened to me? Is it really over? Can I go back?* I did not want my dream trip to end.

Prince was gracious enough to grant me the right to use his song, but that wasn't the greatest permission he extended. With his very presence, his wild sense of individualism, and his determination to define himself in a world eager to do that for you, Prince stood for self-ownership. He stood for conscious and full-throated defiance. He stood for freedom and creative expression, for rule-breaking, rule-making, and imagination. And that summer as I stepped onto the grandest stage of my lifetime, Prince stood, in spirit, with me.

# 6

## WORLD STAGE

### CLIVE DAVIS, LEGENDARY RECORD EXECUTIVE AND ALICIA'S MENTOR

In February 2001, a few months before the release of *Songs in A Minor*, I hosted my pre-Grammy gala, the three-hour show I put on every year. It's the hottest ticket in town, filled with A-listers from across the entertainment world. "I've got good news and I've got bad news," I said to Alicia before the gathering. "The good news is, I don't traditionally include new artists at my gala, but I'm going to create a best new artist category and ask you to sing." She was thrilled. "And what's the bad news?" she asked. "Angie Stone is performing right before you, and one of her selections incorporates a sampling of 'Neither One of Us,' the great Gladys Knight song. Gladys will be in the audience, and I'll ask her to come up and join Angie on her rendition of the song. The bad news is that I can't let Gladys leave the stage without doing 'Midnight Train to Georgia.' I'll of course introduce Gladys as one of the all-time greats, right up there with Aretha and Streisand, and after she sings, it seems to me a wonderful time to go from a legend to a brand-new artist. So you're going to follow Gladys Knight." It's a measure of Alicia's confidence, grace, and maturity that she said, "I get it, and I'll just have to do the absolute best that I can. I'll give you my best." Gladys, of course, brought down the house. And then Alicia got up onstage and gave a riveting, breathtaking performance of "Fallin'" that brought the crowd to its feet. Not only was she creatively brilliant—she was also her own best ambassador.

Classical music has always given me the shakes. Even as a child, whenever I had to perform an intricate Bach or Chopin or Brahms composition, I'd work myself into a tizzy, rehearsing feverishly for hours, the whole time fearing I'd freeze up at showtime. Once on stage for the recital, there I'd sit, hands quivering and feet shaking on the pedals, racing through the labyrinth of opening notes as Mom and Nana and Fafa held their breath and willed me to stay on course. After I made it through the first measure, I could usually relax a little. And over the years during any performance that included a classical piece, I even learned to breathe my way through the full experience and enjoy it. But in June 2001, as I stepped onto the stage above all stages—the set of *The Oprah Winfrey Show*—my tremors returned.

Just a few months earlier, "Fallin'" had been released but soon ran into resistance. We first released it to R & B—but even in the urban market, the song wasn't getting nearly as much airtime as we'd hoped. And it had to break through in urban before pop would even consider it. The reception among listeners was mixed: People didn't quite know what to make of my sound, which had a retro soul, throwback feel to it. My opening measures of "Fallin'" brought a certain visual to mind: a jazz crooner from a bygone era, maybe a Billie Holiday or Etta James type, singing about a long lost lover. Radio DJs didn't quite get it, and they played the song less and less as time went on.

Clive moved quickly to intervene. He had every incentive to ensure that my lead single and the forthcoming album struck lightning. *Songs in A Minor* was not only the launch of my solo career—it also had the potential to further establish the reputation of Clive's new venture, J Records. A lot was riding on this moment for both of us. So with the combination of zeal and determination that fueled Clive's rise to the top of his industry, he decided to do something he'd never done for any other artist. He asked Oprah to book me on her show.

Clive had known Oprah for years, and yet he didn't just pick up the phone. Instead, he penned a persuasive letter, one in which he referred to me as "so special, so unique and clearly an 'all timer' that I felt I really must personally bring her to your attention." He realized, he explained, that Oprah usually showcased established artists, which was understandable. But he proposed that she do for up-and-coming musicians what she had already done for so many first-time authors: provide them with a platform for connecting with her millions of viewers. And yes, he wanted her to feature me, the twenty-one-year-old classical pianist with shaky hands, right at center stage.

Clive realized that, like others, Oprah needed to see me perform in order to truly take in my whole vibe. So along with his letter, he enclosed a video, one that featured me at the piano with my full passion and artistry on display.

In response to the letter, the show's executive producer called Clive. Oprah had watched the video and wanted to have me on the show, the producer explained, but her team was developing the show's concept. As they talked through possibilities, Clive suggested building an episode around the crop of rising neo-soul artists like Jill Scott, India.Arie, and me. He hadn't worked with Jill or India but admired them both greatly. The producer, who liked the approach, later widened the scope by adding some gospel singers to the lineup: Yolanda Adams and Mary Mary.

Meanwhile, I had no idea the stars were aligning in my favor. On the afternoon Jeff told me that Clive had booked me on *Oprah*, and that my performance of "Fallin'" would close out the show, I just about passed out.

"I'm playing my song on Oprah's show?" I kept asking, to be sure I'd heard him correctly.

"Yes," he said, beaming. "And it's next week."

Let me take you back to 2001—the year when Oprah's show was already fifteen seasons into its twenty-five-season run at number one in the ratings. There was no stage more powerful, no cultural touchstone that compared. Movements were launched on Oprah's set. The book publishing industry was revolutionized. Wild dreams took flight, ugly tears were shed, Favorite Things were handed out to scores of squealing audience members. And stitched right into the show's DNA was a quest for truth, for lightbulb moments and epiphanies that altered the trajectories of those who tuned in. It was a daily collective gathering at the well, an hour when mothers, daughters, sisters, friends, and more than a few woke men came together from every corner of the globe.

I'd grown up watching Oprah after school, in between homework and piano practice, and it was always on at my Nana's house. But you didn't need to see the show every day to feel a part of its magic; it spilled over into the headlines and reverberated through kitchen-table conversation and hair salon gabfests. And I was about to become part of that phenomenon. *Heart, be still. Fingers too.*

The universe was clearly on my side because it sent me a small miracle: I got to meet Oprah before showtime. When Clive had first connected with Oprah's producer, she'd asked him, "How good is Alicia in person?" Clive assured her I was a compelling live performer. She took him at his word, and as a result, Oprah invited me to sing at a dinner she was hosting for a group of her major national advertisers. The gathering in Chicago was a few days ahead of my big appearance. When I arrived, Oprah's warm "Hey, girl!" greeting immediately took the edge off my nervousness—but only the top edge. I made it through that evening without a hiccup, and the crowd embraced my performance, and yet the real test awaited soon after. More than anything, I wanted to rise to the moment—to honor the opportunity I'd been given with a performance worthy of Oprah's stage.

Still a tomboy at heart, I pulled together my version of a Sunday-best outfit: a tux jacket with satin penguin wings. I'd had my hair freshly done for the occasion, in my signature zigzag cornrows, finished off with beads cascading down my back. In my sparkly Cesare Paciotti sneakers, I stepped foot on the set, one of the first I'd been on. I peered around, hardly stopping to blink, with one thought reeling through my head: *I'm literally inside of the television right now.* That's just how brand-new I was.

As I took my seat at the piano and placed my hands on the keys, the shakes made their debut. I was smiling on the outside, but my insides were screaming, *What the hell is happening?!* I inhaled deeply and began with Beethoven's "Für Elise," doing all I could to stave off the trembles. With each passing measure, I could feel the stress exiting from my fingertips as I thought, *Just get through one more bar.* And then another. And then another. I hit the opening chord for "Fallin'" and a momentary hush fell over the audience. I then leaned back, closed my eyes, summoned my first note from the farthest corner of my soul, and sang into the microphone, "I keep on fallin' . . . *iiiiin* . . ." That's when the universe took over.

Something supernatural happens when you give in to the energy of a song. You momentarily forget you're performing and you just lean into the music's vibration. There you sit, curled up in the notes, allowing them to lift you heavenward. That was my experience. On Oprah's public stage, I had a private hallelujah moment. Never mind that millions were watching; I was just gone, ascending to someplace beyond the stars. As the spirit took hold, it transported me back to my mother's living room, to an afternoon when I played at my battered upright, amazed at music's inexplicable power. What pulled me back to the present was the audience's applause.

Afterward, Oprah joined me onstage.

"You've been writing your own music since you were fourteen?" she asked me.

"Fourteen," I repeated. "Definitely. There was no other path for me. I knew this was my path. I had to follow it."

"I noticed that you wrote and produced every single song on that CD, except for Prince's," she said. I nodded and grinned.

"That is *amazing!*" she declared with her trademark enthusiasm, sprinkling her fairy godmother stardust in my direction. "Your first CD!"

I blushed. "It's important for me to properly express how I feel at the moment and not have it filtered through other people," I told her. "It just feels natural for me to just say how I feel at the moment. . . ."

"And to be in charge of your life!" Oprah responded. "Oh, you're a woman after my own heart!" She then threw her arm around my shoulders and faced the red blinking light of the camera. "Okay, Alicia Keys!" she said as the credits rolled and the audience cheered. "Thanks, Clive!"

Not long after, the heavens parted. *Songs in A Minor* debuted at number one on the charts, selling 263,000 copies in the first week, another 450,000 copies in its second, and eventually more than 16 million copies around the world. "Fallin'" went from struggling at radio to climbing into the top position on the charts. During the show, Oprah was spotted singing along to "Fallin'." The world took her cue and gave the song a place in the sun. And I, the Hell's Kitchen girl carrying a dream twice my size, stood in gratitude as the wonder unfolded.

———

"Aren't you Alicia Keys?" an eightysomething-year-old white man leaned in and whispered to me. I was on my flight home to New York after Oprah's show, still in my dream state and floating high above the thirty thousand feet our plane had climbed to.

"Yes," I said, trying to recall where I'd met this man. He cleared up the mystery: "I just saw you on the *Oprah* show!"

That sentence heralded my entrance into the strange land called Fame. There was no easing into this new country; the transformation was at once rapid and surprising. The morning before my *Oprah* appearance, I'd been a relatively unknown artist who'd spent years composing and polishing my album. The very same day, my stroll through the airport spurred a hundred head turns as I wondered why people were suddenly staring at me. It felt like the moment in *Dreamgirls* when, seemingly overnight, the group leaps from obscurity to center stage. What happens in the movies isn't supposed to happen in real life. And yet it is exactly what happened to me.

If I'd been under the impression that only a certain segment of the world's population tuned into Oprah's show, that notion was flatly overturned. The variety of people who approached me proved just how enormous and varied the show's cross-section of viewers were: young and old, male and female, Latina and Asian, black and white, rural and urban. Some just gawked but didn't say anything. Others asked for my autograph. Many more came up to me exclaiming, hand over mouth, some version of the refrain I'd hear repeatedly in the coming months: "Oh my gosh—I just saw you on *Oprah*!"

I remember the first time I tried to walk around my old neighborhood. At Mom's apartment, I threw on my sweats and wandered out onto Eighth Avenue, probably in search of my fake ID place because I (still) hadn't reached my twenty-first birthday. I got two steps out of the building's revolving door before a deliveryman, there to take up someone's lunch, stopped, set down his bag, and exclaimed, "You were on TV last week!" From that moment to the time I arrived at the little shop, seemingly every person did a double take upon spotting me. The zigzag chunky braids were a giveaway, and once I got hip to that, I tried disguising myself under a hat and big sunglasses that covered two-thirds of my face. The ploy didn't work, and in fact, it made it super obvious I was hiding. One woman marched up to me and said, "Is that Alicia Keys under that hat?" Busted.

This sea change felt as thrilling as it did humbling. On most days, I glided around in a happiness high, a giddiness brought on by triumph's sweet elixir. The accolades poured in, each one more incredible than the last. That September, I was invited to perform "Fallin'" at the Metropolitan Opera House in Manhattan's Lincoln Center for the *MTV Video Music Awards*. For its November issue, *Rolling Stone* hailed me "The Next Queen of Soul" and put me on its cover in a cropped T-shirt proudly displaying my city's name, as a tribute to New York right after 9/11. The following January, my album's second single, "A Woman's Worth," made it into the top ten on the charts.

For me, the utter elation of this whole period came from the world's embrace of my creation, my music. No feeling compares to having others love what you love, and then enthusiastically sharing it with others. Fame for the sake of fame had never been the dream. But spreading light is a pleasure I'll always live for.

Kerry was on cloud (forty) nine. Even prior to the six years we'd spent creating, shaping, and refining *Songs in A Minor,* he'd been in search of his own unique place in music's universe. The year the album hit, he was overjoyed to at last celebrate the strong sense of fulfillment brought on by his work on the album.

"You know that song you wrote with Alicia?" fans would often say to him after noticing his name in the credits. "That song changed my life." What's far more satisfying than being known is feeling purposeful. That was true for both of us.

————

Soon after *Songs in A Minor* dropped, I went on tour with Maxwell, the neo-soul prince with the buttery-smooth vocals. Our twenty-five-date, fourteen-city tour kicked off in New York and looped its way through cities including Chicago, Atlanta, and Minneapolis. Maxwell, of course, was the main event. I, the newbie on the ticket, warmed up the crowd by opening the show with a medley from my album.

When your album rockets to the top of the charts, you're not instantly loaded. While on the Maxwell tour, I was still living on the advance money I'd received years earlier upon signing with Columbia. I'd also gotten a payment when I transitioned to Arista, but because Clive had to spend so much to get me out of my old deal, my second advance was relatively modest. With my earnings from the Maxwell tour, as well as my own tour to follow in the spring of 2002, my income had increased enough to make me financially comfortable. But not as wealthy as some might imagine.

Enter the world of commissions—that percentage of royalties that managers, lawyers, agents, and other handlers earn as part of their professional partnership with an artist. At the time, I had no idea just how much of my pay wasn't making it into my savings account. In part, that was because I was allowing others to commission me on my pre-tax, pre-expense gross income. So if I made 100 dollars, 30 or more of those dollars might go to commissions. With the 70 dollars I had left, I then had to cover all expenses that came with managing my tour and my business, plus settle up with Uncle Sam. You've heard the tragic stories of musicians whose tours grossed millions, and yet they somehow end up without a pot to piss in. How does that happen? It happens when you take your eye off the intricacies of your business; and when you know better, you hopefully do better. Those early years taught me how to do better real fast.

I've always been financially conservative. My mother worked hard for her money and spent it carefully, and she taught me to do the same. The music equipment that I'd invested in after signing the deal with Columbia had been my first major purchase. Later, after finally getting my driver's license at eighteen, I leased a gold Mazda 626 in order to get around. A few years into our work on the first album, Kerry and I had outgrown his one-bedroom crib, not to mention that our three a.m. jam sessions were annoying the hell out of the neighbors. That reality coincided with my desire for some space of a different kind: a little breathing room in our relationship during a time when we were working through some challenges. So Kerry kept the apartment, and I moved over the bridge to Jersey.

I immediately regretted that decision, because the daily toll to cross the George Washington Bridge took a big bite out of my budget at the time. A few months later, I moved into a family's basement in Ozone Park, Queens—and that gave me a toll-free ride over the Queensboro Bridge. I stayed there for a hot minute before Kerry and I reconnected and, together, relocated to a small house in Rosedale, Queens. I used my Arista advance to purchase that house, which had enough space for us to both live and work. The equipment, the Mazda, the home—all were smart investments in getting my album off the ground.

*Songs in A Minor* improved my financial picture, but it didn't significantly change how I handled my money. Every *ka-ching* triggered in me a long-held fear, followed by a question: *If all this suddenly goes away, have I saved enough to be okay?* I'd seen how quickly circumstances could shift, as fast as they once had when my mother lost her father and the family's breadwinner. And I was determined not to end up as the penniless bag lady, the former star whose downward spiral left her in dire financial straits. So in the early days of my career, I was very, very careful with cash. And when I did buy something for myself, I never went for flashy; in place of $5,000 designer boots or Bentleys, I opted for white T-shirts and Timbs I could get for cheap on 125th Street.

I'll never forget the first time I went to Bergdorf Goodman, the luxury department store on Fifth Avenue in Manhattan. Erika, my childhood friend who later worked on my team as my day-to-day manager, was with me. Following the album and tour, I'd just received my first major check; I deposited it and didn't touch it for weeks.

"You should go shopping!" Erika urged me. I reluctantly agreed. *It can't hurt to look,* I figured. And maybe it was time for a small indulgence.

If you've ever roamed the aisles of Bergdorf's, then you understand how forcefully desire can grab you by the throat. You quickly go from swearing you don't need a single thing to lusting after designer sneakers you hadn't even known existed before the moment you spotted them. Within a half hour in the store, I'd picked out a pair of shoes, a leather jacket, a scarf, and a killer belt. When the lady at the counter announced the total—"That will be $3,482," she said without blinking—I looked blankly at her.

"I'm putting all of this back," I whispered to Erika as I scooped up the items and left the register. "This is ridiculous," I said. "I can't pay this much."

"Come on," Erika pressed. "You should do something nice for yourself for once." I stared at her but didn't respond. "Do you love these?" she asked, picking up the sneakers I'd just propped back up onto their display stand. I nodded. "Well, if you really love them," she went on, "you should buy them. It's time to celebrate a little."

I ultimately bought two of the five items—the high-top sneak-ers and the leather jacket—and for days after the purchase, I was in turmoil. Not just because I'd still spent over a thousand dollars, an insane amount, in my view. But also because I should've gotten that belt. Months later when I went back for it, the item had been discontinued.

Erika wasn't pushing me to live beyond my means. Rather, she was nudging me toward a different mind-set, a mentality that was foreign to me. I'd grown up in survival mode, clutching tightly to every dollar that came my way. And when you spend from a belief that every cent you earn will be your last, you operate from a place of scarcity—a context that runs counter to the energy of abundance. Money, like all life, is an energy exchange. You give yourself over to whatever you're passionate about, and what comes back to you is en-ergy in the form of monetary compensation. You attract more or less of what you want by how you choose to interact with it, as well as what you believe about yourself. Do you truly feel you deserve what you're asking for? Are you worth it? How you answer impacts what comes your way.

None of this means you should foolishly squander your paycheck in Bergdorf's. Rather, it's about seeing money through a spiritual lens rather than a physical one. Erika, who'd always been as connected to the spiritual side of life as Kerry is, understood this principle. Her parents were entrepreneurs who ran a successful headhunting firm and had exposed her to smart spending and investing strategies; as an adult on her own journey, she'd also come to understand money management based on the universal law of attraction: What you fo-cus on expands. If you focus on the goodness in your life, you create more of it. And if you live with an open palm rather than a closed fist, you leave room for immeasurable blessings to flow through your hands. It was one of the strongest lessons Erika passed on to me in the classroom my life was becoming.

Speaking of lessons, I collected another one during my first tour: Let your mother be your mother and never your assistant. When I brought Mom on board to help me on the road, she was so fiercely protective of me that I began jokingly calling her my bulldog. She'd go off on a publicist who was insisting that I do one last round of interviews after I'd already done ten of them. She clearly wasn't aiming to collect a Miss Congeniality award; her sole mission was to guard my space. I appreciated her mama bear instinct, but to keep from offending everyone in the industry, I had to ask her to chill.

"So am I fired?" she asked, grinning. She wasn't, at least not right away. For me, the turning point came when I watched my beautiful mother crawl into one of those tiny lower pods on our tour bus. *Why the hell do I have my mom in a bunk bed?* I thought. It didn't feel right. Nor did our arrangement as mother and assistant. We eventually both realized that we were better at being family than we were at being colleagues. And that meant hiring an assistant who hadn't given birth to me.

———

In December 2001, I received an early Christmas present: I was nominated for not just one Grammy, but six of them, including one for "Fallin'" as Song of the Year. Jon Stewart was tapped to host the ceremony at the STAPLES Center in Los Angeles. And I, still floating someplace above the atmosphere upon hearing of the nominations, was asked to perform.

I was battling the flu on the day of the show, but I willed myself out of bed. I wasn't about to miss my first Grammys, even if my face crashed right down onto the piano keys. My voice was hoarse, much too raspy to make it through the opening notes of "Fallin'." I was freaking out. So that morning, a doctor gave me a vitamin B12 shot right in the ass, the long needle stinging me so badly that I cupped my hand over my mouth as he pulled it out. I don't know whether the dose of B12 had anything to do with it, but my voice was restored, at least temporarily.

Even with the recovery of my voice, my brain felt caught between a sick fog and a dream fog throughout the whole day, a heady exhilaration mixed with the haziness brought on by meds. The iconic stylist Patti Wilson dressed me. Even with my foggy brain, I held on to the clear idea I'd had from the beginning: I wanted to mix a dress with jeans, a combo of street and glam that reflected my vibe. Patti got my vision immediately. She draped me in a sea-foam green Christian Dior slip dress overlaying a white T and jeans. My makeup artist finished off the look by super-gluing jewels on my eyelids. I loved the touch of bling, but those fake diamonds were heavy as hell! If you look closely at the footage of me onstage, I looked like I'd developed a sudden case of sleepy-eye. I could barely keep my lids open.

My trip down the red carpet shifted the day's surrealism into fifth gear. As I made my way through, I couldn't believe I was there. All around me were the stars, including powerhouse artists Celine Dion, Mary J. Blige, Patti LaBelle, and Gwen Stefani. For years I'd been inspired by their work, and it felt so strange to have them greet me with "Hey, Alicia!" I was like, *How do you even know who I am?* The entire experience was as if I were suddenly being inducted into a society club that I'd never officially pledged. I have no clue what I said to anyone. My body was there, but my head was someplace else. I had that same inside-the-TV-feeling I'd experienced on Oprah's set.

Pure bliss—that's the only way I can describe performing "Fallin'" as some of the greatest musicians of all time sang along from the audience. My flamenco-infused performance medley was lifted by the talents of Joaquín Cortés, who danced alongside me as I played and sang, struggling to keep my lids from snapping shut, half high from the mix of adrenaline and flu meds—and pretty sure I was forgetting some of the dozens of flamenco steps we'd practiced so hard beforehand. We all come into the world blessed with a unique gift. And I've always known that dancing will never be mine. I can move, I can groove, I can float, I can vibe, but I was never meant to be out there on stage doing dozens of orchestrated moves with twenty dancers behind me. It's not my thing. Yet there I was, sharing the stage with a world-class flamenco badass, and though I flubbed a few moves, I was *not* about to mess up my moment.

Before the ceremony, I'd already won two awards off camera. And then, in the arena that night, my name was called again. And again. And again, for a total of five of the six Grammys I'd been nominated for. When my name was announced as the winner of the Best R & B Album award, I rose and walked to the stage, both ecstasy and sheepishness on my face. What new artist wins five awards after just one album? Given the extraordinarily talented musicians who were nominated alongside me, my series of wins felt unbelievable to me, even otherworldly.

"This award right here, I'm very honored for," I said with my hand over my heart and my palm clutching the golden gramophone. "I would like to dedicate this to just thinking out of the box—to just not being afraid to be who you are no matter what anybody says."

Coloring outside the lines is what had led to that stage, along with another force far greater: providence. Part of my journey, as I see it, has been guided by Spirit. It's a rickety upright that suddenly becomes available in the spring of 1987. It's a vocal coach who spots a girl group and mentions them to his brother. It's a teenage dreamer, roaming the streets of the Village and crossing paths with someone who will share in her musical destiny. Some might call it coincidence. I call it divine order.

# 7

## DIARY NOTES

**LEIGH BLAKE, COFOUNDER OF KEEP A CHILD ALIVE,
ALICIA'S FIRST NONPROFIT**

Music, not fame, has always come first for Alicia. When she and I sat together on a plane ride back from South Africa, we talked a lot about the madness of celebrity—the mobs of screaming fans, the onslaught of attention. She appreciated the world's embrace of her music, but she was struggling with what that meant for her personal space. Keep a Child Alive, the nonprofit we started in 2003, gave Alicia a way to use her extraordinary platform as a force for good. To travel to Africa in your early twenties, to meet people there who radiate incredible strength and kindness amid such great suffering, and then to return home with a strong mission for how you can have an impact—that fed Alicia. It also imbued her fame with a profound sense of purpose.

Fame comes in many colors. One is an electric purple, the shade of vibrant euphoria that fell over me when *Songs in A Minor* reverberated. That initial rush of exhilaration eventually morphed into another color, a drab gray, a sense of overwhelming intrusion and the slipping away of privacy and stillness. I vacillated constantly between the two hues: the exultation and deep gratitude that came with people connecting with me and my music, and the frenzy brought on by the applause. Amid this seesaw of realities, my instinct was always to hide my gray zone from the world. Until now.

Sometime between my first album and my second, I began grappling with an existence that felt so strange to me. Imagine if, for two decades, you'd been going to the same grocery store, filling your cart with produce while minding your business. Now imagine one afternoon going into that same store and having literally every person, from the shoppers to the cashiers, staring hard as you pick out your strawberries. At first, you might stand there feeling a mix of delight and disbelief at others' curiosity. But if that scene played out month after month, not just in your supermarket but in every public place you visited, the novelty would soon wear off. You'd be no less thankful for the love, but you might find yourself yearning for sweet anonymity, that time when you'd been able to roll out, undetected, in your raggedy sweats, blissfully oblivious to all but the beats pumping through your earbuds. This loss of anonymity became my new normal—my gray zone.

Every person who lives under this microscope deals with this reality, this grayness of the glory, in his or her own way. I was the girl accustomed to disappearing for hours in Joplin's ragtimes or immersing myself in my diary, and I initially pulled back from the recognition. And yet that desire to step away was at odds with an urge just as powerful in me: the desire to be liked, to be seen as the nice girl, to accommodate others even if that meant dismissing my own needs. That tendency had been years in the making, sprouting up in two very fertile conditions: a childhood spent as a chameleon, shifting constantly to keep my mother more calm than fiery; and a world in which women, for generations, have been conditioned into voicelessness where their opinions are cast aside dismissively, the expectation being that they accommodate others and put their own needs last.

My boundaries were weak during this period. When my team filled every possible space on my calendar and left me hardly any personal time, I didn't know how to push back, to say no, to advocate more strongly for myself. If a fan asked me for a photo after I'd already taken thirty, I almost always agreed, mostly because declining felt selfish. How could I turn away from the very people who'd so wholeheartedly supported my work? Not easily.

The spotlight came with another unexpected glare: self-scrutiny. After the first album's success thrust me into the public square, some began questioning my sexuality.

"Man, she's got such a hard edge," one commentator remarked. "Is she gay?" If I were, I'd be proudly waving my rainbow flag. In fact, though I am not gay, I wave that flag in solidarity. And yet others' assessment led me to question how I came across. Few people ever consistently see their own reflection mirrored back, in full color, on television. It can be jarring at first. I'd sometimes view my press interviews, like my first appearance on Jay Leno, and dissect my performance. *Could I have spoken more softly? Should I have put on a dress or worn my hair straight? Would that have made me look more feminine?* The impulse to change myself—to try to tuck in a backside that clearly didn't conform to someone else's expectation of how I should appear—awakened from its slumber.

The image on the cover of *Songs in A Minor* captures my essence. I'm rocking a green wide-brimmed hat (hats have always been my thing—they just work for me), my head cocked to one side, rows of big beads adorning my long braids, hands on my hips, a black leather coat and green-striped cropped blouse. When I arrived at the shoot for that cover, Patti Wilson, the same iconic stylist who'd dressed me for the Grammys, had assembled all this chiffon and bows.

"I don't wear bows," I told her. I was clear about who I was. I got myself. So we went in a direction that reflected my vibe. It's '70s bohemian with an urban twist. It's hippie 'hood, the concrete jungle version of a free spirit, a flower child minus the flowers. I'm dressed, but I don't look like I've tried too hard. It's simple and never over the top. It's raw and real and fresh and The Original Me, edition

1.0. And it's a visual truth that, in the coming years, I'd find myself drifting away from little by little, a half centimeter at a time.

———

Leigh Blake orchestrated two seminal experiences of my twenties. First, she connected me with Bono, the one-name rock legend with a heart even more golden than his pipes. Second, Leigh lifted my gaze toward a world, over the horizon, that I knew little about.

Leigh is an unstoppable force, a mighty hurricane of passion. The feisty five-two South Londoner has, for decades, possessed a fervor and resolve to halt Africa's AIDS pandemic. She'd first befriended Bono back in 1990, during her creation of *Red Hot + Blue,* the first AIDS benefit to be aired on US television. In 2001, Leigh had a fresh idea for how she and Bono could partner on another campaign. Why not shine a light on the AIDS crisis by bringing together a group of successful musicians to remake Marvin Gaye's 1971 hit classic "What's Going On"? Bono, of course, loved the concept. Proceeds from the single, which were to be released just ahead of World AIDS Day that December 1, would help fund health clinics across Africa. A who's who of more than forty artists—from Justin Timberlake, Christina Aguilera, and Michael Stipe to Jennifer Lopez, Nas, and Destiny's Child— agreed to take part. After *Songs in A Minor* debuted, Leigh invited me, through Peter Edge, to participate. *For a great cause involving a version of one of my idol's all-time most riveting social anthems? Sign me up.*

At the studio session in New York, I adored Bono from our first hello. That man just exudes coolness. The way he holds your gaze, the ease and humility with which he pokes fun at himself, the warmth and graciousness of his manner—it all made him immediately feel like the brother to me that he has now become. Once our recording session had ended, I stuck around to talk with Leigh about her and Bono's work in Africa. Leigh spoke with zeal and conviction about how HIV was threatening the existence of an entire continent, and how we, a community of artists, could change that. I was so moved by her words and warrior spirit that, as I left,

I said to her, "Anything you want me to do for this issue, I will do."
I don't know from where, inside of me, that sentence rose up. I can
only tell you that I meant it.

I soon got swept up in my tour, but Leigh and I stayed in touch.
In 2002, as my time on the road was winding down, MTV invited
me to be part of *Staying Alive,* an HIV awareness initiative and char-
ity concert in Cape Town, South Africa. The event was to be recorded that November and broadcast on World AIDS Day. Ahead of
the trip, I told Leigh I'd be visiting Africa for the first time.

"Mind if I join you there and show you what the AIDS pandemic
has done on that continent?" she asked. I agreed.

What I witnessed on that trip will forever be seared in my memory. Leigh guided me through a series of clinics nestled in the Soweto
townships just outside of Johannesburg. As we entered the first clinic,
a group of young mothers, each stricken with the dual scourges of
HIV-positive status and extreme poverty, sat cradling their newborns. In their villages, none of these first-time mothers had been
taught that their own breast milk, the gift nature had graced them
with for nurturing their young, carried the same incurable virus that
had wreaked havoc on their immune systems. In these women's eyes,
I saw desperation. I saw fear. And I also saw hope. Hope that I—a
singer from the other side of the planet, from a land of extraordinary
wealth—would surely offer them help.

"What can I do?" I asked, though the answer seemed obvious.
One mother stared at me, tears brimming in her lower lids, and
whispered, "We just need the medicine. That is all. Please help us
get the drugs." Only the wealthiest South Africans could ever dream
of having access to the antiretrovirals that reduce the risk of mother-
to-baby transmission. Without these medications, the women and
their children would die. They could barely afford consistent meals,
much less medication that can cost hundreds of dollars per dose. I
was in total shock that medicine that could save someone's life would
be available, but just not to the people most in need of the help. That
injustice pissed me off. It still does. It's a human rights issue.

On another stop, children who'd lost their parents to AIDS gathered around me by the dozens. With their mothers and fathers gone, the eldest orphans—some just seven or ten or fourteen—had been forced to raise and provide for their younger siblings, even as they struggled with the physical hardships of living with a disease that comes with a crippling social stigma. I, then just twenty-one, saw my younger self in their innocent brown faces. *What if this was happening to me? What if no one cared or listened or helped?* I learned that 50 percent of all the world's children who live with HIV have no access to treatment. And after watching one or both of their parents succumb to AIDS, these children are left with even more agony: raising themselves and their brothers and sisters while grappling with the overwhelming loss.

In Soweto, Leigh introduced me to Carol Dynasty—or "Mum Carol," as she is affectionately called by the scores of children who rely on her as a surrogate mother. Witnessing the heartache brought on by AIDS is what first moved Carol to tears, and then to action. She and her classmates were once among those who marched, rallied, shouted, and prayed in the streets of Soweto during the 1976 antiapartheid student uprisings. Years later, after training in community development, she felt the call to channel her fire in a new way: opening her arms to the thousands of children devastated by HIV/AIDS. When a child loses his or her parents, how can that child financially support a family? The lack of money makes these children prime targets for sexual exploitation, as both girls and boys are forced into prostitution; many of them also become homeless. Mum Carol's heartbreak over these children's predicament is what eventually led her to create Ikageng Itireleng AIDS Ministry, a Soweto-based AIDS center that has opened its doors to more than two thousand vulnerable children. It's more than a ministry. It's a community where these girls and boys can be seen, heard, and nurtured as their tiny shoulders buckle under the weight of an unfathomable burden.

I will always remember Cecy. On the evening when I met the

fourteen-year-old girl, she was gathered in a small circle, the kind of group Mum Carol brings together frequently. These circles come from the African tradition of gathering around a tree to solve problems together. Mum Carol's circles provide a place where children can openly share their problems, their fears, their hurts. In life, most are completely on their own, but in these circles, they are for once not alone. "Both of my parents are gone," said Cecy. Her voice trembled as she spoke. Her eyes filled with water as one tear slid down her smooth, dark brown cheek. "I don't have money," she said, squelching back sobs. Then, without a single word or the need for one, Mum Carol, who was sitting at Cecy's side, clasped the girl's hand and drew her close, the way my own mother and Nana often did when I was a girl. In that moment, this pandemic became personal for me. Mum Carol hadn't been able to turn away from these children's suffering. And in the presence of sweet Cecy, and amid all the other powerful stories I heard that day of those who'd lost loved ones, neither could I.

Being there with those women and children broke my heart even as it forced open my eyelids. I knew I had to intervene. I couldn't un-see what I'd seen. I couldn't just fly home, carry on with the conveniences of my world, and choose to forget the way those women and children looked at me. Leigh told me she'd already been exploring how to get antiretroviral drugs into the hands of Africa's poorest residents.

"If you can create a blueprint for how to do that," I told her, "I'll be with you all the way."

Keep a Child Alive (KCA) opened its doors in 2003. Even before my adventure through the foothills of Jo'Burg, Leigh had been working on both the concept for a nonprofit and a television campaign— one that would rally Americans to donate just one dollar a day, less than the price of a cup of coffee, toward the cost of nutritious food, medicine, and basic care for impoverished families in Kenya. That crusade caught fire, and within months, the Kenyan clinic we'd partnered with had adequate resources to care for their community. The effort became our case study, our proof that this kind of intervention works. It was based on that model of success that Leigh and I launched KCA.

As we set up partnerships with clinics across the continent, I returned to Africa on many occasions. And each visit to this land of unparalleled beauty brought me face-to-face with some of the most spiritual, creative, and resilient people I have ever encountered. I learned more about how this disease had altered life itself in sub-Saharan Africa: Seventy percent of those living with HIV are in this region, which also represents 66 percent of the 5,700 new infections across the continent every day.

The frightening numbers extend well beyond Africa, and they disproportionately affect women. A young woman becomes infected with HIV Every. Single. Minute. According to the World Health Organization, AIDS—not cancer or heart disease or stroke—is the number one cause of death globally for women of reproductive age. Many of these women leave a legacy of heartbreak and infection to their orphaned children.

Treatment can dramatically alter this picture—that is what working in this space has shown me. KCA has teamed up with nine grassroots organizations throughout Africa and India, another continent devastated by AIDS. But it's not enough for us to just drop off medicine and food. To have the kind of long-term, ongoing impact that we're working to create, you've gotta treat not just the disease, but the whole person. You've gotta teach women how to reduce the risk of transmitting the virus to their beloved newborns, because when you empower a woman, you lift her entire family and community.

While I was finding my way into the music business at age fourteen, thousands of girls that same age had already had their communities nearly wiped out by HIV. Thousands more, still children themselves, were heroically rising up to save the babies left behind. Fame, it has been said, is a trip. But it's a journey worth taking if its ultimate destination is service. This spotlight of fame is about more than me and my music—it is also about using the megaphone I've been handed to advocate, with everything in me, for the voiceless. It's about spending my celebrity currency on a cause greater than my own comfort. It's about remembering that the greatest joy comes not in receiving, but in extending grace to others.

————

Even when you're using your platform for good, there's enormous pressure to keep that spotlight burning strong. Success is a hungry tiger, always growling for its next meal. And the more that tiger eats, the more ravenous it becomes. That's the dynamic in play when a new musician releases a successful record. Fans inhale that music in one sitting, and even before the next round of songs can be prepared, the public is already standing by, panting and sniffing for a fresh plate of dinner. The record companies understand this, and they're of course eager to capitalize on the public's craving by pushing artists back into the studio. I got my biggest shove at the start of 2003, soon after my return from South Africa. Time to put away my passport and scoot up to my keyboard.

While still on tour for *Songs in A Minor,* I had started working on my second album, *Diary.* Sort of. When you're cramming in four or five live performances a week, often traveling hundreds or even thousands of miles between each show, you don't have much energy left over to create new music. Also, you need to rest your voice. In that window between boarding the tour bus and passing out on my pillow, I had managed, a little at a time, to write "Feeling U, Feeling Me," a jazzy interlude. But when the tour wrapped in the fall of 2002, that was all the music I'd completed.

There was already talk of the so-called sophomore slump, that jinx that can hang over an artist's second release. This slump seems to show up most frequently for musicians who, under their label's thumb, weren't able to stay musically true to themselves on the first album. And what happens when they're given more freedom on the second go-around? Boom—the music sounds nothing like the sound that initially whetted listeners' appetites. None of this had anything to do with me. My greatest battle for authenticity had already been fought years earlier at Columbia, which is why *Songs in A Minor* represented my unique musical thumbprint. So the pressure I felt wasn't driven by the fear of a slump, but by both the desire to prove that I had artistic staying power, and a loudly ticking clock. It has been said that you have your entire lifetime to make your initial body of work. But you have dramatically less time—in my case, until the end of 2003—to deliver your second.

My crew got popping. By this time, Kerry and I had launched our own small production company, KrucialKeys. We had a vision to assemble a variety of artists, some of them personal friends, all of them with musical aspirations of their own. Taneisha, my girl from our EmBishion days, was one of the first. On *Songs in A Minor,* she cowrote "The Life" with me. Another artist was my childhood friend Erika. Her uncle Norman, the New Kids on the Block percussionist, told me she was working on her own music and suggested we get together. I loved that idea, and we eventually teamed up to create some music. But it was on this second album that our heaviest collaborations began. Kerry and I also brought in talented artists such as Paul L. Green, Illz, and Kumasi. We offered each the opportunity to build a musical platform, with the goal of eventually releasing their work under the Krucial Keys banner. Meanwhile, as each laid the groundwork to go out on his or her own, we'd add them into the mix of creating my albums.

In spring of 2003, I wrapped myself in a musical cocoon to get my album done. My core production team, including Kerry; my sound engineer, Ann; another, Tony Black; as well as some of the Krucial Keys artists, hunkered down at Kampo Studios in NoHo. For eight months straight, we worked around the clock. I rented two spaces, Studios A and C, and I basically lived there. Between creative bursts inside the sound booths or plucking out melodies on the piano, we shared take-out meals, fine-tuned lyrics, and traded concepts for new songs. I often stayed overnight, collapsing onto a cot and propping my baseball cap over my eyes. I'd wake up three or four hours later, blurry eyed but ready to hit the keyboard again. It was intense, but such an uninterrupted creative flow ultimately gave the album a different vibe. *Songs in A Minor* was recorded in so many different studios over seven years. With *Diary*, there was continuity. There was a unified sense of rhythm. And there was a magic I could sense even as we were creating the music.

A revolving cast of artists came through to partner with me. Musicians like Steve Jordan, Wah Wah Watson, and D'wayne Wiggins showed up to play. Kanye stormed through and laid down beats for "You Don't Know My Name," as John Legend—long before he was a household name—sang background vocals. Dre and Vidal, two of the producers who worked with me, joined us in the studio for days at a time. Peter Edge sent me a continuous stream of Brazilian and African beats. I'd have multiple songs cooking as I floated between the two studios, working to incorporate a hodgepodge of flavors and sonics and beats from around the globe. I'd be in the control booth, Timberlands untied and arms thrown up, reveling in the sounds we were mixing. It was major exhaustion but one thousand percent joy.

The label planned to release our new material by the fourth quarter of 2003, just in time to capture holiday sales. By that fall, a few singles were ready, including "Karma" and "Diary" as well as "You Don't Know My Name," but the rest of the album was a long way from the finish line. And yet because of the imminent rollout, I had to begin promoting the album in both America and Europe. So right in the middle of writing music, my operation was relocated overseas. Jeff had to come down there to Kampo and practically drag my ass out of the studio and onto my flight.

Paris became our base for several weeks. I'd be up at six a.m., preparing for a bombardment of interviews with journalists from

England, Germany, Sweden, Holland, Spain, and just about every other country in Europe. I'd sit there for twelve hours straight, through back-to-back conversations in thirty-minute increments.

"Can I at least sit in a spot where I can see the Eiffel Tower?" I'd asked my team ahead of the trip. Thankfully, they'd arranged for me to do all the press bookings on the top floor of a restaurant, one with a distant view of the lattice-iron beauty. After shoveling down dinner, I'd drag myself over to our rented studio space and work until three a.m. Then it was up at six for another dizzying series of pressers, followed by feverish music creation into the wee hours.

Back on American soil a few weeks later, I wrote "Harlem's Nocturne"—a song that begins with a classical piece and crescendos into a stack of harmonies and hip-hop vibes. It's the first song on the record and yet the last one I completed. I intended for it to be more than just an introduction at the top of the album. Rather, the piece is my way of adjusting the listener's ear for the songs to follow and framing the album's sonic. By making it the opener, I established a trend that has become my signature: starting my albums with a piano solo, just as I'd done with *A Minor*'s "Piano & I." I was still fine-tuning "Nocturne" right up until the very last second before our deadline. As I pushed to finish up, Dave Kutch, the mastering engineer, was down at a recording studio called the Hit Factory, rushing to complete a process called mastering, a form of audio post-production.

In total, my team worked on more than ninety songs for *The Diary of Alicia Keys*. We ultimately gave the album that title because it describes exactly what these songs are: a peek into the pages of my life. It's very personal. Every song, from "If I Ain't Got You" and "Wake Up" to "Slow Down" and "Nobody Not Really," reflects some aspect of what I was experiencing at the time. The album was my way of opening myself up, of letting the world inside my head, even if only briefly. Even now, to my ear, the album feels so intimate. That's because it was written from a space of vulnerability and truth. And also, you tend to get real honest when you're creating on fumes in place of sleep.

When the last note of the last song had finally been submitted, you'd think I might've popped open some champagne. But I wasn't very good at celebrating much of anything, so in place of a glass of bubbly, there was a momentary exhale. *I made it through that,* I thought. *Better get on to the next thing.* That's the mind-set of a New York hustla. There's no time for sitting around. Your next payday or project, that next plate of dinner, is always just around the corner.

---

*The Diary of Alicia Keys* dropped, and in December 2003, "You Don't Know My Name," the first single, glided its way to the top of the R & B charts and remained there for nine weeks. Also in December, the full album debuted at number one, selling more than 600,000 copies in its first week and exceeding the label's commercial projections. If *Songs in A Minor* had been a wild ride, *Diary* was a voyage to another galaxy. The album garnered four Grammys and led to a thirty-six-show tour across North America and Europe.

The title track caused a bit of a stir upon its release. During the writing stage, "Diary" was one of those songs that was a challenge from the start. The chords showed up first, tumbling from my fingertips. I'd sit at the piano for hours at a time, playing these beautiful chords over and over, but no lyrics or melody would come. Then one evening I watched *The Bridges of Madison County,* a movie about two lovers with secrets. Feeling inspired by the film's title and story line, I tried to work it into some lyrics.

"Just think of me as your bridge to Madison County," I wrote. That clearly wasn't working.

"What is this damn song supposed to be?" I said to Kerry. I rattled off a few of the lines I'd been struggling with, and he responded with, "Just think of me like the pages in your diary." That clicked. The next day, I sat down at my piano and wrote the entire song, and in verse two, I cleverly slid in an old phone number—one I'd recently had disconnected. At the time, I thought it'd be so dope if I recorded a voice mail on that number, so that when people dialed in, they'd hear a message from me. Not long after the song debuted, calls poured in. But my lyrics hadn't included an area code. Oops. So when fans around the country dialed the number, they called using their own states' area codes. A Georgia resident who happened to have the exact digits I'd weaved into my song took me to court when his phone began ringing off the hook.

"Is this Alicia Keys?" callers would ask each time he picked up. To say he was mad is an understatement. I'll never make that mistake again.

I didn't hit the road for *Diary* right away. In spring 2004, I teamed up with Beyoncé and Missy Elliott for the Verizon Ladies First Tour, the first-ever three-act concert to be headlined by a trio of female R & B musicians. The show was designed to entertain, yes, but it was also intended to deliver a few powerful messages: Women can compose and produce. Women can command their own stage. And despite cultural messages to the contrary, women can band together in support of one another. Even before the tour, I'd known and admired both these ladies. Beyoncé and I had connected years earlier, behind the scenes at the many showcases Columbia Records had set up for both of us. She was then part of Destiny's Child and I was still finding my voice as a solo artist. Missy and I go almost as far back, first meeting through industry circles. During our thirty-stop tour across America, our bonds grew tighter.

The *Diary* tour started in 2005, just days after the Grammys. Kerry had helped me in the weeks leading up to the tour, tweaking the musical selections along with me, bringing in new stage elements, being an extra set of eyes and ears, and making sure I felt great on stage before we parted for several weeks. A tour can be tough on a romance, and ours was no exception. Kerry, at times, would fly in to meet me, and we'd be so happy for the brief reunions. But a tour is a strange thing. As a visitor, you can find yourself sitting around backstage thinking, *What am I doing here?* When you don't have a defined role—a job like tour manager or lighting director or background singer—you can start to feel like you're in the way. Kerry came when he could, and we reached out to each other every day that we weren't together. Back in Queens, his life carried on in a parallel universe: managing the artists on Krucial Keys, caring for his sons, working on lyrics, and generally setting the stage for our next creative push.

Though Kerry and I had been together for years by this point, we'd never officially announced ourselves as a couple. That was intentional. Early on, we'd decided we'd keep our relationship to ourselves, mostly because it was no one's damn business, and also because I didn't want to hear everyone's mouth about our age difference. Once the limelight fell heavily in my direction, my instinct for privacy grew even stronger. The public was already prying into my personal affairs—that just comes with life in the gray zone—so why add a romance to the mix? And Kerry wasn't angling for attention. He has always been super low-key. He wasn't the guy who elbowed his way onto center stage. Yet even with our lips so tightly glued shut, many speculated that we were more than just co-producers. When journalists quizzed me about whether we were lovers, I'd smile coyly and sidestep the question.

Oprah, who had by then become my wise friend and Aquarian big sister, reinforced my inclination to keep quiet about my personal life. In 2004, I returned to Oprah's set during the Verizon Ladies First Tour. Following the show, we shared a pivotal conversation.

"Keep your love life to yourself," she told me. "Keep some of you for you." One of her greatest mistakes, she said, had been allowing her own relationship to become fodder for relentless tabloid coverage. "That kind of media attention is unfair to anyone who hasn't committed to life in the public eye," she said. Also, she'd interviewed one too many women who'd swooned about being in love, only to be left looking fickle and foolish when the romance was over a few months later. Best to hold your tongue from the beginning. Best to hold tight to Oprah's wisdom.

———

The *Diary* years were life in fast-forward. There was a nonprofit to manage. A relationship to keep right side up. The Ladies First tour.

My own tour, followed by a new milestone in the summer of 2005: recording my first live album, *Unplugged,* as part of the *MTV Unplugged* series. The project brought me a third chart-topping debut and earned me five more Grammy nods, including one for "Unbreakable." Then in 2006, I got another surprise: John Mayer called to tell me that Bob Dylan had included me in the lyrics of his 2006 song "Thunder on the Mountain." I was bugging out.

"Really?" I said, incredulous that Bob Dylan would write about me. Sure enough, he did. In the lyrics, he wrote, "I was thinkin' 'bout Alicia Keys, couldn't keep from crying / When she was born in Hell's Kitchen, I was living down the line / I'm wondering where in the world Alicia Keys could be / I been looking for her even clear through Tennessee." I'm still not sure what prompted those lyrics, but it was humbling to be recognized by such an icon—particularly since I still considered myself Baby Keys, a newcomer to the music world.

Throughout 2006, my calendar bulged at the seams. I auditioned for and began working on *Smokin' Aces,* an action thriller and my first major film role. Between photo shoots and press appearances, live performances and increasing demands on my time, I didn't know whether I was coming or going. And in the middle of the chaos, my nana became ill. A throbbing numbness set in—that feeling you get when you're in the room but not really present. You're doing the work, but your spirit isn't engaged. You're charging through your daily tasks, but the whole time, you're praying for the moment when the world will stop spinning. You blink back your sorrow and stuff down your fear until one afternoon, in a dressing room in New York City, the universe sends you an exit ramp.

I've never been much of a crier. In fact, the harder things get, the less I tend to show emotion. It's probably the survivor in me, the part of my personality honed by my mother's own steadiness and refined by the streets of New York. You don't show weakness or vulnerability. You clench your fists and carry on. In retrospect, that's what made my breakdown that day so unbelievable, even to me. I sat there feeling the weight of my nana's illness, feeling overwhelmed at the sheer exhaustion of my pace, feeling the fear that I couldn't keep up with the incredible opportunity I'd been given. *Would I let others down— and would I let* myself *down?* And then, before I could throw up another wall to hold back all those years of stored-up tears, the dam broke.

# 8

## PILGRIMAGE

### BONO, IRISH SINGER AND ACTIVIST

There's a duality to Alicia. When we met on the *What's Going On* project and I recorded her in the studio, I sensed her feistiness. She was polite but firm. There's a don't-eff-with-me aspect to her. As I've spent time with her over the years, I've realized she's also a solitary person. And it's from that well of solitude, from the deep and quiet part of her soul, that her songs arise. She relished that stillness during her time in Egypt and was keen to discover the country's richness. The trip became a critical moment that crystallized so much for her. She has always had such a royal sense about her. She returned home with a deeper connection to herself, her value, and her artistry.

How may I help you today, Ms. Keys?" the travel agent asked me.

I swallowed hard. "I want to get away," I answered.

"Sounds great," she said. "What kind of trip do you have in mind?"

I paused. "I want to go sailing," I said.

Through the receiver, I heard the feverish *click-clacking* of her fingertips on the computer keyboard.

"There's a special vacation package to Key West," she said, "and I think there's a tour to—"

"Actually," I interrupted, "I want to sail down the Nile."

The tapping halted.

"You mean, like, the river in North Africa?" she asked.

"Yes," I said. "I want to go to Egypt."

Egypt had not stuttered on the day that it first called to me. As I'd sat there in my snotty mess in the dressing room, wondering what would happen if I just walked away from everything, the pull toward the motherland and toward my African ancestors couldn't have been stronger. When I told Erika about that pull, she encouraged me to follow it. Why I felt compelled to escape to that country in particular, I may never fully understand. All I knew was that I needed to flee as far away as I could from the pressure cooker my life had become. A few days at a local spa would not suffice. My spirit was demanding a complete and total eject, a force powerful enough to propel me five thousand miles across the Atlantic. In fact, this was not a vacation. It was a prison break.

I had to go alone. My world was so filled with the steady clanking of cymbals, of appointments and appearances and press interviews and pandemonium, I could no longer even hear my own thoughts. I longed for solitude, for space and breathing room without the thought of how someone else might be impacted. Traveling with others comes with a daily series of negotiations: Is the room temperature okay? What sites should we visit? What time should we have dinner? Can I sit quietly and read while you go out shopping? On and on. By default, I cater. And rather than feeling the need to accommodate, I wanted the beautiful freedom to choose, to please only myself. Mom, who will forever be my staunchest protector, urged me to at least travel with security. I resisted at first but finally agreed to take along one guy, just to help me navigate airports and transfer from site to site. Other than those brief interactions, I'd still be on my own.

Given the intensity of my breakdown, you'd think I would've booked the next flight to Cairo. But I needed time to meticulously plan my three-week itinerary, as well as to fulfill a few contractual commitments that had been on my calendar for a while. Also, a month earlier, I'd booked a trip to Greece to run a marathon. Yes, a full one. We modified my flights so that I'd stop in Athens before going on to Cairo.

In early November, I flew into Athens, laced up my sneakers, and lined up at the start line. Halfway through the race, there was a moment that I didn't know how I was going to make it to the end, physically. I kept saying to myself, *Just get to the next traffic light*. It was a metaphor for what I was experiencing on so many levels. After about five hours, I finally crawled my way to completion, cupped my hands over my face, and wept in both exhilaration and exhaustion.

The next morning, I boarded my flight to Cairo. My strongest initial memory of Egypt isn't the pyramids I spotted from my plane window. It's the fire raging through my entire body and especially my thighs. As I hobbled down the aisles of the plane, I looked like a limping mummy.

My adventure began at sunrise on the Nile. I'd never thought of myself as an early bird. I, like many artist night owls, experienced my strongest surge of creativity after midnight, while the rest of the world slumbered. But Egypt's mango sun, peeking over the mountains in the distance, lured me onto my private terrace at daybreak. The vast sky, dappled with clouds, stared down onto the river's mighty currents, sweeping our cruiser north toward the Mediterranean. I breathed in the silence and basked in the sun's rays, the wind tossing my mess of curls to and fro. For hours at a time, I did not move. I lay there on my deck, delighting in the stillness, reading and napping for however long I felt like it. As day melted into dusk and my lids gave in to sleep, I dreamed right there under the stars. The next morning at the first light of sunrise, I woke up to the faint sound of the *adhan,* the Muslim call to prayer.

I lost my voice to laryngitis on day one. I'd brought my keyboard with me, hoping to make music my only companion. The chords I played indeed spoke to me, but as the universe would have it, I couldn't speak back. Nothing fine-tunes one's ability to listen, to deeply hear, like forced silence. I took in the sounds around me, playing the ancient, pentatonic chords of the Egyptian scale. Each note was a meditation, tranquility wedged between the keys. I'd wondered, before I left New York, if I'd get lonely. I did not. In place of isolation, I felt peace. I felt brave and strong and proud that, for the first time in my life, I'd followed my inkling to unplug from the world and restore my spirit.

After three days on the Nile, I headed inland. In Luxor, I visited the Karnak, a stunning collection of temples with the Great Hypostyle Hall at its center, boasting row after row of 134 massive sandstone pillars stretched skyward. The monument, which is the largest religious temple ever constructed, was slowly built over two thousand years. I stood there craning my neck up, incredulous of the masterful work of those who, across so many centuries and kingdoms, erected the massive pillars. I felt at once small—a single speck of sand in humanity's evolving story—and yet inextricably connected to a magnificent, unfolding narrative larger than my one life. I also felt a strong sense of my own capacity. If the Egyptians had so capably built their temples and pyramids without the benefit of modern architectural tools, then I, a daughter of this great civilization, must be capable of more than I knew. We all are. Anything we can conceive of can be built. Perhaps not through our efforts alone, but also by the generations of dreamers whose feet will rest on our shoulders.

I climbed the stairs inside the Great Pyramid of Giza. In a crawl space at the top, I felt an urge to sing, though my voice still hadn't returned. There, amid walls etched with centuries of secrets, I crouched and hummed the chorus of a gospel hymn my nana loved:

> I sing because I'm happy.
> I sing because I'm free.
> His eye is on the sparrow.
> And I know He watches me.

I marveled at the pyramids. I was struck by how, without the benefit of pulleys or cranes or bulldozers, the Egyptians built such elaborate tombs and temples, the handiwork displaying their genius. I could not comprehend how mounds of rock, hard and seemingly impenetrable, were carved and painted and molded into structures withstanding millennia. Each is a testament to the power of the human spirit and a reflection of its Creator. Each is proof that we can sculpt the dust and boulders of our circumstances into fine art. At the foot of Giza, I felt that power and limitlessness.

I did not want to leave Egypt. I wanted more. More silence. More time to vibrate on my own frequency. More time to play my music while gazing at the horizon. More time to think of my nana. I spent my final week in Italy, the homeland of my mother's parents and a country I'd never visited. Mom, Erika, and Erika's mother met me at a resort tucked into the lush rolling hills of Tuscany. On the tail end of full solitude, I eased my way back into humanity surrounded by loved ones. Over tea and tears, I shared much of what I'd experienced: the colors and chords. The mesmerizing sounds and sunrises. My spirit's deep rejuvenation.

When I arrived home, my voice had fully returned. So had my will to forge ahead, now with the intention to create a different reality for myself.

———

I lost beautiful Nana shortly after my return from Egypt. Even in her transition, she left all of us who loved her with a sweet offering— a reminder to get on with filling our lives with what matters most. Death is a gift meant to wake up the living, to nudge us toward a life of purpose and intention.

My nana had always been the most perfect summer day—not too hot, just the right amount of breeze, no jacket required. When I was small, I'd nuzzle up right next to her on the couch, smushing my face into her bosom, taking comfort in her warm embrace and big laugh. Even now, whenever someone tells me that I have a spirit like my grandmother's, it is the greatest compliment I can be paid. Nana was love in human form. Her presence was as soothing as jasmine, her favorite flower. Her generosity knew no bounds.

Nana's dining room table served as proof. Its round oak surface stayed covered with the personal letters, love notes, and greeting cards she was always preparing to send to friends and family; next to that stack lay mounds of coupon clippings, bills, receipts, and junk mail. The house itself, like the table at its center, served as a kind of community headquarters. She was the unofficial mayor of Uniondale in Long Island, beloved by the stream of neighbors who showed up at her door. That doggone doorbell was constantly ringing, chiming more loudly than Big Ben. Everyone knew Vergeil, the woman with the old-school name and the wide-open arms. They'd sit for hours at her side, trading stories and drinking her ice-cold Crystal Light.

Ali is what Nana always called me. That's the nickname all my loved ones use when they speak to me, but especially her. Over summers when I stayed with her and Fafa, she talked to me constantly.

"Ali, I need you to run next door and ask Miss so-and-so if I can borrow a little salt" (for the irresistible butternut squash and mashed turnips she'd make on the weekends). "Ali, come in here and set this table" (which of course meant first clearing it). "Ali, don't be out in the street in that dress" (until the year I stopped wearing them). And I learned better than to ever tell her I was bored. "Oh, you're bored?" she'd say, smirking, hand on hip. "Okay, good. I need you to do six pages in this here workbook and show it to me when you're done so I can check it."

Then there were the gems she passed on to me, whenever she took a notion.

"Never leave the house without some cash in your pocketbook," she'd tell me. "And always keep gas in your car." Nana was my ace, a friend I talked to nearly every day. We became even tighter after we lost Fafa.

In the fall of 2005, I had approached Nana with a proposition.

"Why don't you move in with me?" I said. "I could buy a home large enough for you to have your own space." By this time, Kerry and I had moved on from the house in Rosedale, Queens, into a home on Long Island. We'd opened the doors to our own state-of-the-art recording space nearby, called Oven Studios (so called because we couldn't use the AC during sweltering summers in Queens or else its sound would be picked up in our recordings, and also because the music we were cooking was fire). Nana, who was still in that same one-level ranch-style home Fafa had moved her into years earlier, was getting up in age, and I wanted to have her closer. She loved the idea. To help me out during the daily earthquake my schedule had become, Nana reached out to a real estate agent. Together, they rounded up a few potential homes that would give us both the space we needed.

One afternoon, her real estate agent took us to see one of the places. As Nana crouched down to step into the front seat of the agent's car, she let out a loud shriek.

"What's wrong, Nana?" I asked, rushing to her side.

"My back," she said, leaning over onto my shoulder with the full weight of her statuesque frame. A pain, she said, had shot up through her spine. I suggested we postpone the showing, but after a few moments, Nana insisted she was okay. The discomfort had passed.

We drove to the home, a two-story beauty in Syosset, Long Island. It seemed perfect: spacious enough for Nana to enjoy her own private wing. Within hours of the viewing, I put in an offer and eventually purchased it. We were preparing to move into the new space when Nana's back pain resurfaced, this time more intensely. My mother and I urged her to see a doctor; she was so uncomfortable that she booked an appointment for the next day. After a week of tests, she finally received a diagnosis that still punches me in the gut: She had spinal cancer. The large tumor, surgeons told us, could not be safely removed because of its proximity to her spine and the possibility of paralysis. Oncologists would instead attempt to shrink it using oral medications, chemotherapy, and radiation treatments.

On the day Kerry and I moved Nana into the house, she could no longer walk. This elegant woman, one whose queenlike stature cast light into every corner of my world, was now confined to a wheel-chair as we rolled her through the front door. We turned the library on the main floor into her bedroom and brought in a hospital bed so we could make her as comfortable as possible. I can only imagine the devastation she must have felt as we set up her room. One day, she'd been up walking around, delighting friends and strangers alike with her gracious hospitality. The next, she was flat on her back, her entire world shrunk to the length and width of a hospital bed.

I built my life around Nana's care. So did my mother. Each evening, I'd leave my studio session, where I was working on my third album, and drive home to check on her. By the spring of 2006, my life had settled into a rhythm where I was checking on Nana multiple times a day, and working in the studio in between. I helped Nana bathe and changed her bedpans, and I'd do so again in a heartbeat. Meanwhile, Mom managed Nana's doctors' appointments and organized her medications. We also hired a nurse who came in periodically to assist. This was my first opportunity to be a nurturer, and I embraced it with gratitude. I hoped to offer this great woman who'd mothered me just a tiny portion of the love I'd received at her hands.

Craig flew in to see Nana when he could. He and I hadn't been in each other's presence in years, since that summer when I'd cut him off by letter. We'd talked briefly by phone after *Songs in A Minor* took off. Word had somehow gotten back to me, perhaps through Nana, that Craig was excited about my success.

"I'm so proud of you," he told me during our phone conversation. I froze. In hindsight, I can see why it would've been thrilling for Craig to watch my star rising. I am his firstborn child, his only daughter. And yet his words sounded to me like nails screeching across a chalkboard. I thought, *Proud? You have no right to be proud. You did not contribute.* After my mother had pulled off the Herculean task of raising me on her own, Craig seemed to be stepping in to take credit—and after that call, I'd decided I'd hold on to my vendetta. But Nana, as only she could have, nudged me in a different direction.

"I just want the family to come together," she whispered to me one evening after we'd moved in together. "I don't want you and Craig to be at odds anymore. Please." Out of my deep love for Nana, I honored her request. My father and I were restrained but cordial.

As Nana struggled through the nausea brought on by her chemo treatments, I noticed certain people close to her didn't come around as often as I thought they might.

"Where is everyone?" I asked Nana.

"Baby," Nana would say, shaking her head, "you've gotta accept people how they are." Life would eventually teach me the wisdom of her perspective.

One evening, I drove home, as usual, to check on Nana. I cleared a spot on the bed—by this time, a king-size Tempur-Pedic had replaced the hospital bed—by scooting aside some papers, the same stacks of notes and coupon clippings that had once covered her dining table.

"I want to play something for you," I told her.

Nana's face brightened. "What is it, baby?" she asked.

For weeks in the studio, I'd been composing a song for her. I'd finished the song that very evening and had rushed home, eager for her to hear it, hoping it would express the sentiments that only music can. I put headphones over her ears and pushed the play button:

Imagine there was no tomorrow / Imagine that I couldn't
see your face / There'd be no limit to my sorrow / So
all I can say / I wanna tell you something / Give you
something / Show you in so many ways / 'Cause it would
all mean nothing / If I don't say something / Before it all
blows away / Don't want to wait to bring you flowers /
Waste another hour / Let alone another day / I'm gonna
tell you something / Show you something / Won't wait
till it's too late.

Nana's eyes filled with water as we sat together, our fingers interlaced as closely as our lives had become, the melody and words settling over her like a soft blanket. We were so present in that moment. So aware and awake. I began to cry, and Nana, herself tearing up, reached over and wiped the tears from my cheek. It was a private moment together, the most special moment we'd ever shared. I didn't know it would be one of our last.

A week later, I stopped in for my evening check on Nana.

"How was your day, baby?" she asked as I flopped across her bed.

"It was good," I said. "How are you, Nana?"

"I'm all right," she said. "I'm having a hard time taking my blood pressure."

I sat up. "Really?" I said. "Can I help?"

"No, no, no," she said. "I'm going to do it. I'll just wait a little while and try it again. But don't tell your mother." She smiled.

I looked at her, a little confused about what she meant.

"Why would I tell my mother?" I said. She smiled more broadly.

"Just don't tell her," she said, laughing. Nana, who'd always had a silly side, seemed to be in the mood to play. We cracked a few jokes back and forth, and it made me so happy to see her face lit up, her cheekbones high, her eyes gleaming. As I rose to say good night, I said, "Are you sure you're okay, Nana? Is there anything I can help you with?"

"I'm fine," she said, smiling.

The next morning, I poked my head in her door to find her sound asleep. Her face looked so peaceful. *I'm glad she's sleeping in a little,* I thought. *She needs the extra rest.* I quietly closed the door and returned to my room, grateful for a few more hours of rest myself.

When I looked in on her again, she was still sleeping. *Strange.* She'd occasionally slept past her usual wake time, but never this long. I tiptoed in, crouched down to the side of her bed, and shook her softly.

"Nana?" I whispered, feeling suddenly terrified. She didn't respond. Minutes later, the scream of sirens sliced through the morning air and a medical team rushed in to transport Nana to the ER. She'd slipped into a coma.

That evening before, when she'd seemed so cool and happy and full of jokes, she'd been in the early stages of delirium. Doctors had put her on a medication intended to shrink the tumor, but the med had a side effect: it spiked her blood sugar. By the time I stopped in to check on her, her elevated blood sugar had begun making her incoherent.

Craig and my brother, Cole, flew in immediately. The medical team did all they could to revive Nana from her glycemic coma, but she didn't regain consciousness. Even if she were to come out of the coma, doctors told us, she would be brain-dead.

I had to escape. I have never felt more raw pain, even in the years since. I struggled to breathe. The devastation bore down heavy on my chest, threatening to suffocate me. As Craig sat at Nana's bedside in the ICU, I took my brother, then fifteen, out of the hospital and away from the horror unfolding. In an attempted distraction, we fled to the movies, sitting numbly in the dark theater. Just as we left the theater, my cell rang. It was Craig.

"She's passed," he told me, sorrow heavy in his voice. I dropped the phone and sobbed. My nana was gone.

The following days were a blur. I don't even remember the funeral. Every cell in my body ached. I was wracked with guilt, an overwhelming feeling that I could have saved her. I could have intervened that evening. How could I not have known something was truly wrong? Why hadn't I, someone gifted with an artist's powerful sensitivities, been able to intuitively feel that Nana was slipping away? Why did I go back to sleep that morning? There were no answers. There was only an unrelenting agony, a sadness that swallowed me whole. I stopped going to the studio, and on many days, I did not get out of bed. I lay there weeping, replaying in my head those final moments with Nana, and most of all blaming myself. My only consolation was that she might've passed peacefully. She'd at least been spared the torment of a painful transition.

For weeks after Nana slipped away, a heaviness lingered over me. Though Kerry was with me, the house felt eerily empty. I'd pass

Nana's room and descend into overpowering sadness that she was no longer there. One evening when Erika and I were in the attic upstairs, a space I'd once dreamed of renovating for Nana, I told my friend about the heaviness. She listened intently. We sat there in the dark for a long time, the shadows draping over our shoulders.

"You'll see Nana again," Erika finally whispered. I stared at her but did not respond as her words washed through me. For the first time since Nana's passing, I felt relief. Nana and I would meet again. Not in this lifetime but in another. And somehow in that moment, I realized that every lifetime we've lived, we were in each other's lives. Our bond is that enduring.

I often dream of Nana in heaven. There she stands, proud and majestic, taking her place among the angels and ancestors. Her presence, even from up there, is still so strong here on earth. I feel it in my every breath, in my every song, in the hint of jasmine or the laughter of my children. When they were first born, I felt her especially close by. She is right here with me, pulling me close, stroking my hair, whispering her wisdom, and showing me the way.

PART TWO

# CREATING

---

*Music is life*
*Captured in a bottle of sound*
*Set free to be felt*
*Until the end of the song*
                    —Alicia Keys

# 9

## GROUND SHIFT

### KERRY "KRUCIAL" BROTHERS

When Alicia returned from Egypt, she wanted a fresh start in every area of her life. I told my friend Nick that I wanted to begin pricing engagement rings. But by then, things were already shifting with Alicia and me. I'd taken so long to propose because I was waiting for the perfect moment. I wanted to have things in place, like a certain amount of money to bring to the table, to show that I was worthy. As a man who'd been resourceful from a young age, I never wanted to ride her coattails. I think she sensed the proposal was coming. She told me, "Let's just go back to dating again." For a while, we lived in separate rooms in the house. Maybe she felt, *If I'm going to possibly be with this man for the rest of my life, I need to be sure.* We tried the dating thing, but we eventually ended our relationship before I got to propose. In hindsight, the whole reason we might've been in each other's lives was for the songs to come through us. That couldn't have happened in the way that it did if we hadn't been so close. Maybe we were brought together for a specific purpose: to make music history.

Most of us take about sixteen breaths per minute. That means we typically breathe 960 times an hour, or around 23,000 times a day. During my two glorious weeks of silence, I had more than 322,000 opportunities to breathe my way into a new existence. One exhale at a time, I let go of the urge to twist myself into a pretzel, trying to live up to others' expectations. I let go of the belief that, if I stepped away, nothing would be there when I returned. And in place of that notion, I inhaled liberation. I inhaled the boundlessness and brilliance that once guided the Egyptians in crafting monuments of greatness. That's what fourteen days of solitude can bring: space to breathe. Time to reflect. A chance to reimagine what your life can look like.

When freedom tapped me on my shoulder, I answered loud and strong. Back in New York, my team immediately noticed a shift in me. "I need two weeks to myself before and after every tour," I announced. And when, ahead of a press day in Japan, my manager showed me the proposed schedule—one crammed with wall-to-wall interviews—I pushed back. "I'll need a fifteen-minute break after every hour to keep from turning into a robot," I said. I began using the single most powerful word a pleaser can ever speak: No. It took practice. When pleasing has become your MO, it's tough to consistently begin holding your boundaries. But it gets easier the more you do it. You start to realize that the earth doesn't fall off its axis because you turn down a speaking engagement or even a movie role. The world keeps right on spinning. And the gift you give yourself is more energy to do the work you actually want to be doing. Saying no doesn't make you less of an artist or human being. It makes you a stronger and more purposeful one.

My new spirit also showed up during studio sessions. I'd already been creating in the air space of full expression, but after Egypt, I removed all safety nets and opened myself up to different ways of collaborating. I'd been so inspired by the pentatonic scale that I began implementing that sound. I even brought in sitarists to play the ancient instrument and compose with me. The songs we wrote never made it onto the next album, but they marked the start of my exploration. My desire for playfulness and newness. My intention to both color outside the musical lines and build my very own crayon box.

On my first two studio albums, I'd mostly written with Kerry. I'd always felt nervous about composing with others because the process is so vulnerable. You're sharing your greatest insecurities with someone when you write a song with them. You're revealing the most sensitive parts of who you are, because that is the only way to make the lyrics feel authentic. After Egypt, I felt brave enough to try writing with others. I connected with Linda Perry, the prolific songwriter and former lead singer of 4 Non Blondes. She has created epic songs for artists like Christina Aguilera, Adele, P!nk, and Gwen Stefani. When we first sat down together, side by side at the baby grand, I was scared to expose myself. But Linda was so open, so secure in her space while being tender with mine, that I quickly felt comfortable enough to peel back the layers. She encouraged me to create by blurting out, stream-of-consciousness style, phrases that didn't always seem to make sense—but that expressed feelings under the surface. And when my subconscious spoke, we flowed with it. That unvarnished truth comes through on "Sure Looks Good to Me," one of the songs we wrote together: "Life is cheap, bitter sweet / But it tastes good to me / Take my turn, crash and burn / That's how it's supposed to be." In every crack and tremble of my voice, you can hear the rawness.

Linda also worked with me on "Superwoman." Steve Mostyn, another great songwriter and musician who'd played with me on tour, and I had already started the song. All three of us were a part of creating the song: "Even when I'm a mess / I still put on a vest / With an S on my chest / Oh yes / I'm a Superwoman." Before that song, I'd never publicly acknowledged that I can be a mess. But post-Egypt, it was time. Linda, Steve, and I started with that chorus and built the full song from there. I wrote "Superwoman" not because I felt like one. The lyrics were what I needed to hear, words that affirmed that, even in my brokenness, there is strength.

*As I Am,* my third album, is a blend of bold tempos and musical textures, each reflecting my experimental zone. When I listen to the album now, I hear the funkadelic sounds of the clavinet and the strum of the harpsichord. I hear the '60s influences, alive and reverberating, on "Teenage Love Affair." I hear my voice, tinged with emotion, on "Tell You Something," my tribute to Nana. On the lead single, "No One," I hear the fever pitch of the Jupiter, the vintage keyboard. And on the album's cover, I see my face on full display, up close and intimate with the world.

I also see a gang of hair flowing down my back, which is prominent on the front of the "Superwoman" single as well. The white T-shirt and door knockers are so me. But those layers of long locks, blown back by the wind from a fan brought in during the photo shoot, were a step toward a girly look. On my second album, *Diary,* I'd edged in that direction a tiny bit, trading 24-7 cornrows for hair braided in the front but down in the back. And alongside *As I Am*'s deeply honest lyrics, there is another small pivot—from hippie 'hood to hippie glam. At my core, I'm still myself—just exploring and experimenting with how to express that truth visually.

———

Losing Nana had given Craig and me something in common: grief. He was a heartbroken son. I was a devastated granddaughter. Our shared sorrow served as a gale force, pushing us toward each other even amid our tensions. During those months when Nana struggled through her chemo, I'd witnessed a side of Craig I hadn't seen. He sat near the edge of Nana's bed, his voice soft, his tenderness apparent as he stroked his mother's hair and spoke words of comfort. In those moments, I saw Craig not as the father who'd let me down, but as the child of a woman he loved deeply. His obvious care for Nana softened me. It also paved the way for a conversation we had soon after her passing.

For eleven years, I'd put Craig on mute. In fact, even before then, I'd never asked him to tell me his story, or to explain how he and my mother's paths had crossed. One evening, with the shadows of dusk settling over my neighborhood, we walked side by side. I listened quietly as he explained to me, for the first time, what he'd experienced. He and my mother had been lovers, yes, but not in love with each other. I'd been conceived in an act of passion, a rush of desire that resulted in the unexpected. By the time my mother told Craig she was pregnant, she'd decided she was keeping me. Craig, who had no say in this huge life choice Mom had already made, was simply not ready to opt in to fatherhood. I realized that probably left him with some difficult questions: *Where do I fit into this scenario? How do I express what I'm feeling to this strong-headed Taurean woman? And how do I connect with a child I never intended to have?*

As Craig shared his perspective, it rang true. And during my childhood and beyond, it was this very narrative that had filled me with such resentment. What's crazy is, while the poison of anger was corroding my insides, Craig seemed oblivious. On the other side of the country, he carried on with his life and other family while I stewed in my misery. I wasted so much energy nursing my bitterness, trying to get back at him and hoping he'd experience as much heartache as I had. But the whole time, I was the one hurting. I was the one who, by living in that negative energy, drew even more of it to myself. It was so backward.

That night, as Craig spoke, I came to a realization. He did not have to be my daddy. He could just be Craig. The years he'd missed were already in our rearview mirrors. Right there, in the present, we could get to know each other not as father and daughter, but as two adults. All my life, I'd been carrying around this notion of who Craig should've been for me: the doting father who showed up. The dad who read me stories at bedtime or cheered me on at my piano recitals. It was normal for me to want those things; most kids do. But that just wasn't our situation. And it dawned on me, more than a decade after I'd ended my communication with him, that looking back wouldn't change a thing between us. I could not rewrite our complicated story. But what I could do was create an entirely new one.

"Can we start from this point on?" I asked him. The question itself, like Craig's nod of agreement, marked a pivot—the pause of a comma in place of my letter's final punctuation mark.

An aha moment is not a happy ending—it's an open doorway, one you have to choose to walk through. After the lights came on for me, I didn't suddenly set aside all my hard feelings. That's not the way it happens in real life. But the conversation gave Craig and me a new place to enter. And on the other side of that entryway, we discovered there was a lot more work to do. That work is still being done.

———

It was a complicated time for Kerry and me after my first few albums took off. He worked hard on great music behind the scenes, only to later get just a small slice of the affirmation that I regularly received. That dynamic, that inequality in our experiences, swayed our relationship off-balance. Even for someone as laid-back as Kerry, the lack of acknowledgment had to be rough. Yes, being listed in the credits on my albums brought him satisfaction. But, like any ambitious and talented artist would, he longed to be recognized for all of what he brought to the table.

Yet Kerry's contributions were often overlooked. We'd be out celebrating at an industry gathering when someone who'd already met him fifteen times would ask him, "What's your name again?" I would then feel badly and try to compensate. I wanted him to be seen as an equal, to feel validated.

"You know my partner, Krucial, right?" I'd try to say when others approached us. On the occasions when I didn't introduce him because the moment just wasn't right, he'd notice. Later, at home, he'd sometimes mention it. It was an awkward situation, made worse by the fact that I was anxious about being judged. I was still Baby Keys, the new artist with a strong urge to bolt whenever I heard my own music over the loudspeakers at an industry party. I'd find myself standing nervously across from a heavyweight in the business, struggling to hold my own while pretending I knew more than I did. And in that headspace, I wasn't always focused on making sure Kerry was recognized.

Our extended separations added another level of stress. For months while I was touring, we lived apart and lost some of the intimacy that only an in-person connection can bring. Though Kerry visited, he wasn't able to drop his whole life to stay with me on the road. So in our Long Island studio, he spent countless hours writing and producing while I was gone. He also guided the artists on our production label, Krucial Keys. That became its own challenge, as we'd taken on more than we could handle with our team. Every one of our artists was so brand-new. In a way, we all were. Kerry and I were like the blind leading the beginners, and over time, that got heavy. Our goal had been to provide all these different artists, most of them our dear friends, with a creative outlet. But as we learned, it takes an enormous amount of energy and investment to launch an artist. They each put in serious effort but still couldn't get much traction. And the only work that seemed to be producing any financial gain was our collaboration on my albums. It was both overwhelming and unsustainable.

Meanwhile, Kerry was experiencing some success with writing and producing his own music. In 2001, he'd locked down a publishing deal with Broadcast Music Inc. (BMI), as well as composed and produced music for the soundtracks of *Doctor Dolittle, Shaft, Drumline,* and *Ali*. He also set up Krucial Noise, his own production company, and earned strong royalties through that brand. When it came to his independent releases (Kerry was always driven to create his own music), he definitely established a following. And yet the music didn't have quite as much commercial impact as we'd both hoped. That lit an even stronger fire under him, and around 2006 he began working around the clock on his material. During late-night studio sessions that stretched to sunrise, he and his crew would be in the studio, banging out beats and trying to lift their creations to the next level. That's around the time he found himself drinking a little too much.

Kerry would typically have a beer during his studio sessions. But over time, that once-in-a-while beer turned into a daily habit as he dealt with our extended separation, helping others in their careers, and the difficulties that come with the creative process. The liquor seemed to loosen his tongue. Kerry was ordinarily kind, complimentary, cool; but when he drank, he was, at times, belittling. He never raised a hand to me, not once, but he could get loud. In one session when we were collaborating with some other artists, he talked over me, implying that I didn't know what I was doing. I excused it. In those days, I was an expert at playing down or ignoring conduct that I should've spoken on directly.

"No, he didn't mean it like that," I said to Jeff when my manager later asked me about the incident. I knew Kerry was drunk. I also knew there was alcoholism in his family. But instead of immediately saying to him, "I never want you to speak to me that way again," I tried to calm the situation by minimizing his behavior.

In 2006, while I was on the road, Kerry called my cell.

"I just got in a bad car accident," he said, breathing heavily into the phone.

I froze. "Are you okay?" I asked.

He was. And though thankfully no one was hurt during the incident, his Escalade was totaled. He'd been driving home that morning after spending the whole night in the studio, creating and drinking over the course of the evening. It scared me that he'd let his habit go far enough to put his life in danger.

Our relationship, which was already strained, deteriorated from there. I retreated to the patterns I'd had in place from the beginning of our time together: I didn't communicate my frustrations. I played the same record I'd played throughout my childhood, staying silent and pulling back in an attempt to keep things cool. When you don't speak the truth for years at a time, the words left unspoken slowly leak the air out of your connection. Even if, years later, you are ready to say what you couldn't earlier, the moment has passed. The details and circumstances have faded from memory, and yet the emotions linger. And then the day finally comes when you no longer recognize the person you first loved.

That day came for me at some point in 2006, around the time I slid into depression over Nana's condition. Kerry and I were still together, but I'd never felt more disconnected from him. *Who are you—and who am I?* I'd often stare at him and think.

I realized Kerry was looking at rings. I can't recall whether he told me that or if it was just in the ether. Whatever the case, it made me nervous. Not just because our relationship was already on shaky ground, but also because I wasn't sure I *ever* wanted to get married. I definitely was not a girl who'd always dreamed of a fairytale wedding. And at twenty-six I wasn't ready to make such a big commitment.

"I don't want any diamonds," I said to Kerry one evening. Blood diamonds were used to finance war and oppress the poor, and I wanted no part in it. But that's not the only reason I mentioned it to Kerry. Rather, it was my backdoor way of telling him: Don't bring me an engagement ring.

I eventually told Kerry I needed space so we could begin again, and we started sleeping in separate rooms. I had hoped that by backing away I could rediscover, with fresh eyes, all the incredible things that first drew us together. We were both holding on to the amazing memories and music we'd created, as well as the space of comfort and familiarity we'd shared for so many years. But I felt clear that I needed to transition. One evening that fall, sitting across from Kerry on a couch at my mother's house, we ended things.

With the passing of time comes perspective. And from where I stand now, more than a decade after Kerry and I moved in different directions, I deeply cherish and acknowledge our relationship for what it was: a safe space to experience love and music. It was also yet another opportunity for me to see myself in full. A chance to recognize all those places in me that still needed to grow, all the ways in which I'd swallowed my truth rather than voicing it. We don't draw loved ones into our lives coincidentally. They're there to shine a light on our unfinished emotional business, to reveal to us our deepest tendencies. And as my life is proving to me even now, those patterns appear time and again, often cleverly disguised. And they'll keep right on showing up until we're willing to truly look at them.

———

In November 2007, *As I Am* debuted at the top of the charts, making it my fourth consecutive number-one release. Fans—or "my fam," as I call them now—were still embracing my music with wide-open arms. In its first week, the album sold 742,000 copies, the highest for any female R & B artist. The lead single, "No One," also secured the top spot on the charts and became that year's most-listened-to song. *As I Am* ultimately went triple platinum and earned me three more Grammys. I'd established myself as a musician with lasting momentum, and it felt unbelievably amazing.

I'm often asked which one of my albums is my favorite, which is like asking a mother which one of her children she most adores. Even if she has a clear preference, she'll never admit it. For me, *As I Am* will always be one of my top three most-beloved albums, mainly because of the season in my life that it reminds me of. While writing those songs, I was just beginning to discover my true self. Before then, my life had been kicking and screaming, trying to get my full attention. And on a deck drifting down the Nile, I finally tuned in and took inventory. Once home, ready to work on *As I Am*, I had cleared my voice and my space, creating room for a miracle I couldn't have known was coming.

# 10

## SUNFLOWER

KASSEEM DEAN, AKA SWIZZ BEATZ, GRAMMY AWARD–WINNING
SUPER PRODUCER, COFOUNDER OF THE DEAN COLLECTION,
AND ALICIA'S SOUL MATE

"In the beginning, Alicia thought I was super obnoxious—because I was. I was so obnoxious that I couldn't even talk to myself. I was in Ruff Ryders mode, part of that whole aggressive DMX hip-hop scene filled with Rolls-Royces, diamonds, gold watches. The excess was a way to celebrate finally getting some artistic freedom. But all that flash didn't resonate with Alicia, who has never been about material things. Years later, when we started getting to know each other, our conversations got real unpredictable real fast. And that's when she realized there was more to me than the cars and the jewelry. I wasn't out here just popping bottles and collecting Ferraris, trying to feel important or compete with my crew. I was sleeping on the floor in the studio, completely focused on making music history."

It's crazy how long Swizz and I have known each other. He was sixteen when we first met, which meant I was about fourteen. Nikki, my friend and an emcee, went to school with him.

"Yo, you've gotta meet Swizz," she kept saying. "He's doing his music thing, you're doing yours, and y'all should work together." One afternoon we stopped by the school they both attended, Truman

High in the Bronx. As Swizz now recalls, I was standing out front rocking a purple puffy jacket, looking tomboyish but still kind of cute. We talked for a minute about nothing deep, and then as I walked off, he asked if we could exchange numbers. I was like, Nah, I'm good. *I'll just see you when I see you.*

And see him around I did. In 1998, rapper DMX stormed onto the scene with his first album, *It's Dark and Hell Is Hot,* which was on the Ruff Ryders label. Swizz—who'd been working with that label alongside his uncles, who owned it with Swizz's aunt—created the iconic beat for "Ruff Ryders Anthem," which became DMX's number-one hit single. Once that album exploded, we ended up in the same circles at various awards shows and industry events. He'd usually pull up in some fancy car, rolling deep with his Bronx crew and shining with diamonds. He couldn't just have on one fresh chain; he had to have *five* of them. I wasn't feeling the vibe. It was so ostentatious, so over the top. And I wanted nothing to do with that scene or with Swizz.

Years later, I read an article Swizz had been interviewed for. In it, he claimed he could create a beat in ten minutes. *So annoying.*

"Why would somebody be bragging about producing music that fast?" I said to Jeff. *What I'm doing is real music,* I thought. *You're supposed to craft it from scratch, take your time with it, and really care about it.* I was so friggin' righteous then. And after that story, I was also even *more* turned off by Swizz.

Fast-forward to when I was wrapping up some new music I'd been working on. I was feeling creatively burned out after months of poring over it.

"Why don't we bring in Swizz for a collaboration?" Jeff suggested. "It would add another flavor to the album." Even before he could get that last sentence out of his mouth, I stopped him. Not only did I refuse to work with another artist on the tail end of partnering with a whole series of them, I told Jeff, I also had zero interest in teaming up with Swizz, the self-proclaimed ten-minute beat master. I liked his music well enough to dance to it, but I couldn't see how we'd ever be a good match in the studio. "It's cool if you don't want to work with him," Jeff told me, "but why don't you just meet him? There's no commitment." I reluctantly agreed.

Swizz was finishing up his own session when I arrived at the studio.

"Hey, what's up?" he asked.

"I'm cool," I said in a tone that made it apparent I'd rather be anyplace else.

"Hey, look," he said, glancing down at his shirt and then over at mine. "We're both wearing yellow." *Eye roll.* We chatted briefly but didn't work on any particular song that day; we just hung out and talked to see how things flowed. And despite my funky attitude at the start, it turned out to be cool. By the time we parted, he'd moved up a half inch in my book—from totally irritating to only slightly annoying, and actually a bit funny. A few weeks later, our managers set up another studio session.

When the day rolled around, Swizz flaked at the last minute—and my bad attitude came rushing back. Once he did arrive at the studio, I was working on a song.

"Whatever you're doing in here," he said, "keep doing it. There's some magic happening in this room." I thanked him, and he left to go to another room we'd work in as I stayed and finished the vocals. Later, when we began experimenting with some beats and lyrics, the energy was incredible, and I found myself laughing and enjoying the process. He was definitely in his zone, opening himself up to the music without overthinking it, and just allowing the vibe to carry him. That's how he flows. It's also how, as I saw for myself that afternoon, he could create so quickly. Next thing I knew, we'd written a whole song using this sick house beat juxtaposed with my piano playing. You won't believe how long it took us to put it together—about ten minutes. *My bad.*

The more we talked, the more I noticed how his mind worked. He clearly didn't fit the stereotype of the rapper who was only about diamond medallions and showboating. Outwardly, he seemed to be all those things. But beyond the baggy jeans and the arm tats, there was depth. He once casually mentioned, for instance, that he'd bought his first Ansel Adams photograph when he was just eighteen. And he was so aware of what was happening in the world, so curious about not just art and music but also about business, entrepreneurship, and current events. *Interesting*.

"Can we grab something to eat?" he asked me one afternoon. We were becoming friends, but I politely declined. He was cool and everything, but I'd never been busier. With my crazy schedule, getting together was out of the question. "Well you've gotta eat, don't you?" he said. "What about just a lunch?" I finally agreed, on the condition that I'd only be able to take a forty-five-minute break from a photo shoot I was doing. I made a reservation for noon at an outdoor restaurant in downtown Manhattan, a place close to my set location.

I arrived at twelve on the dot. Swizz was nowhere in sight. Fifteen minutes later, I was still on that patio waiting and asking myself, *Why did I set myself up for this foolishness?* My schedule was crazy, and one late moment led to a whole day off track. When he finally came strutting in at 12:20 p.m., I was in no mood for an excuse. He tried to hug me, but I brushed him off. While apologizing profusely, he handed me a bag. I opened it and lifted out a pair of sunglasses.

"You're late and you're giving me Louis Vuitton glasses?" I complained. He grinned, which cooled things off just long enough for him to sit. As he did, I looked more closely at the bag. On its front was a beautiful art replica.

"Wow, who did that piece?" I asked.

"That's Erté," he said matter-of-factly.

"*Who?*" I said.

"Erté, the French artist," he said. "You don't know Erté?"

"I don't," I said, studying the image. "But I like the bag better than the glasses."

"Well, I'm going to introduce you to Erté," he said. "His work is phenomenal."

I shrugged and set the bag aside, still feeling annoyed. We put in an order and began talking, and as much as I wanted to stay mad at Swizz, he lifted the mood with a steady stream of humor and fascinating conversation. Even before we'd finished our meal, I rose to leave, reminding him I had to get back to my photo shoot. He insisted that he walk me out. As we approached my car, I noticed something enormous attached to its top.

"What's *that*?" I said, walking closer.

He smiled. "That's why I was late," he said.

Swizz lowered the large item, removed the big bow tied around it, and held it up to reveal a painting of a grand piano with paint brushes attached to the keys.

"When I saw this," he explained, "it seemed like the perfect representation of our friendship. You're the keys, I'm the brushes." When he'd purchased it from a street vendor a few days earlier, he explained, he'd planned to give it to me. But in order to prop it up on my car roof, he had to arrive at the restaurant *after* me so that my car would already be there. It was such a nice gesture. To this day, Swizz is generous like that: If he meets a budding photographer and has a camera on him, he'll hand over the camera on the spot. And he brings thoughtful gifts to those he has just met all the time, to make them feel special. That's his style. I tried to play it cool, but I was impressed. And yet nothing in me suggested this would be anything more than a friendship. So I thanked him for the painting and we moved on.

We ran into each other off and on, and every time we connected, we realized how similar our stories were. We'd each been successful at a young age. We were creators of our own sound and lyrics. And we each shouldered major financial responsibilities in our families. Stylistically, he and I couldn't have been more different, yet when it came to our experiences, we were kindred spirits. And each time the universe brought us face-to-face, an ease and understanding surrounded our conversations. Even still, we didn't connect much. He was traveling. I was traveling. We were just living our own lives with little time for anything else.

———

One evening, Swizz invited me to dinner and a surprise. I accepted. "Just meet me after you're done with your day and we'll go from there," he told me. He met me downtown at a building that, from the outside, looked closed. But when we stepped through the front door, I entered a brave new world of art: a gallery filled with some of the most exquisite paintings I'd ever seen. With the help of his longtime friend, David Rogath—an art connoisseur and the gallery's owner—Swizz had flown in from France an entire collection of Erté pieces. He'd also arranged for David to close the gallery, just so Swizz could give me a private tour. "I told you I'd introduce you to Erté," he said. I couldn't believe it.

As I wandered, wide-eyed and stunned, through the gallery, Swizz walked at my side, explaining every painting—from the year the work had been completed to its artistic and historical significance. He was so knowledgeable. Not just about Erté, the father of art deco. But also about the dozens of master artists whose names he referenced with such ease, from Chagall and Dalí to Basquiat and Warhol. As he spoke, his eyes danced with childlike delight. I'd realized, months earlier, that he had more than a passing interest in art. But his deep awareness of the art world proved he was as much a student of the subject as he was an avid collector. At the end of the tour, we rounded the corner into a room with a gorgeous, candlelit table already set for two. Swizz knew I didn't eat meat, so he'd brought in a chef who'd prepared a scrumptious vegetarian meal. It was the most special thing anyone had ever done for me.

The Erté surprise stirred something in me I'd never known was there. *Is this real? What does it mean? And where do we go from here?* Over dinner that evening, we spoke openly about what was happening between us. The magnetism was so unbelievably strong that

neither of us could dismiss it. I've never experienced that kind of pull toward another human being.

———

As I was preparing to leave on another tour, Swizz and I went out for Japanese food. He paid for dinner, but for some crazy reason, he got home later and found my credit card in his pocket. He called and told me that.

"There's no way you have my card because I never took it out of my purse," I said. But sure enough, the card was mine. "Damn, I'm gonna need that card while I'm on the road," I said. "Can I pick it up from you at the studio tomorrow?" He agreed.

The next evening when I arrived, Swizz met me out front and handed me the card. I had an hour to spare, so we decided to hang out a little more before I left town.

"Take us someplace quiet," I said to the driver, who was new. He drove us to Battery Park—to the very spot where Swizz and I had often met up.

We walked and talked about what the future might hold for us. And right there on our path was a book, turned upside down. I knelt and picked it up. It was called *Old Turtle and the Broken Truth,* a children's story about a "Truth" that once fell from the sky. As it fell, one half blazed through the atmosphere while the other half tumbled to the ground. Someone found the fallen piece and kept it only for his tribe. Wars broke out among the tribes about who would own the Truth. In the end, they discovered that their broken Truth fit together with its other half to form a golden heart—and only once those halves were rejoined could there be peace.

After reading the story, Swizz and I stared at each other, flabbergasted. It felt like a sign. Then as we were walking out of the park, we noticed on the sidewalk a children's chalk drawing of some large sunflowers. "Sunflower" is the nickname Swizz had given me.

"Your energy is so bright," he'd say. The drawing, the book, the credit card—each, it seemed, was providence pulling us toward each other. As we left the park that evening, the sun descending over the Hudson, we both recognized the truth. The magic between us was so powerful, so undeniable, that we knew we were meant to be together.

———

A few months after Swizz and I had been together, it was my turn to do something special for him. I brought together four of his biggest passions: Art. Fast cars. Louis Vuitton. And music.

I told him to dress up but offered no other clues.

"Just meet me at seven p.m.," I said. I'm sure he thought I was planning a nice dinner out. When he showed up, dapper and excited, I said, "I've got a little surprise for you." It actually wasn't so little.

The Louis Vuitton store in NYC is on Fifty-seventh Street and Fifth. Swizz stopped by the store so frequently, like he was dropping in for a quart of milk, we began jokingly calling it "the bodega." Ahead of the celebration, I got in touch with the managers and arranged to rent the entire store. And on that evening, I ushered him into the front door of the bodega, which had been transformed into a dining room for a private party. A master chef prepared a delicious meal, a difficult feat because there was no kitchen on the premises. Swizz's grandmother was there. His parents were there. Some of his aunts and uncles and close friends even flew in to join us.

Dinner was just the beginning. Swizz had always been a big fan of the Gumball 3000, an event in which drivers race fancy cars thousands of miles across Europe and other continents. Swizz talked about it nonstop. I rented a slew of high-end cars, and when we exited the Vuitton store, the line of vehicles, from Lamborghinis to Porsches, and with enough room for every guest, awaited. Our destination? The Guggenheim on the Upper East Side. Swizz cut over to Madison Avenue and sped uptown in his Porsche, an enormous grin on his face the whole way. Once we arrived at the museum, which we had to ourselves, we partied to the beats of Angélique Kidjo, an African artist and dear friend of mine. He was floored—maybe even more shocked than I'd been on the evening of the Erté surprise. And he couldn't believe I'd been able to pull off such a big event without him ever having an inkling of it. I have his friends and family, the coconspirators I'd enlisted, to thank for that.

For years before I met Swizz, I'd never understood the old cliché "You just know when you know." *How can you ever be sure that you're destined to be with someone?* Only after crossing paths with Swizz did I grasp the truth in that saying. A soul mate connection isn't just an awareness. It's a deep sense of knowing, a wave of intuition that permeates your every pore. All the cells in your body rise up on their tiptoes. You don't see this feeling coming. You can't prepare for it. You might even try to push it away, as I did. And yet it always surges back, each time with greater force, sweeping you up in its mighty current, thrusting you toward a beautiful shore unknown.

# 11

## EMPIRE

**JAY-Z, GRAMMY AWARD–WINNING ARTIST AND ALICIA'S FRIEND**

I got a call one weekend from a music publisher, Jon Platt, also known as Big Jon because he's like six-seven. He had this song by two writers, Angela Hunte and Janet Sewell-Ulepic. He played it for me and I was like, "I'm ready to do it. Send me the files." I took off the verses and added my own but kept the chorus. When it was done, I listened back to it and knew it was going to be special. You get those feelings, and sometimes you're wrong, but I knew this song was going to be impactful. For the chorus, I thought, *Who embodies New York?* Mary J. Blige came to mind first. But there was something about the piano part that made me feel like it had to be Alicia. I kept picturing her, in her braids, playing those piano stabs. So I reached out to her and started overselling it. "This is going to be the biggest record about New York since Sinatra's," I told her. After she heard it, she was like, "Cool, let's do it."

When I heard her vocals, something was a bit off. Her full swagger wasn't there, and I wanted all those little ad libs she does. I can be OCD, so it bothered me a little. But I'm reluctant to make a call like that, especially with people I'm fond of. I drank some water and thought, *Here goes nothing.* When I asked her to do it over, there was an awkward silence for about three seconds. She was like, "Huh?" But then she recorded it again and even wrote that beautiful bridge—"Put your lighters in the air, everybody say yeah!'"—which took the song to another level. I recently performed "Empire" in South Africa for Global Citizen Festival. From the stage, I looked to my right and there stood Big Jon, the guy who brought me the song, with the biggest smile on his face. It was the perfect full-circle moment. And it was Alicia's bridge that tore the roof off the stadium that night.

"Empire" was on my album called *The Blueprint 3*. My original idea for that album was to go all around the world and produce different sounds, like Paul Simon did with *Graceland*. It was going to be this global album. What's crazy is, a song about my hometown ended up being the biggest song, worldwide, that I've ever made. That's why I believe in the power of intention. My intention was to have a global album, and even though that didn't happen exactly the way I initially thought it would, the universe heard my intention and delivered on it.

Empire State of Mind" almost didn't happen for me. In early 2009, when JAY-Z suggested that we get together on a song in tribute to our hometown, his idea never made it around to my ears. For weeks, Jay had been reaching out to my manager about the collaboration, and when that went nowhere, he nearly gave up and called on another artist.

"But I kept feeling like you were the right person to do it," he said, "because you're from New York and you get the whole vibe." Which is why he finally dialed me up directly.

Jeff had been my gatekeeper from day one. Everything related to my career flowed through him. When *Songs in A Minor* took off and my world suddenly spun out of control, I loved having Jeff on the front lines. It brought me an older-brother kind of comfort, one I appreciated since I was still so young. I felt protected and taken care of, like someone had my back while also keeping an eye on the front door. But as I grew into myself, both as an artist and a woman, I started realizing that was way too much power to hand over to another person, even to someone as trustworthy as Jeff. All those who wanted to reach me had to contact Jeff first and he then got to decide whether I should hear about a pitch or project. I don't know why, but Jeff didn't mention Jay's idea.

In the studio, Jay played me the bones of the song. "Please call Jay's team and tell them I'm for sure doing the song," I told Jeff soon after. Right away, Jay and I began trying to sync up our schedules to record in the same studio, but given our crazy calendars, we couldn't make it happen quickly. Meanwhile, I came down with a cold. Jay, who was on a tight deadline to finish the song for his eleventh studio album, suggested that I do my part on my own. So I recorded the first version of my vocals in an L.A. studio and sent it to him. He called me after he heard it.

"Hey, A," he said, "thanks for the vocals. But, uh . . . can you record it again?"

*Silence.*

"Huh?" I said, laughing. "You mean, you want me to do the whole thing *over*?"

"Yeah," he said. "I just think you could cut that one a little better."

I couldn't argue. My head cold was so bad that, while I was recording, I'd worked my way through a whole box of Kleenex.

"And you know how you always do that ad-lib talking in your songs?" he said. "I need you to do some of that on here."

Once my cold had passed, I recorded the second cut in my Long Island studio. Jay seemed thrilled with it. My vocals were added to the full song and we were both excited about the sound.

"Do you think it's too New York?" he asked me.

I paused. "Yeah, it's pretty New York," I said, "but I think that's cool." Jay wondered whether listeners would get it, whether the lyrics were so tied to life in our city that it wouldn't resonate with anyone who wasn't from here. He didn't change the song—he simply asked the question.

The world answered in unison after we released our ode to the City of Dreams that October. "Empire" topped the charts for five consecutive weeks. It roared across multiple continents, pushing past language barriers and joining Frank Sinatra's 1979 rendition of "New York, New York" as one of the city's best-loved anthems. In fact, it was such a potent force that it crushed all music in its path, including my own—radio DJs were already giving so much airtime to "Empire" that two of the singles I put out ahead of my fifth album, *The Element of Freedom*, weren't getting as many spins. That's when we came up with the idea of creating my own broken-down take on the song, with me at the piano, singing all the verses. That move allowed me to perform my version on any stage around the world, and Jay didn't have to be there to rhyme. It also appealed to a wide radio listenership that extended beyond hip-hop. To this day, "Empire State of Mind, Pt. 2" is one of my all-time biggest-selling records.

The following year during The Element of Freedom Tour, I performed in Paris. I stood backstage, thinking, *Is "Empire" going to make sense to this audience? Will it translate?* Man, did it. From the opening note to the final verse, those beautiful French people stayed up on their feet and sang every. Single. Word. They belted out the lyrics at the top of their lungs, nailing each turn and nuance. It was so visceral, so passionate, and so on point that I didn't even have to open my mouth. They performed the song for me as their energy soared up from the seats and filled the air above. That happened time and again in my later tours. In Brussels, Berlin, and Barcelona. In Lisbon and Zurich. In Tokyo and Sydney. In Kuala Lumpur and Manila. When thirty thousand people are stamping their feet, singing along to songs you've helped create, the complete awe and spine-tingling energy of that experience never gets old. It is more than just a concert. It's a spiritual communion, a bright, pulsating vibration that uplifts everyone in its presence.

After that Paris performance, I had an epiphany. "Empire" isn't just about New York. It's about hope. No matter where we're from, we all want the opportunity to work hard and breathe life into our ambitions. My hometown, more than any other city, represents that possibility. Millions have arrived on New York's shores, inspired by the sight of Lady Liberty, her torch lighting the way for dreamers.

This city will always be the port of entry for risers and idealists, a place where potential dances in the streets and wafts through the air. A place where the seemingly impossible feels worth attempting. And that feeling isn't just about a location. It's about aspiration, imbedded in the human spirit, transcending all geographical barriers.

No one could've predicted that "Empire" would become the kind of worldwide phenomenon that it did. Artists often think we know what songs will strike a chord as we work in the studio, but no one can ever be sure. When a song becomes part of the culture in the way that "Empire" has, there are so many factors involved. No promotional plan can bring that about; it cannot be re-created, because it's a mystery. And when it occurs, all you can do is enjoy the miracle even as you give thanks for it.

———

Bliss is a beautiful destination, but you can often only reach its shores after a turning point. It's as if the universe is testing you to be sure you are strong enough to make it through the murky waters, not just the serene ones, so that you can move to a new and unknown place in yourself. In 2009, life sent me exactly such a transition.

The year began on a high note, with Barack Obama becoming president. On that brisk January morning, our nation's first black commander in chief placed his palm on Lincoln's Bible while Michelle, graceful and resplendent in that gorgeous Isabel Toledo dress-and-coat outfit, looked on with enormous pride. As I watched from the stands, I felt honored to be seated next to civil rights activist Ralph Abernathy, one of the many brave pioneers who marched and fought to make possible the moment we were standing in. Anticipation echoed from the steps of the Lincoln Memorial to the top of the Washington Monument, reverberating through the millions who'd gathered to witness history unfold. Following the ceremony, the only thing left to do was party. I had the privilege of performing "No One" at our new president's inaugural ball. Then, following Beyoncé's rapturous rendition of "At Last," Mary J. Blige, Shakira,

Mariah Carey, will.i.am, Sting, Faith Hill, Maroon 5, and I joined Stevie Wonder on stage to sing "Signed, Sealed, Delivered (I'm Yours)" as the first couple and the entire audience danced along.

As the year got underway, my connection to Swizz continued to surprise me. We seemed like such opposites, both artistically and personally. He'd often show up at the studio hours after the start of his session, and then work only a short time before heading out to a dinner, a gallery, a this, a that. He allowed the energy to guide him rather than the other way around. If the spirit was moving, he stayed with it. If it wasn't, he left and returned. My style was so different. I grew up with the kind of focus and discipline and structure honed through strict classical training. I'd arrive in the studio with a plan of execution, and if the vibe wasn't there, I dug in, the way I once did at Kampo for the *Diary* album. If I was an hour late to the studio, I freaked out, whereas Swizz would run four hours behind. He's a free spirit, a superdreamer with his head in another galaxy. That difference is part of what drew us together. And over time, his spontaneity loosened my rigidity even as my sense of structure rubbed off on him.

We also stood shoulder-to-shoulder as equals in the music industry. When we attended events together, I didn't need to introduce him to anyone or rush to be sure he felt acknowledged; I could just exhale and enjoy myself. Swizz is an established artist in his own right, already widely known and respected. Upon entering a room, people were immediately drawn to Swizz. His words and ideas, his vision, his vibration and charisma—they seemed to compel others as strongly as they'd enraptured me. In public, the buzz was no longer just about my arrival. It was about both of us, two energetically equivalent lights burning side by side in separate but equal musical spheres.

That sense of equality brought understanding. If Swizz told me he had to go on the road, my response was usually, "Of course you have to be away next week, and I'll have to be away the week after that." Neither of us was ever leaving the other behind, feeling guilty about the constant travel that comes with being in our positions. There was an ease and effortlessness in our relationship. It also felt intellectually stimulating. Swizz was always scanning for new ideas, keeping his eyes on everything from internet blogs and podcasts to the *Los Angeles Times* and *Cultured Magazine*. On long Sunday afternoons, we'd get lost in hours of conversation, on everything from the rise of the Black Panthers during the turbulence of the '60s, to the master works of photographer Gordon Parks. At every turn, Swizz and I challenged one another, widening each other's perspectives.

The year came with another ground shift, this one between Jeff and me. When he and I had met all those decades ago at the Police Athletic League in Harlem, I was fourteen and still the brightest shade of green; he was an industry vet with a don't-eff-with-me demeanor. In many ways, it was a perfect pairing. His strong-mindedness balanced out my youth and vulnerability. He was outspoken when I didn't yet have the voice or courage to be. That formula worked well for a long time. And then I sprouted wings.

I'd felt the push and pull between us even in the early days. When I launched Keep a Child Alive, Jeff supported the idea of helping impoverished families battling HIV, but he didn't think I should be the one to spearhead that effort. Stay in my lane—that's what he wanted me to do. In his view, musicians created songs, activists launched movements, and those two spaces didn't need to overlap. Why dilute the artist's core brand?

"Your music is what makes you most relevant," he'd tell me. "Focus on that." Jeff hadn't changed; he'd always been forthright. I was the one who'd outgrown our dynamic. While I respected his viewpoint, I didn't agree with it. Activism flows through my veins as strongly as artistry does. That mix is who I am. And the more I rallied for the important causes of our world, the less tolerance I had for any pushback. My involvement in social justice doesn't downplay my musicianship. It enhances it.

At every turn, Jeff had been my greatest advocate, protecting me in an industry known for its mafia-like culture behind the scenes.

But once you finally take sail in your life, you no longer crave a captain. You simply want a consultant, someone who can advise rather than steer. At fourteen, I was still too young and afraid to trust myself, to direct my own course. At twenty-eight, I was finally becoming brave. And as I grew more courageous, Jeff and I grew apart. But even with my newfound strength and clarity, it was scary to move away from someone I'd depended upon for so long. Was I fearless enough to depend on myself?

I now see transitions for what they are: the dawn of a new chapter. As miraculous as beginnings can be, they can also be excruciating. My new space with Jeff was preparing the way for all the heart-opening experiences still to come.

———

As the curtain fell on 2009, I celebrated a highlight. *The Element of Freedom* became my first album to reach number one in the United Kingdom, even as it claimed the number two spot on the US charts. It went on to be certified platinum and sold more than four million copies worldwide. The single "Un-Thinkable (I'm Ready)" rocked into the top spot on the R & B charts and stayed there for twelve consecutive weeks, making it the longest-running single of that year and beating the previous ten-week record set by "No One" in 2007.

And yet with all the awesome moments the year brought me, I look at the cover of *The Element of Freedom* and notice that my eyes are lowered, my spirit heavy. Even the album's title says a lot about the state I was in. For many years, I've understood the power of words, and when I titled the album I thought the phrase was super empowering. It's not. The word *element* suggests one small piece of freedom, a single morsel rather than the full experience. Both the title and the image reflect how that time was for me. I definitely wanted freedom, but I wasn't yet ready to step into it, embody it, breathe it, own it. You can hear those growing pains in the mood and lyrics of *Element*. The album has a somber sound. *Element* turned out to be one of my biggest albums, particularly because it included my version of "Empire." But vibrationally, the image on the album's cover is my most muted. That had everything to do with the transition I'd been navigating.

That tough passageway came with a surprising revelation. When life forces you to face yourself, what awaits in the mirror is a gift: vulnerability. Your heart is pierced. You're broken open. You're hyperaware of what you're feeling. The song "Un-Thinkable (I'm Ready)" is an expression of that kind of rawness. I wrote it with Drake, who was then just starting out in his career. The flow was a conversation with myself: "I was wondering maybe / Could I make you my baby / If we do the unthinkable / Would it make us look crazy / Or would it be so beautiful / Either way I'm saying / If you ask me I'm ready." The song resonated with so many because it came from a genuine place. The lyrics were a statement, not to the world, but to myself. I can show weakness. I can be real. And when I reveal my true heart, not everyone is going to approve. What I know now is that I don't need them to.

# 12

## CORSICA

SWIZZ BEATZ

Alicia and I were in the South of France, hanging with our friends Dessi and Katia. I woke up early and said to Dessi, "Bro, I'm doing it today." He was like, "You're doing *what*?" I said, "I'm getting engaged." I hadn't planned it. I just felt it was the right time because Alicia and I were so head over heels. While she was still sleeping, Dessi and I rolled out and got a two-carat ring, one I could use that day until I had another one designed later. That afternoon we went on a boat ride. While Alicia was out swimming, I began orchestrating the moment: where I'd stand, where Dessi could position himself to capture the surprise on camera, how he could get the mountains in the background. That's the Virgo in me—precise. I finally went out on deck, got on one knee, and said, "Will you be my wife?" She was bugging out. In fact, she was so shocked that she dropped onto her knees. I'm like, No, stand up—I'm the one who's supposed to be kneeling! After she said yes, I slid the ring on her finger. For years, she wouldn't take that ring off, even after I presented her with the upgrade. Come to find out she actually loved that damn ring and never wanted to trade up. That's Alicia for you—less is more.

Swizz has never been an early riser. So when he woke me up with a peck on the lips at 8:45 a.m. on a Sunday while we were on vacation, that should've been a flashing-red siren that something was up.

"I've gotta go out for a bit," he said. He was fully dressed. I, wrapped in a tumble of white sheets, slid open my eyes and glanced around the dark room. The night before, we'd pulled down the shades so the Mediterranean sun couldn't disrupt our plan to sleep in.

"Where you goin'?" I murmured.

"Just running an errand," he said. I nodded, pulled the duvet over my head, and drifted back to sleep.

Swizz and I were on a getaway to Saint-Tropez. Every morning, we'd wake up late, hang out on the water all afternoon, party all night, and then stumble home to sleep off the hangover. Before I met Swizz, I thought I knew how to truly enjoy myself. I definitely didn't. He was constantly introducing me to new places, new friends, new ways of seeing the world. With him, everything was about dreaming up these vivid, colorful ideas and then charging ahead on an adventure without a blueprint or worry. In many ways, he taught me how to live. How to throw out the rulebook and make my own rules. How to jet over to the French Riviera, last minute, for some fun. On the weekend when we arrived in Saint-Tropez, Dessi and Katia, this cute Bulgarian couple we rolled with a lot, hosted us in their home.

When I got up around eleven, Swizz hadn't returned. Dessi had gone with him, Katia told me, so the two of us lounged by the pool and had some breakfast.

"When will you be back?" I texted Swizz. We were planning a boat ride for that afternoon.

"Almost done," he wrote. "You and Katia can just meet us at the marina at three."

Swizz and Dessi were already onboard the boat when we arrived.

"Wow, I love it!" I said as Katia and I settled into a couple of chairs on the front deck. That's when I noticed a funny look on Swizz's face. "What's up?" I said. "You okay?"

"I'm fine," he assured me. Moments later, our boat left the dock.

After an hour out on the water, we pulled into a cove surrounded by mountains. The sun lent the sea its rays, highlighting flecks of brilliant turquoise blue.

"I've gotta get in," I announced. If I weren't an artist, I'd be a mermaid. That's how much I love the water. I jumped right in from the edge of the boat and then stayed out there for a long time, alternating between swimming and floating around on my back, soaking in the beauty around me. Once it got chilly, I climbed back onboard. The others weren't around; I figured they were hanging out indoors. So I dried off, took up the spot back in my chair, and vibed to the Bob Sinclar album that was playing. Swizz always brings along his own symphony.

Swizz walked out on deck. "Come on," he said, playfully pulling me up from my seat and leading me to a rail near the bow. "Let's look at this beautiful sunset." We stood there in an embrace as the setting sun gave the water a pinkish-blue tint. We reminisced about the specialness of our connection, and how nothing has ever felt more electric or natural. And then suddenly, Swizz knelt down as if he'd dropped something.

"What's happening?" I said, getting down on my knees beside him.

"Stand up, girl!" he said, laughing. I stared at him for a second, still clueless about what was unfolding. "No, seriously," he said, "stand up." I rose. "Will you be my wife?" he asked. He opened a little black velvet box, revealing a silver band with a glistening diamond heart.

"*What?!*" I squealed.

"Will you marry me?" he asked again.

The tears came flooding down my face.

"Yes!" I said. I dropped down beside him again as he slid the ring onto my finger. I hugged him hard as the tears kept flowing, Dessi and Katia snapping photos from behind us. "This is *crazy!*" I kept saying. "Are we crazy? Yes, we're crazy." Moments later, our friends met us on the deck, eager to share the backstory of how the spontaneous proposal had come together. Who wakes up one morn-ing, decides to get engaged, goes out ring shopping, and then sets up a perfect proposal? It's classic Swizz.

I absolutely love that ring. Every year, Swizz tries to outdo himself by presenting me with a flashier one. "Will you stop?" I finally told him. Bling is not my thing. Simplicity, in the shape of a heart from the man who captured mine, always will be.

———

Soon after our engagement, my birthday rolled around. This one marked the beginning of our "birthday wars"—the annual attempt to outdo each other in celebration. Some years, we go all out; other years, we keep it low-key but no less memorable.

For this birthday, my twenty-ninth, it was an all-out year. Swizz took me to Kauai, the Hawaiian island covered in lush tropical rainforests—otherwise known as paradise for a nature lover like me. Around noon on my big day, Swizz said, "Let's go for a drive." We loaded into a two-seater Jeep, curving and winding our way through the forests until we pulled up, an hour later, at a little house. The home sat on stilts, looking out over the pristine waters of the North Pacific. We climbed the steep stairs, admiring a small garden out front, and then entered the house. There, on a table in the living room, sat an enormous box.

"Open it," Swizz said, smiling as he slid the box toward me. I lifted the cardboard flaps and looked inside to see several large canisters.

He pulled me close. "I've always wanted you to be my canvas," he whispered. The canisters were full of body paint, in every vibrant color imaginable, and Swizz had had them shipped to the guesthouse ahead of time. Later, stroke by stroke in the shadows of dusk, he turned me into his masterpiece, covering me in swirls of yellows, reds, and purples. Afterward, my body still tingling from the sensa-tion of cool paint on my warm skin, we walked out to the garden, where he photographed me. Never have I experienced anything more sensual.

Which is why, when I missed my period a few weeks later, I wasn't exactly surprised. Swizz was with me when I took the home pregnancy test, but even before it confirmed that I was expecting, we'd both sensed it. The pregnancy wasn't planned—it was inevitable. We were so deeply intertwined on every level, from the soul to the cellular, that even if we hadn't conceived that weekend, it probably would've been a matter of when, not if. As that winter gave way to spring, we relished our two pleasures: the engagement and the pregnancy.

———

In February, I began the Freedom Tour: forty-three shows across North America and Europe. Talk about a crazy time to get pregnant. The child I was carrying became my respite, an escape from the whirlwind. After every performance, I'd crawl back to my room feeling exhausted, and yet somehow rejuvenated by the presence of this gift growing inside me. Swizz was my other quiet place. During our moments together between tour stops, I felt at peace inside the intimate bubble we'd built around ourselves. Nothing else seemed to exist or matter when we were with each other.

We chose not to reveal the pregnancy or engagement right away. I wanted to carve out a sacred space for my child and myself. And yet keeping my news private came with a trade-off: I didn't get to revel in that outward display of joy that new moms normally experience. Then again, there was nothing normal about my life— living in tour buses and hotels, on and off, for months at a time. I was in such a heavy work cycle, just trying to keep up. Even if others had known I was pregnant, there wouldn't have been much opportunity to bask.

Only a tiny circle of people initially knew Swizz and I were expecting: my doctor, my mother, Swizz's parents, and Erika. I didn't even tell my road crew and manager for the first several months. My dear friend Wouri, who was styling me on the tour, might've suspected. In an effort to disguise my developing baby bump, I repeatedly asked him to bring in these long necklaces and loose-fitting tops, but I never told him why. I'm sure he thought I was crazy. Or maybe since we have a friendship dating back to junior high, Wouri figured it out and kept quiet.

I'm fortunate that I didn't have morning sickness. There was only one night when I almost lost my dinner during a show in Lisbon. I was at the piano, pumping the foot pedals, rocking my medley of creations. Right in the middle of the second verse of "Superwoman," a wave of nausea washed over me. I could feel the vomit gathering in my throat. I looked out over the thousands in that stadium and said to myself, *You will not throw up all over this piano, Alicia.* Between the end of that verse and the next, I leaned to my left side, drew in a long breath, closed my eyes, and willed every bit of that vomit back down into my stomach. I then sat up and kept right on singing. Mercifully, the feeling subsided, because if it hadn't, it would've been one nasty moment. I can just visualize the headlines.

Back at the hotel that evening, I told Erika about my close call. As the conversation turned toward what was ahead of me in the coming years, I also admitted the questions I'd been carrying around: *What if I'm not cut out for motherhood? What if I fail at being responsible for a child—a life? What if I can't do this?* There's probably not a parent on earth who hasn't asked those questions in some form at some point in time. I had to be so strong outwardly, but inside, I felt afraid and emotional. The fear was real. And, I found, so was the whole nesting instinct. I think of it as nature's way of prompting a mother to vacuum every corner of her emotional and spiritual house. Even in the earliest months of my pregnancy, I felt a powerful desire to clear my space of all negativity. A similar instinct once carried me to Egypt. But this urge, one on behalf of my baby, was twelve times more forceful. I felt determined to do for my child what I'd once struggled to do for myself: rid my life of all circumstances that no longer served me.

When I told Jeff I was pregnant and he seemed less than thrilled, his response confirmed what my spirit had been whispering for months: We were on two vastly different planets. The old me would've continued anyway. But the woman I was becoming, one with a clear voice and viewpoint, knew a shift had to be made.

By the time I told Jeff we needed to transition, we'd been backing away for months. He'd traveled on tour with me less and less, and in fact, we seldom saw each other in person. Ahead of our final conversation, I'd spent months untangling our legal ties. An artist–manager relationship is similar to a marriage, and ending it can be just as difficult. For fifteen years, Jeff had been the point of contact for every aspect of my business, from contracts and collaborations to serving as the primary liaison between me and the record label and the rest of the world. Loosening those massive knots came with a major lesson. In any partnership, whether business or personal, no one individual should hold all the reins. A year earlier, I'd launched my own company, AK Worldwide, with that wisdom in mind. My organization became the command center for every branch of my business. All matters flow in and out of that central office, and all roads lead back to the owner: me.

———

I had never seen myself getting married, maybe because I didn't grow up in a home with marriage at its center. And if two people loved each other, why did they need to sign a legal contract to make that official? In my mind, a government-instituted document could never be the glue that actually held a couple together. Only a day-to-day commitment of the heart could do that. Falling in love with Swizz shifted my perspective—a little.

"I have an idea," I told Swizz one evening over the phone. "Instead of getting married, what if we just dedicate our lives to each other? We can create our own document, stating what kind of relationship we want, and sign it ourselves."

The line went silent. "What do you mean?" he finally said.

"I mean, we're the ones who should define our relationship, right?" I said. "We can even hang our document in the living room to remind us of why we came together. It would be so beautiful and so poetic."

For all of his bold ideas and out-of-the box visions, a tiny piece of that man is surprisingly conservative. He didn't want to hear about some hippy-dippy arrangement; he wanted traditional. And though he didn't say that during our call, he did ask a question that melted me: "You don't want to marry me, do you?"

"I do!" I said. "That's not what I'm trying to say, babe. I just want us to do things our own way." But Swizz thought that was an excuse, my way of wiggling out of a full commitment to him. In the following days, when I noticed him getting down about it, we revisited the conversation and agreed on a compromise: We'd marry the old-fashioned way. But we'd put our own spin on the vows.

We finally announced our engagement. We also shared news of the pregnancy when I was about four months along, and the public declaration seemed to cause my stomach to pop. We made plans for an intimate ceremony in Corsica, France, near the end of July.

A spirit of positivity—that, more than any other detail of my wedding day, was most important to me. I wanted Swizz and I, as well as our child, to be encircled by good vibrations. That's why we created our guest list so intentionally. We invited loved ones who were truly pulling for us as a couple, those who celebrated and respected our union and would continue to uplift it. Twenty-six people received an invitation, and once their guests were added, the total was less than fifty. My brother Bono was there. My dear friend Queen Latifah attended. My girls Erika, Taneisha, and Kat were invited. So were our families, including my mother and father, as well as Swizz's parents and grandparents.

Swizz wanted to do something special for me. He decided to go big by asking Deepak Chopra to officiate our ceremony. We both admired his insights, which were in line with the theme of our vows. It turned out that Puff and Deepak lived in the same building, and through Swizz's brotherhood with Puff, Swizz was able to ask Deepak to preside over our nuptials. He graciously agreed. Our friends, Alex and Laura, offered us their house as a venue. The cliffside home, with its breathtaking view of the Mediterranean, could've been pulled right from the pages of a *Travel + Leisure* spread.

On the evening before the ceremony, we all gathered for dinner outdoors at a local restaurant. Not long after we were seated at the banquet tables, I felt a sprinkle. Then a shower. Then a downpour that forced us to scramble indoors with plates in hand, only to return outside later in the evening when the storm had passed. Thankfully, the rain wasn't a sign of weather to come. The morning of our wedding dawned bright and clear.

Mom helped me dress. I slid into the one-shoulder Grecian-inspired gown that Vera Wang designed for me, with its ivory silk georgette fabric draping gently over my baby bump. I also wore a headpiece, two strands of intricate jewels that adorned my swept-back hair. Swizz had already made me feel like a goddess. I now glowed like one.

A half hour before the ceremony, Craig put his head in the room where I was getting ready. His expression brightened when he glimpsed me. As he started to close the door, Mom said, "Where are you going? We want you to walk Alicia down the aisle with me." Craig teared up. I don't recall how my mother and I made the choice to include him, but it felt right. As complicated as my relationship with Craig has been, he will always be the one man who gave me life. Having him walk me down the aisle was an acknowledgment of that.

With Mom on my right arm and Craig on my left, I clutched the bouquet of purple calla lilies. We made our way from the house and onto a steep and winding cobblestone path, and with every step, even in my flats, I prayed I wouldn't fall. I rounded the corner where the guests and groom awaited. Swizz beamed when he saw me. There he stood, so handsome in his tux, so hopeful about the path ahead. He led me onto a platform near a glistening pond.

Our exchange of vows was the pinnacle. Face-to-face, with the world around us seemingly silent, we made our promises. We vowed that full freedom would forever live at the center of our union. That we'd never seek to own each other, but rather to love and liberate, like birds always free to fly. In place of a mandate to be together, there stood a choice, one we'd continue making every single day on our journey. Nearly a decade after we spoke those intentions, we're still holding them—and each other—close.

# 13

## ON FIRE

**DJ WALTON, PRESIDENT OF AK WORLDWIDE
AND ALICIA'S LONGTIME FRIEND**

I've witnessed Alicia's evolution. Before she had her first son, she was hard-core Hell's Kitchen Alicia. She was as incredibly heartwarming as she is now, and yet she also didn't play. She got that hustle and drive from her mother, as well as from the environment she grew up in.

Her work ethic was unsurpassed: constantly touring and promoting on very little sleep, handling a grueling schedule that would've tested even the most dedicated. She took her career so seriously that all of us in her camp had to stay on top of our game—and she inspired us to do that because she led by example. Even when she was pregnant and not always feeling her best, she'd go out on stage and kill it. She never missed a show.

After she had Egypt, I saw a dramatic shift in her. She was still hard-working and ambitious, but she went from intense Alicia to kumbaya Alicia, at one with the earth. The change came overnight. She lightened up. She had new priorities. If a gig didn't work in her schedule, she'd just move on. She was much more relaxed in her approach and much more at peace with herself.

I wanted our baby's gender to be a surprise. For the first few months of my pregnancy, I got my wish. And then I got a sonogram while on the road.

"You should keep on top of your checkups while you're traveling," my New York doctor told me before I left on the Freedom Tour. "Your sonogram results can be sent to me." So around the five-month mark, while I was in London, I made an appointment with an ob-gyn I didn't know, this chatty Brit who joked the whole way through the procedure. I lay horizontal as he slowly glided a small sensor across my stomach. He stopped just above my navel, studied the monitor on my right, and grinned.

"Looks like your baby has a third leg," he said. It was hysterical. It also blew the lid off a surprise I'd been determined to keep.

What's crazy is that I knew it was a boy. On the road, I was in and out of hotels, by myself a lot in the evenings. I employ fifty-plus people on a tour, but it can be very lonely. Once the show is over and I'm back in my room, it's just me and my jet lag. In the middle of the night, I'd often feel the baby's spirit—and that spirit was definitely a *he,* a masculine energy. At certain moments, I felt as if my son were already born and walking alongside me, bringing me comfort and companionship.

After our wedding, the countdown to joy intensified. With about three months until my delivery, Swizz and I took a baby-basics class a friend recommended. A mother's instincts tell her some things about nurturing a newborn, but not everything. Fresh off my course in breastfeeding and swaddling, my ob-gyn, this incredible female doctor who'd mastered old-school birthing techniques like delivering a breech baby naturally, turned me on to the Marie Mongan method of HypnoBirthing—a way to manage pain, using a state of focused attention (aka hypnosis) during natural childbirth. In the weeks leading up to delivery, Swizz and I practiced being relaxed and open, because when you're stressed, you're clenched and closed. We also rehearsed putting Swizz's voice in my head, so that when he spoke during the birthing process, his words and vocals would prompt deep calm for me.

HypnoBirthing is a next-level, beautiful concept that I found incredibly empowering. For years I've understood how the words we choose and repeat can frame and define our experience. Hypno-Birthing incorporates that principle. When you change your vocabulary around the birthing process, our instructor told us, you alter how you relate to the process. So instead of using the word *contraction,* which sounds harsh and excruciating, you'd use the word *surge,* which accurately describes the rolling vibration, peaking into a wave of discomfort, that I felt during my birthing process. I was also taught how to protect the space around the baby and me. As any pregnant woman can tell you, everyone seems to have a labor horror story to share, and I learned to interrupt storytellers midsentence. "I'm sorry you experienced that," I'd say, "but I want to keep my thoughts clear and positive."

On the morning of October 14, 2010, a surge woke me up at two a.m. I didn't recognize the sensation, so I ignored it and drifted back to sleep. When another one hit an hour and a half later, I got up, turned on the light, and waddled over to a rocking chair in our bedroom.

"Baby, please wake up and start timing these," I said, recalling my doctor's instructions to keep track of the amount of time between surges and head to the hospital when they were an hour apart. My man sleepily pulled out a pen and paper and wrote down the first time. He then blacked out again. This went on for several hours before I finally insisted that he show me the paper. There, scattered across the sheet, were numbers all over the damn place: some upside down, others crooked, none of the times listed in order. My water hadn't yet broken, but it was time to get moving, as best as I could tell by my inner surge clock.

With Swizz at my side and his voice in my ear, I surged my way into motherhood. The doctor placed my miracle right onto the warm skin of my chest, my son's heart beating in rhythm with my own. Weeks before he arrived, we'd chosen his name.

"The Egypt trip was such a defining moment in your life," Swizz said. "Wouldn't that be amazing as a name?" It felt right the moment I heard it, as did adding in Swizz's middle name, Daoud. Two days later, I left the hospital cradling Egypt Daoud Dean, my constant reminder of a life-altering pilgrimage that taught me what liberation feels like.

Soon after I arrived home, one of my mom's dearest longtime friends, my Aunty Elaine, stopped by to see us. After she cuddled Egypt for the first time, she and I sat together in the kitchen.

"You've got on your big-girl panties now, don't you?" she said, smiling. It was true in every way. I'd literally gone from wearing tiny thongs to these big cotton drawers, but I'd also stepped squarely into a space that felt at once divine and daunting. This little soul, this child lying swaddled in my arms, was now my responsibility, just as I'd once been my mother's.

Becoming a parent involves more than just bathing and feeding and changing, though there's a lot of that involved. It's also a sacred assignment to teach and love and celebrate. And it is, for Swizz and me, a commitment to raise a boy. A son. A king. A man.

———

When Egypt was three months old, I returned to the studio fiercely focused. I took control of my schedule—with far greater force than I had upon returning from those two weeks of silence in Egypt. For me, motherhood came with a litmus test: *Is what I'm doing important enough for me to spend time away from my baby?* If the answer was no, the task went the way of the Walkman cassette recorder—phased out. Gone was the era when I'd spend days at a time in the studio, not just burning the candle at both ends, but melting it right down to a messy puddle of wax. Parenting, complete with its two a.m. feedings and pumping in the studios to ensure Egypt always had enough milk, pulled me toward a new frequency. I was intent on doing what was best for my child, which, by default, was best for me.

I called this new focus "Girl on Fire" energy. The lyrics to that song just tumbled out of me, as if the universe had written it on my behalf. I'd been thinking about the powerful women around me: my mother, my godmother, my sister-friends Taneisha and Kat, and the many others I'd crossed paths with over the years. The world can be a challenging place for us women to navigate. We often find ourselves feeling burned out, incapable, and lonely, and yet we're still so resilient. I'd carried that thought around for a couple of weeks when the words flowed out of me while we were in the studio one afternoon: "Hotter than a fantasy / lonely like the highway / She's living in a world and it's on fire / Filled with catastrophe but she knows she can fly away / She got both feet on the ground / And she's burning it down." The lyrics perfectly captured what I'd been feeling—the idea that women, even in our vulnerability, continue trudging forward. We still make our moves. We still rise to the moment. Like the words of "Superwoman," the message was as much a celebration of others as it was a reminder to me.

We wrote the lyrics before putting them to music. I'd brought in two awesome producers for that part: Jeff Bhasker, a Grammy Award–winning songwriter (who also wrote lyrics with me), and Salaam Remi, who has worked with artists like Amy Winehouse and Nas. I slipped out of the studio session for a restroom break and I just had to call Swizz. The sound of the chorus thundered through the walls as I dialed my husband: "This . . . girl . . . is on *fi-yah!*"

"Babe, something crazy is happening here," I told Swizz when he picked up.

"Seriously?" he said.

"Yes," I told him, "and I don't know how to explain it. You've got to hear it."

It might be rare that an artist can predict what will resonate, like with "Empire," but that song right there? I knew "Girl on Fire" would hit. I felt it in every fiber of my being. During the creative process, I never know how a song is going to come to me, but every now and then, the universe sends me a gift: the lyrics and melody seemingly just appear—and I'm grateful whenever that happens.

By this time, I'd relocated my studio. Ann Mincieli, my sound engineer, business partner, and friend, approached me with the idea.

Ann and I go way back. In 1997, she and I met at Quad Studios in Times Square. She was an assistant sound engineer then, and I was a newly signed artist mostly still doing vocals in the closet of Kerry's Harlem apartment. In many ways, Ann and I have grown up together in the industry. We vibe because we're both sky's-the-beginning visionaries. In 2010, Ann purchased two commercial condos in Chelsea. She transformed the space into Jungle City Studios, a state-of-the-art, seven-star artist haven offering the best in vintage and modern technology.

When Swizz and I returned from our honeymoon in Saint-Tropez, Ann told me about the project and showed me the space. I was blown away.

"What would you think about moving your studio here?" she asked. I loved the idea. On the building's east side, Jungle City provides space for the thriving community of musicians who regularly book there; on the building's west side, I purchased the two condos mirroring Jungle City and moved my Oven Studios from Long Island to the new space. It has since become my personal playground, one that allows me to create on my own terms; no one can ever tell me when, whether, or how to make music because I own the place. What a long road from walls soundproofed with comforters to a top-of-the-line studio.

This new space next to Jungle City was where I recorded much of *Girl on Fire*. Making the album was like throwing a big house party, one filled with the dopest guests. The collaborations abounded, from Maxwell's sultry contributions on the slow jam "Fire We Make" and Bruno Mars's writing and background vocals on "Tears Always Win" to the Babyface collaboration "That's When I Knew." In 2011, I took my party to Jamaica and turned it into a writing camp at Geejam Studios in Port Antonio. John Legend, Miguel, and Babyface flew in. These two awesome producers and writers Pop & Oak came, as did producers and writers Antonio Dixon, Stacy Barthe, and Jamie Smith of The xx. Rodney Jerkins, the hit maker for artists like Michael Jackson and Lady Gaga, joined us. Our time in Bob Marley's homeland turned into a whole series of circulating sessions. It was sick.

The renowned British artist and singer-songwriter Emeli Sandé partnered with me on several of the album's songs, including one of my favorites, "Not Even the King." The lyrics tell of a ruler who lives in a castle, surrounded by people, but who has not a single friend who isn't on the payroll. He has wealth and power but is missing what's priceless: real relationships. I wrote that song after watching a couple I know, two great-hearted people, walk through a soul-wrenching time. From a financial standpoint, they were set: mansions, cars, vacation homes. And yet despite their enormous wealth, they were experiencing deep emptiness—a condition no amount of money could cure.

As I watched my friends struggle, I thought, *If striving for billions comes with that kind of emptiness, then I'm straight.* The point isn't that wealth should be feared or disregarded; my family is successful and we plan to build on that. But as we move in that direction, I work to stay mindful of what I most value. For me, it comes down to capacity: *What kind of life do I want to build and what sacrifices will that require? What commitments can I let go of so I can remain a conscious partner and parent?*

What works for me is extreme weed-pulling on my to-do list. Clearing out the unnecessary creates the space and conditions for me to nurture my connection with family. And the soil beneath it all is acceptance. I do everything I can to be a present mother and partner, and then daily, I make peace with what has had to go undone. It's all any of us can ask of ourselves.

"Brand New Me," another song I did with Emeli, reflects the zone I was in while making the album, and the lyrics showcase that: "It's been a while, I'm not who I was before / You look surprised, your words don't burn me anymore / Been meaning to tell you, but I guess it's clear to see / Don't be mad, it's just the brand new kind of me / Can't be bad, I found a brand new kind of free." In fact, when you look at many of the titles—like "Girl on Fire," "New Day," and "That's When I Knew," a song inspired by my relationship with Swizz—the theme is as obvious on this page as it was in my life. My senses were sharp, my energy sparkling. I was open, a wide clearing for the songs to come through me. I was a channel of free expression.

———

On the magic carpet ride of my life, I've shared the stage with some of music's greatest icons, one highlight being the incomparable Stevie Wonder. During the months when I was completing *Girl on Fire* and feeling bathed in that energy, Stevie and I performed at the 2012 Billboard Awards. Our duet included "Higher Ground" and "Overjoyed"—which sums up the immeasurable excitement I felt during the experience. At the close of the show, Stevie, who'd recently celebrated his sixty-second birthday, made a request.

"I want you to give me a birthday gift," he said. "I want you to sing 'Empire State' *a cappella*." Still high on the energy of our duet, I pecked around on the keyboard to find my opening note.

"Will y'all help me?" I yelled into the mic. The crowd applauded. I cleared my throat, reached down into a far corner of my diaphragm, and pulled out the first line of the chorus: "In New York . . . concrete jungle where dreams are made of . . ." Stevie swayed and clapped. "Happy birthday!" I said to the man who, in 1981, gave the world the most soulful version of that song.

This wasn't my first time singing with the Grammy Award–winning legend, nor my second. Before our group jam session at President Obama's 2009 inaugural ball, I performed with Stevie and Lenny Kravitz at MTV's 2004 Video Music Awards. Ahead of the show, the three of us planned to rehearse at Lenny's studio in Miami. I arrived before Stevie did, and Lenny warmly greeted me at the door.

"Come on in," he said.

Everything about Lenny—his style, his artistry, his swag, the spaces he curates—exudes badassery. That man is the epitome of cool. And his studio was as eclectically fascinating as you'd expect, starting with, in his entryway, a massive mural done by Jona Cerwinske, the artist known for creating elaborate images using only the stroke of a black Sharpie. As we awaited Stevie's arrival, Lenny and I began practicing our parts for "Higher Ground." An assistant popped her head in our door a few minutes later.

"Mr. Wonder will be here in twenty minutes," she said. Right then, one of my singers, Whitney, who'd been rehearsing with us, stepped out for what I thought was a quick run to the ladies' room. When she returned fifteen minutes later, she was completely dolled up in a dress and heels.

"Um, you know Stevie won't be able to see you," I joked.

"Yes," Whitney said, "but he'll be able to *feel* if I'm not right." We cracked up. I don't know whether Stevie could sense her appearance, but I do know one thing: her energy was on point for the rest of that session.

Stevie arrived with that trademark grin on his face and a harmonica in his pocket. I tried to disguise the tremor in my voice as we warmed up. There I sat at my keyboard, playing and singing alongside one of the world's most creative geniuses, the artist behind an immense catalog that extends through more than a half century. Decades before my existence was even the tiniest seed of a thought, Little Stevie—who was just eleven when Berry Gordy signed him to Motown back in 1961—was already captivating the world with hits like "Fingertips" and "Uptight (Everything's Alright)." That was only the beginning. With amazing songs like "As," and "Boogie On Reggae Woman," and the song that will forever give me goose bumps, "They Won't Go When I Go" from *Fulfillingness' First Finale,* Stevie's creations serve as a backdrop for our lives, both marking time and reflecting it. And for me, he is an example of what a true musician should be: a boundary pusher who values artistic growth, at times even more than commercial success.

So on the afternoon when Lenny and I jammed with Stevie for several hours straight, my body was there but my head was someplace else. It was even more surreal when, in addition to our "Higher Ground" performance, Stevie pulled out his harmonica and played along as I sang "If I Ain't Got You." It was one of the greatest pinch-me moments of my life, right up there with meeting Prince—the other artist who has had a profound impact on my artistry. Both Stevie and Prince have provided me with a powerful blueprint of what creating outside of the lines looks like.

———

Prince and I stayed connected long after that day, in 2001, when I had nervously awaited the sound of his voice over the phone. And with every encounter after that, I was no less tongue-tied. During my *Songs in A Minor* Tour, Prince came to one of my shows. He took a spot near the soundboard, the place in a theater where the sound quality is usually the best. I'd heard Prince might be there that evening, which made me nervous. Afterward, he met me backstage.

"Good show," he said, "but I didn't like the sound." I stared blankly at him, not sure how to respond.

"You don't like the sound?" I finally said.

"The balance is not good," he explained. I didn't love hearing that, especially from someone I held in such high regard, but I received the critique as he'd intended it: as a teaching moment. Also, I knew he was right: The engineering had thrown off the sonic. Ultimately, the feedback let me do some fine-tuning to elevate my production quality. Better—that is what Prince and all others who achieve excellence are always pushing toward. They rise. They insist upon meticulousness. And in so doing, they alter the very space they inhabit.

In 2004, when Prince offered me the great honor of inducting him into the Rock & Roll Hall of Fame, I spoke of that idea.

"There are many kings," I said as I stood at the podium. "King Henry the Eighth. King Solomon. King Tut. King James. King Kong. The Three Kings. But there is only one Prince—only one man who has defied restriction."

No matter where in the world I was, Prince always knew how to get in touch with me. I might not see or talk to him for months and then, boom, someone on his team would dial me up.

"Prince would like to talk with you," I'd hear. Many times he'd just call to encourage me. After he heard "You Don't Know My Name," he told me, "I really love that new song." I can still feel the electricity surging through me. Years later, he came to another of my shows, and by then, I was playing in big, seven-thousand-seat arenas.

"Your audience doesn't look the same anymore," he told me backstage after the show. I just stood there. I never knew quite what to say to Prince. "That happened with me," he went on. "Over time, my audience became much more diverse." I'm sure he could see the question splashed across my face: *Isn't that good?* To this day, I am amazed at the diversity of my audiences, how sixty-seven-year-old white men come to concerts with their fifteen-year-old grandkids. Prince didn't offer a conclusion that day; he was just pointing out the similarity.

In the following years, Prince and I talked more about the natural shifts that come with evolving as an artist. I didn't always understand what he meant at the time, but I do now. When you put out your first album, you strike a chord with a certain group of people. That chord is so genuine that the group rallies around you. Your music both speaks to and reflects them. Their applause becomes the water for your growth. You feel free to expand and experiment with new sounds, and the resulting music widens your audience to include new groups that hadn't paid you much attention in the beginning. There may then come a moment when your original crew doesn't like your new direction.

Prince masterfully pulled off a juggling feat that some musicians find impossible: He continually widened his audience and his artistry without ever alienating his core group. That is my own intention. I want to superserve my most committed tribe—those like-minded listeners who've been with me from the start—even as I push myself artistically and expand my fam. This is one of the great lessons Prince passed on to me. His legacy, like Stevie's, has lifted me and countless others onto higher ground.

———

Becoming a mother opens a new wing in your heart. You think you've always known how to love, and you have. But it's only after your child arrives that your love takes on new shades and textures you hadn't even known existed. Your capacity for care expands. It's a love not based on reciprocity or conditions, but on existence alone. You care for your child simply because he or she is yours. And that love can't help but spill over into other spaces in your life. It's a revival of the senses, one that can be heard in every measure of the *Girl on Fire* album.

"Girl on Fire," the lead single, blazed a path around the globe and back again. The song is still one of the biggest records in my catalog. It crossed over in every way, with millennials and boomers, gay and straight, soccer moms and urban hipsters, schoolgirls in Africa and grandmothers in Dubai. It became the definition of viral. My youngest son would one day, at age four, be able to recite every single word of "Girl on Fire." There's just something about that song that resonates. That probably has a lot to do with the catchy and memorable chorus.

And the image on the album's cover? I call that my *hell yeah* pose. What a drastic difference, energetically, between that photo and the one on *Element*. I stand with my hands on my hips and my eyes on the truth, unflinching in my gaze and courageous in my resolve. I'm no longer on simmer, relegated to my life's back burner, pushing everything and everyone out front in place of me. I am radiant and determined, wild and untamable, and, at long last, woke.

# PART THREE

# AWAKENING

---

*Just wonderin'...*
*When will we fly above the mess*
*The confusion, the hatred*
*The lies that untie us*

*Just wonderin'...*
*When will we see each other as golden*
*And children as innocent*
*Meant to be protected*
*And color as irrelevant*
*And love as everythin'*

*Just wonderin'...*
*'Cause I know we are more than the tragedy*
*But every day there's another*
*To the left and right of me*
*With unanswered questions*
*And unaccountability*

*When I look at us*
*I see what we could be*
*Free from the mess and slumberin'*
*But I'm just wonderin'*

*When will we fly above the past*
*Those things we were taught*
*The confusion, the hatred*
*The lies that untie us*

*Just wonderin' . . .*
*When will we see each other as golden*
*And children as innocent*
*Meant to be protected*
*And color as irrelevant*
*And love as everythin'*
*Just wonderin' . . .*

—Alicia Keys

# 14

## NEW VISION

### BONO

It's not every day you have lunch with the president of the United States in his private dining room. It was just the three of us: myself, Alicia, and President Obama. There was a guitar in the corner. I picked it up and began playing and singing "Norwegian Wood," the Beatles song. Alicia sung along for a few bars. Just by way of ragging the president, I asked, "Do you and Michelle ever do karaoke?" "Michelle does," he said. "Not here in the White House but at Camp David. And actually, Michelle is pretty good on karaoke." "And what about you?" I asked. "Oh, I don't do karaoke," he said. "How come you don't do karaoke?" Alicia said playfully. "Is it beneath you, Mr. President?" "Oh no," he said. "I don't do karaoke 'cause I can actually sing." "Prove it," I said. Then in this perfect baritone, he began singing a Bill Withers song. Alicia looked at me. I looked at him. And we were like, "C'mon, dude! It's not enough to be the leader of the free world and to have a wife like Michelle. You can also *sing*?!" He had this big, big smile on his face. At the end of the lunch as we walked out, I said to Alicia, "Look, you and I should never tell this story because if we do, people are going to ask him to sing again." She said, "You're absolutely right. Let's just keep it to ourselves." Not long after, without us saying a word, the president seemed to be singing *everywhere*! It was like he'd woken up to that side of himself.

The White House hums majesty and whispers glory. Beneath the crystal chandelier of the Yellow Oval Room, along the West Wing Colonnade walked by world leaders, history and grandeur intersect. Lincoln once resided in these walls. JFK Jr. played under his father's Oval Office desk. President Johnson signed the 1964 Civil Rights Act into law. And following that November day in 2008 when the people spoke, President and Mrs. Obama began the transition out of their Chicago home and into America's story line. During the Obamas' eight years in the White House, I had the privilege of visiting more than once. And each time, I grew to respect the First Family more and more.

One of my first visits came in March 2009—only two short months after the inauguration, yet long enough for Mrs. Obama to begin lifting girls into the spotlight. In celebration of Women's History Month, the First Lady brought together twenty-one female trailblazers like astronaut Mae Jemison, the first African American woman in space, and Olympic gymnast Dominique Dawes. She also gathered artists such as Kerry Washington, Sheryl Crow, Tracee Ellis Ross, and Phylicia Rashad. I was honored to be among the group. The plan was straightforward: We'd first gather in the Diplomatic Reception Room near the front of the White House before dispersing to share our stories with girls in several DC-area schools; we'd then return that evening for a celebratory East Room dinner with some of the students.

"Our job is simple," Mrs. Obama said to us before we set out. "Just be open, be honest, be real, be clear, and have fun." In essence, she was asking us to be who she'd already been for us: one million percent authentic. That morning when I'd arrived at the White House, Mrs. Obama—the perfect combination of a refined First Lady and your coolest, most down-to-earth sister—immediately put me at ease with a warm embrace and welcome. Even in such a lavish setting, she somehow made me feel like I could drop my shoulders.

I'd met Mrs. Obama before. In May 2005 I visited Oprah's home, an awe-inspiring estate tucked between the hills of Santa Barbara and the Pacific. If heaven has a representation here on earth, it might just be The Promised Land, the nickname for Oprah's Montecito home. Down the cobblestone pathway known as Hallelujah Lane, a dozen mighty oaks—the Twelve Apostles, as Oprah calls them—raise their arms in sweet surrender. Just beyond a fountain, her neo-Georgian house sits, atop a hill, with its head held high. It was in that magic kingdom that Oprah hosted Legends weekend, a monumental three-day celebration of twenty-five extraordinary African American women whose talent and tenacity have built a bridge from past to present. Oprah also invited forty-five "young'uns," those who, like me, have crossed over on that bridge—everyone from Mariah Carey, Mary J. Blige, and Naomi Campbell to Halle Berry, Natalie Cole, and Angela Bassett.

Joy lit up each face and love lived in every detail: in the words of the young'uns collectively reading to the Legends "We Speak Your Names," a poem penned by Pearl Cleage; the glamorous white-tie gala; and a heart-opening brunch during which BeBe Winans handed the mic to Shirley Caesar, the mother of gospel, and the Spirit took it from there. The whole experience was transcendent, like waking up in paradise and meeting every person I'd ever dreamed of meeting. Coretta Scott King, Diana Ross, and Maya Angelou were on my right. Tina Turner, Chaka Khan, and Roberta Flack were on my left. The phenomenal Cicely Tyson, glowing and regal, sat near me on the couch. At one point, I was so overwhelmed that I took a seat on the staircase in the living room and cried.

"Can I please have some paper?" I asked Oprah. Moments later, she handed me a journal, and I poured my feelings onto the page in a stream-of-consciousness torrent. That's how moved I was, and how humbled I felt to be surrounded by such greatness. It made me want to uphold that legacy of greatness both in the world and in my artistry. Later, when Mrs. Obama arrived at the gala, Oprah leaned in and said to me, "That's Michelle. Her husband, Barack, might one day be the first black president." Three years later, history indeed leaned in that direction, guiding the Obamas to 1600 Pennsylvania Avenue.

After the full-body chills of those experiences came another thrill: Bono and I were invited to lunch with President Obama in 2011. Upon arrival, we were escorted right into the Oval Office. The president stood from behind his desk and walked over to greet us.

"Come on in!" he said. He showed us into a small room adjacent to the Oval Office.

"Where should we sit?" asked Bono.

"Sit wherever there's a chair," said the president, laughing. That's when Bono spotted a guitar in the corner, a campaign memento from a Rock the Vote event. He picked it up and began playing and singing the second verse of "Norwegian Wood": "She asked me to stay / And she told me to sit anywhere / So I looked around / And I noticed there wasn't a chair." All of this, for me, was happening in slow motion, through the hazy filter of surrealism.

On the agenda: the importance of worldwide HIV and AIDS funding. In the previous administration, Bono and I had worked to ensure that President Bush kept America's funding in place; with President Obama, we again stressed the need for our country to stay on the front lines of the pandemic. I talked about what I'd learned in my work with Keep a Child Alive, and yet the lunch felt less like a business meeting and more like a family dinner. During three courses over a full hour, laughter flowed as we shared what was happening in our personal lives. Between the first sip of soup and the last spoonful of berries, I took it all in, wanting to imprint in my memory every story, every expression, every feeling of the day. Even in my dazed, I-can't-believe-I'm-here state, I'd never been more present. For me, this lunch represented the gift that I and every other artist has been given. Our creations have the ability to reach people from all worlds, from those on 125th Street in Harlem to those serving our nation in the capitol. Music is a powerful uniter.

———

An artist's life is a teeter-totter. When you're in the lowered position, you're composing at the piano. You're in the studio. You're breathing sounds and beats and lyrics. Then, when your side of the board goes up, the energy suddenly shifts. You're on tour, performing for thousands most nights. Your focus moves from inward to outward. Between each six-week leg of a tour, there's usually a couple of weeks off, but even then, you're in constant motion, trying to catch up on everything. Then later, when the tour circuit finally ends, boom, you're back in the studio for the next round of creating. You're also back in your kitchen trying to remember where your pots and pans are.

That is the general rhythm of my existence: Up. Down. Up. Down. And the whole time I'm teetering, I'm also holding my family tight. Swizz and I are striving to keep our promise never to go more than two weeks without seeing each other, and yes, we actually keep that vow. Swizz has even flown from New York to Sydney to be with me, in order to keep that commitment intact. Face time and always planning sweet things for each other is what keeps our connection fresh. Our schedules are so hectic that if we weren't intentional, we could *easily* schedule each other out of our lives: He's on business in Shanghai or London while I'm racing through fifty cities during a tour leg. We also set aside one weekend a month to go away together, just the two of us, even if the getaway is only a thirty-minute drive to a cozy hotel in lower Manhattan; we'll check in on a Saturday afternoon, go explore an exhibit and head someplace nice for dinner that evening, and then sleep in on Sunday morning.

I bring my village of support on tour with me, and I'm super deliberate about surrounding my children with family. My son, Egypt, has often been with me on the road, spending as much time as possible with me even as his two grandmothers travel in to lend a hand. I'm insistent that I do most of the caretaking. My albums and tours, as well as the breaks in between them for concentrated family time and other business endeavors, are how I remember the seasons. The seesaw is how I mark time.

After the *Girl on Fire* album hit around Thanksgiving in 2012, the usual flurry of press appearances came with it. I'd agreed to do a photo shoot and interview for a magazine cover story. Just as the issue was hitting newsstands, I saw the cover. I stared at the image, which was a shot of me from the waist up. *Whose arms are those?* I thought, pulling the page closer to study it. My arms and shoulders had been majorly airbrushed to seem smaller than they are. In fact, it was so overdone that it looked like my head had been pasted onto someone else's body.

It stung. It felt like someone's judgment of me had been delivered, in secret, from behind a computer screen. We live in a culture where there's seldom space for imperfection, for celebrating our perfectly imperfect bodies. In this case, someone had decided, at his or her own discretion and without consulting me, that a part of my body that I like was, in their view, a flaw—one unfit for public display. I wish I could tell you that incident was isolated, but that kind of thing happens all the time, just as it had years earlier during that hypersexual photo shoot I felt manipulated into doing. Even when you conduct a shoot on your own terms, someone else chooses how you'll be portrayed.

More time would have to pass before I realized how our society's oppressive standard of female beauty had left deep claw marks in me. It's hard not to begin doubting yourself just a little when, with the stroke of an airbrush, someone slims down your thighs or shaves off half your booty. And if I'm doubting myself, imagine what that does for the young people forced to digest these images of so-called beauty. It was this fake-arms cover that led me to begin taking the stance I take now: I need to approve photographers' images of me ahead of publication. In fact, I am unrelenting about it. I'm supposed to own my body and its presentation—that I know for certain.

The Set the World on Fire Tour began in March 2013. The tour was then my most extensive ever, sweeping through Australia and Asia and the Middle East, as well as through the major capitals in Europe and North and South America. Once home at the start of 2014, the seesaw tipped and I got back in songwriting mode. I began with a list. On the plane ride back from the tour, Erika and I feverishly wrote down everything we were sick of. Like how girls are so often sexually victimized. How boys are raised to believe that being hard and playing with guns make you a real man. How wars are fought more for money than for the good of humanity. How women are evaluated, above all else, for their appearance. How people of color are frequently targets of police brutality. With every observation and headline—like the 2012 death of seventeen-year-old Trayvon Martin, escalating hate crimes, mass shootings seemingly every month—I'd become more and more disturbed. The list became my guide in creating my next album, *HERE*.

This wasn't going to be some fleeting or frivolous project. Every issue was one that had grieved me, dissatisfied me, and stirred me up over the years. That's one reason I brought together a small group of collaborators, all of whom shared my intention to deeply impact the culture, to create a cohesive message and sound. I teamed up with two top-level writers I'd known and worked with over many years: Harold Lilly, who composed with me on "You Don't Know My Name" and "Unbreakable," and Mark Batson, who contributed on *As I Am*. Others would have input, but that remained the core group. I called us The Ill'uminaries—artists committed to spreading light (and also because we are ill, as in amazing). Swizz eventually joined our production and writing team, marking our first full project together.

From the start, it was apparent that this was no ordinary collaboration. The songs came together at record speed; I've never written a group of songs more quickly. That's mostly because our creative process was rooted in our longstanding friendships, as well as in the big questions and conversations we brought to the table. As I began writing "Illusion of Bliss," for instance, I asked Mark and Harold, "What's your illusion of bliss?" The three of us sat around for hours, candidly discussing the things we all can latch on to in our quest for temporary comfort: sexual pleasure, work and ambition, food, financial gain, drugs, and any number of other addictions. Holding our own experiences and illusions up to the light was an exercise in self-examination for all three of us. It meant looking at those places in our lives that aren't all that pretty to stare at. It also eased us into vulnerability, the space necessary for authentic songwriting.

Harold always seemed to have a book with him in the studio. He'd be reading at the console while I was recording and as the writing process was happening. I don't know how that brother did it with all the noise. One evening, I spotted him with Elaine Brown's book *A Taste of Power*. Elaine rose up from an impoverished childhood in North Philly to become the first and only female leader of the Black Panther Party, the '60s political organization formed to challenge police brutality, fight systemic racism, and empower black communities. I had devoured that book when I was around seventeen. In fact, I read books by many Panthers because I was so fascinated by how the movement came together, so drawn to the strength, community, and pride it evoked.

I saw traces of my own experience between the lines of Elaine's story. She is a classically trained pianist; she attended a predominantly white experimental elementary school where she studied both ballet and piano. She was also raised by a single mom and spent a short stint in college (in her case, Temple University) before moving to Los Angeles to work as a songwriter (she eventually recorded two albums, for Vault and Motown). The irresistible pull toward social activism has guided both of us. Just spotting *A Taste of Power* on Harold's control board brought back a flood of emotions and memories and connections.

During our sessions, Harold read aloud some passages, including one about how, in 1967, Elaine began teaching piano lessons to children in a Watts housing project, wanting to expose them to the performing arts. Her work there served as an awakening that eventually led her toward broader activism amid the struggle for racial equality. My crew and I wrote a couple of songs (unreleased as of yet) based on Elaine's riveting account.

"How about if we invite Elaine into the studio?" Ann suggested. I loved the idea.

Ann reached out, but Elaine didn't initially believe Ann was contacting her on my behalf; she thought it was a hoax. Ann persisted, and eventually, the one and only Elaine Brown—the renegade who's as much of a firecracker today, in her seventies, as she was when she ascended to the top ranks of the Panthers in 1974—actually met with us. The day we connected happened to be her birthday. I was in LA at the time, and Elaine traveled down from Oakland to sit with us for hours, recounting her stories, gifting us with her gems. We had a hundred questions for her, and we recorded the entire conversation.

Elaine's presence and energy, her insightfulness and self-determination, served as a backdrop for the album. With *HERE*, I had a point to prove to myself: that I could have a clear artistic vision and then hold on to it tightly, never allowing pieces of it to get chipped away through the compromise that usually comes with commercialism. The album represents everything I was thinking, feeling, living, and breathing during that time. Every lyric, every verse and measure is an invitation to crawl inside my most uncensored thoughts. It's my take on the city that birthed me, the streets that helped form my identity ("She Don't Really Care," "Pawn It All," and "The Gospel," for which the brilliant director A.V. Rockwell created an award-winning short film). It is the lens through which I view our treatment of Mother Earth (in 2017, I'd perform "Kill Your Mama" in Brazil, after the government's attack on the Amazon and its indigenous people); the unrealistic standard of female appearance ("When a Girl Can't Be Herself"); global conflict ("Holy War"); and the hopes, fears, and frailties that tie us all together no matter where we grew up or who we love ("In Common").

In the studio, our flow was raw and real. Every interlude—like "Cocoa Butter," the hilarious real-talk snippet of me and my homeboys Cross and Pic, discussing the insecurities we all have—was part of an actual conversation recorded during our sessions. It all added up to the most profound musical experience I have ever had, a project surrounded by a divine presence. I was so clear about exactly what I wanted that album to be. And I was writing a type of music I'd never before written. Every day, I'd drop to my knees in gratitude to God for sending me this potent spirit energy; I couldn't believe I'd been gifted with it. I was proud of what we had created and fascinated that *HERE* had come through me.

Swizz and I weren't initially planning to collaborate. We'd always loved and supported each other's music, and while we worked on our individual projects, we'd play each other songs and give input. But aside from that first song we worked on and a Whitney Houston song, "Million Dollar Bill," that we'd once partnered on, we hadn't formally created together. That changed a few months into my work on this album. One evening, I was in the studio listening to some music by Miriam Makeba, aka Mama Africa, and thinking about some styles I could experiment with. I do that from time to time: set aside all writing and just bathe in various beats and styles and sonics for a full week. Swizz stopped by at nine p.m.

"Hey," he said, flopping down on the couch across from my chair, "we should work on something tonight." I looked at him.

"That's not what I'm doing right now, babe," I said. "I'm just listening." He laid back on the couch. Two minutes later, with light in his eyes, he popped straight back up.

"I mean, I know you're in listening mode," he said, "but I'm feeling this amazing vibe . . . like we should work on something." I smiled and gave him a look that said, *You're intruding on my personal space.*

"All right, cool," he said, walking out. "I'll just let you do your thing."

At two a.m., I realized he'd never returned. *Where did he go?* I wandered around the studio, first looking in our downstairs office. No Swizz. Finally, I heard some loud music coming from the preproduction room, which we used to call the *bang-out room* because you could lock yourself in there and go crazy creating some songs. I slowly cracked open the door to find him in there, rockin' to music.

"What is *that*?" I said, my eyes bugging out of my head at the electricity in the room. All evening, he'd been putting together "I Just Want the Good People to Win," a song I've loved since that moment.

"I told you we were supposed to work on something tonight," he said, smiling.

We haven't (yet) released Swizz's song, but hearing it that night inspired me, and I pulled out a beautiful Rhodes piano chord progression a friend had sent to me. At three that morning, as my husband drove us up the West Side Highway toward home, we played that Rhodes progression on a loop while we threw possible lyrics back and forth. By the time we pulled into our driveway, we'd written all the words to the song the world now knows as "She Don't Really Care." I hardly slept because I couldn't wait to get up later that day and do it all over. And that is how my husband became the fourth and final member of The Ill'uminaries.

Though our core group was tight, many came in and out of our sessions. Between the four of us, we knew a lot of people, so someone was always having friends come by:

"Can Chris Rock swing by tonight? And by the way, he's bringing David Blaine with him." *Sure.* David, the internationally known magician, would then come in and leave us under his spell. Another day, JR, the French photographer and artist who puts together these incredible, statement-making art displays all over the world, was, at the time, working with the New York City Ballet on *Les Bosquets,* the ballet he had created. He knew us all. So after finishing up his work at Lincoln Center at around nine p.m., he'd call and ask, "Can

I come by?" *Of course.* He'd usually bring along Lil Buck, the mind-bending dancer who rocked onto the world stage with a Memphis style of dance called jookin'; he was a guest dancer and choreographer in JR's ballet.

"It feels like magic in here," JR would say in his thick French accent. He was right. In fact, everyone who walked into the studio felt that vibe, that space of truth and naked aggression we wrote from. And, courtesy of Blaine, some literal magic got added to the mix.

As I gave thanks for the miracle happening in our sessions, Swizz and I received another blessing: He was accepted into Harvard Business School. For years, my husband had sat in meetings where billion-dollar deals were made. In those kinds of rooms, there are two parallel conversations: one related to music and another connected to the business side of our industry. Swizz, being the innovator that he is, wanted to powerfully contribute to both dialogues.

"Look, man, I really want to get the language of our business down pat," he'd told a friend the year before. His friend mentioned Harvard's Owner/President Management (OPM) program, a program delivered in a series of three-week intensives, completed on campus over three calendar years.

Swizz submitted an application but was disappointed to later hear the program was already fully booked. And then, as the universe would have it, a space opened up at the last minute. My man is usually not a crier, but that day, a couple of tears might've fallen. All of us celebrated and toasted to him. Swizz already owned some successful companies, and for more than a decade, he'd been advising others on marketing strategy; he's gifted with golden instincts. Completing the program would now give him the language to have more say around boardroom tables. I was so proud to see my man's journey from the South Bronx to Harvard. No ceilings for either one of us.

While we were on our Harvard high, I received news of a different kind. For weeks, I'd been feeling very tired. In the rapturous experience of creating an album that I just knew would become my

*Purple Rain,* I hadn't stopped long enough to think about why I was so drained. Swizz noticed.

"Something's the matter with you," he said to me one afternoon when I lay in bed. First of all, I'm now the early riser in our family, and second, I never sleep in the middle of the day. So I went in to see my doctor, the same ob-gyn who had delivered Egypt. She gave me a pregnancy test. Not only was I expecting—I was nearly four months along.

I wasn't ready for this, which is what I told the doctor. She looked at me for a long moment and pursed her lips.

"When is *anyone* ever really ready?" she said.

"But you don't understand," I protested. "This is the worst time *ever*. I'm working on my next album. My husband just got into Harvard. And I've been drinking—a lot." She shrugged and took off her glasses.

"Who hasn't been drinking?" she said, laughing a little.

I left her office feeling so torn. The music I was creating felt more important and urgent than just about everything. It had consumed me, requiring most of my energy and focus, even as I nurtured little Egypt. I couldn't imagine setting aside the album. Though the music was damn near finished by then, I'd have to put off its release and the tour for at least a year if I chose to have the baby.

While I was struggling over my choice, I went into the studio one evening and began listening to "More Than We Know," a song we'd written soon after Swizz got into Harvard. The lyrics are about how we're capable of so much more than we can even imagine, how the seemingly impossible is often within reach: "If we just stayed on the ground / Then we would never see the stars / And if you're too afraid to walk in faith / Then you will never know your heart . . .'Cause baby we can do / More than we know." As the truth of those words washed over me, my eyes filled with tears. How could I take away the potential for this beautiful child, this light that might touch others in ways I couldn't dream of?

For me, the song was a powerful message that I should go forward with the pregnancy. Sometimes you write the lyrics you most need to hear. And sometimes, you fit your life around your circumstances rather than the other way around.

———

My stomach popped over the summer, soon after my late discovery that I was pregnant. By August, a few weeks before Swizz's birthday, I was already waddling around with a big tummy as I dreamed up ways to raise my birthday-wars game. One evening while we were on vacation for our anniversary, Swizz and I were watching *Coming to America,* the 1988 Eddie Murphy comedy. That's when I got an idea.

In the movie, twenty-one-year-old Prince Akeem (Eddie Murphy) is the sole heir to his father's throne in the wealthy African kingdom of Zamunda; the prince is so pampered that servants feed him, bathe him, and throw rose petals on the ground everywhere he steps. As any big fan of the classic can tell you, there's a scene near the start of the film when King Jaffe Joffer and Queen Aoleon (James Earl Jones and Madge Sinclair) present their son with his bride-to-be (Vanessa Bell). After a triumphant group of dancers performs, they step aside to reveal the gold-sequin-clad bride, who walks toward the throne where the royal family awaits. Oha (Paul Bates), the king's royal servant, then breaks out into this high-pitched song, "She's Your Queen!" The prince refuses to marry his bride and instead heads off with his servant, Semmi (Arsenio Hall), to the one place he imagines he'll find a wife: Queens, New York.

Swizz absolutely loves comedy. And we'd both watched *Coming to America* so many times that we could recite some of the lines by heart. Which led me to an aha: Why not re-enact that bride-to-be scene, just for fun? I knew he'd never expect it, which would make it a great surprise. So I set out looking for a space. In downtown Manhattan, I found this old bank, one with massive columns and stunning architectural details that made it feel regal. *Perfect.* I then reached out to several of Swizz's friends and family members to help me pull it off while keeping everything a secret.

We set up a birthday dinner—a decoy. All of Swizz's closest boys took him to a restaurant, a spot super close to the party space. Just as they were finishing up, several women appeared and began throwing rose petals on the floor, just like in the film. Swizz was like, "What's going on right now?" He and his friends followed the path of petals all the way into the ornate bank building. When he entered, a crown was placed on his head (and a faux tiger hide draped over his shoulder) as he made his way toward the throne where his parents and grandparents waited. The minute he took his power seat, the African dance troupe I'd signed on began killing it with this elaborate dance number. Swizz was stunned, and then started cracking up.

After one of his close friends began singing, "She's Your Queen!" I walked my pregnant self down the aisle in my sparkly dress.

"Welcome, my king!" I said. "And happy birthday!" That's when everyone got on the dance floor. The party was my way of acknowledging Swizz—the man who both lights me up and lights my way. Even with the crazy pace and busyness of our lives, we make the time to truly celebrate each other. It's how we keep our relationship fresh.

———

On August 9, 2014—four and a half months before my due date—Michael Brown, an unarmed, black eighteen-year-old in Ferguson, Missouri, was killed by Darren Wilson, a white police officer. According to accounts at the time, Brown was shot multiple times with his arms raised in surrender. The killing ignited protests, and thousands gathered in the streets, chanting the slogan, "Hands up, don't shoot!" Law enforcement's response to the crowds, complete with deploying officers in riot gear and toting semiautomatic weapons, was reminiscent of the '60s race riots. That November, a few days before Thanksgiving, a grand jury issued its verdict: Officer Wilson was not indicted.

The killing of unarmed black people wasn't new. What shifted—after the Wilson verdict, as well as the incident with Eric Garner, the unarmed black man who said "I can't breathe" eleven times as an NYPD officer choked him to death in Staten Island—was the public's outcry. Concerned citizens of every walk of life let out a scream, one so piercing and primal that it could not be ignored. The grand jury's decision touched a tender nerve, triggering dozens of demonstrations in what organizers hailed as a National Day of Resistance. And the rage echoed across the nation, from the tens of thousands who marched through Times Square shouting "No justice, no peace—no racist police!"; to the Chicago residents who staged sit-ins at the mayor's office; to the crowds in Cleveland who blocked an intersection; to the throngs of demonstrators who revolted in Los Angeles and Oakland. Fury over the continued inhumane treatment of black people spilled over into the streets as the winds of change gathered force.

And I, carrying one son in my arms and another in my belly, was left with the question a friend posed to me around that time: "Why are we here?" My answer lit a match.

# 15

## RESOUNDING YES

### OPRAH

Alicia came to see me at my home. Over lunch, she shared with me many things she was dealing with, and I saw in her some of the same frustrations I'd lived through: being pulled in myriad directions with others depending on you, needing answers from you, having their own agendas about what you should do. I have lived that experience to the fullest and really exhausted myself trying to please everybody at the same time. When you're doing what you love to do, you don't get exhausted. You get exhausted from trying to fulfill everyone else's ideas and ideals about who you should be. When you do that, you're not being true to yourself.

Pregnant with a peace sign on my belly—that's how my fall of 2014 began. The year ended with me cradling my second son, who arrived two days after Christmas. I showed some skin for both these experiences. And in the middle of them, I got a bold idea.

The revolution might not be televised, but a piece of it may have been spotted forming in an Italian restaurant in Chelsea that summer before. At a brick-oven pizzeria near the studio, me and my writing crew—Mark, Harold, and by this time, Swizz—stopped in for some slices and a little downtime away from that evening's session. As we sat awaiting our order, the conversation flowed seamlessly. And then, in the spirit of the bold-faced honesty we'd been creating in for months, the discussion got deep. That's when Mark put a provocative question on the table: "Why are you here?"

No one had ever asked me that question, at least not in that form. I sat there in silence, allowing his words to saturate. Mark wasn't talking about a place, I understood. He was asking about the big picture: What is the reason we're all here on the planet right now? Up to then, I'd thought a lot about intention and the power of words, and I'd also considered the idea of my purpose, the calling I felt to spread light through music. But this question was broader. This was the enormous *why* beneath every *what*. It was about the point of all of us being here on earth together, in this moment. Around the table that evening, the four of us talked for a long time before we agreed on an answer: We're here for one another.

Our conversation stayed lodged in my spirit for weeks. Though Mark had been asking about our collective reason for existence, his question led me to think further about my personal one: *Why am I here?* At earlier times in my life, that idea may not have struck me so forcefully. But at this juncture—just as society stood at a crossroads, just as I was creating music with the intent to move the culture forward—the question wrapped its arms around me and would not stop squeezing.

That August, a few weeks after our conversation, is when Ferguson descended into mayhem. In the days following Michael Brown's killing, mothers and fathers, aunts and sisters, teachers and nurses, and people from all walks of life joined with the Brown family to raise their voices and their fists. One dad came wearing a T-shirt printed with a poignant question: "Is my son next?" The protests turned violent, and images of officers hurling fiery tear-gas canisters into the crowd went viral. Around the country, so many of us watched in disbelief, sickened by our view from the sidelines.

I think now of that muggy weekend as a major what-the-hell moment, one that preceded the volcano to come. This was still months before the presidential campaign season got underway. This was the time before a fresh batch of sorrow—the Charleston church shooting, Colin Kaepernick under attack for taking a knee, children ripped from their mothers' arms at our border—reeled through our social media feeds hourly. This was before the numbness set in, before the urge to turn away from the heartbreak rooted itself. For me and many others, Ferguson was the jolt that first shook us awake before the whole world seemingly came undone. It was a watershed moment when a lot of young people in particular were dialed in, taking note of how dramatically the times were changing right as we were standing in them. Violence and unrest and bigotry and intolerance had always shown their faces in America. But this felt different. This felt north of horrifying.

Beyond our shores, other harrowing headlines abounded: An Ebola outbreak swept through six countries and claimed more than ten thousand lives. The 276 Nigerian girls, snatched from their classrooms by the extremist group Boko Haram, still hadn't been found, even after Mrs. Obama shined a light on the crisis with her Twitter campaign, #BringBackOurGirls. Around kitchen tables and in living rooms, in community centers and on Twitter, people were paying attention. And in my long discussions with friends about both the global headlines and the Michael Brown and Eric Garner cases, I noticed something that concerned me: there was a sense of resignation. Right there next to the outrage, there was a feeling of powerlessness. Protestors were marching, yes—but would it really change anything? Once the demonstrations ended, how could we effectively channel our frustration into a cause? And how could we move all this talk out of our dining rooms and onto the front lines—and would mobilizing make a bit of difference?

Mark's question continued to linger. For weeks after, I would ask everyone I met a version of my friend's question: "Why are you here?" Some didn't know how to respond, probably because they were as baffled as I was when I heard it. Others gave answers, from the spiritual and political to the career and family related. Those replies led to more thought-provoking conversation, and led my crew and me to make our way into the studio. In a single session, with the brand of rapid-fire energy that had fueled our work together thus far, we wrote "We Are Here." Two lines of the song conveyed the message I most hoped would resonate: "We are here for all of us . . . Our souls were brought together so we could love each other."

On September 9, with the lioness energy of an expectant mother, I took that message to my fam on Facebook and Twitter.

"It's not about me," I wrote. "It's about WE. Let's create a coalition of all of us who want to make a difference . . . It starts with ourselves, and then our families, and then our communities, and then the world. I am here for you. What are you here for? What is your gift to the world? Tell me your answer and hashtag #WeAreHere." Thousands of responses poured in, beautiful messages like "I am here to love" and "I am here to uplift others."

Then, a week later, on the set of the *TODAY* show, I scooted my belly up to a baby grand and performed "We Are Here." And on September 21, I turned up the volume again with an official launch, one held at the UN Foundation's Social Good Summit in my hometown.

"As I prepare to give birth to a new child," I told those gathered at the 92nd Street Y, "I can't help but think about the world I'm bringing my baby into . . . As Mahatma Gandhi said, we must be the change we want to see in the world. We all have a voice. We just need to know how to make it heard. That is why I created We Are Here."

The premise of the initiative was simple: Build a massive army of intenders determined to make our planet better. We'd do that by teaming up with a coalition of trustworthy nonprofits, twelve organizations already doing incredible work in areas like global poverty, disease, and education for girls; racial equality in the criminal justice system and beyond; LGBTQ rights; common-sense gun laws; suicide prevention among teens; and equal pay for women. Leigh Blake, the powerhouse activist who teamed up with me in launching Keep a Child Alive, was also part of imagining this concept. I believe people want to give, but they don't know which charities they can trust or whether their money will be put to great use. We Are Here aimed to provide a solution to that dilemma: We would serve as a one-stop shop for information, resources, and donations, money that we'd pass on to the vetted organizations. During the launch, I wrote a personal check for $1 million and encouraged others to match my donation. Many did.

First came the question. Then came the song and the organization's unveiling. And finally came my naked photo on Instagram. It was a publicity move with a purpose, my way of getting as many people as I could on board with the organization. Mark Seliger, the same photographer who captured that 2001 image of me on the cover of *Rolling Stone,* wearing the New York City T-shirt right after 9/11, photographed me in the (almost) buff for this image. Spoiler alert: The photo shoot was pretty G-rated. In reality, I wore flesh-colored panties, and I think I even had on jeans that were pulled down below my stomach. The final photo only shows my body from the belly up with my hands cupping my boobies. The peace sign, drawn on my belly with white body paint, was crucial to the messaging: We are here to raise our voices in nonviolent protest. Even without me fully disrobed, I knew the picture would grab headlines—and it did.

*The New York Times* and CNN ran pieces about the movement. Several celebrities chimed in: Queen Latifah, Pharrell, Jimmy Kimmel, J. Lo, Madonna, Kelly Rowland, and many others. On social media, my fam responded by donating, as well as by posting their own reasons for being here. And their involvement went beyond simply donating. Some recognized, for the first time, how interconnected many of these issues like poverty and education are. Others volunteered with the organizations we'd featured in the limelight.

On December 3, a grand jury released a verdict that further stoked tensions: The NYPD officer who strangled Eric Garner to death for selling cigarettes was not indicted. Eric was just forty-three on the day he breathed his last breath. Violence and looting erupted in New York. By myself in a room one evening, I created the piano ballad "We Gotta Pray"—a musical outcry to the heartrending news.

"We absolutely feel disregarded as human beings," I told *New*

*York Times* reporter Andrew R. Chow in an interview after the song's release. "There is that New York camaraderie, but it's bigger than that. There's injustice going on, and it seems so blatant. We will continue to be loud. I hope that this is our twenty-first-century civil rights movement."

Through the rest of that holiday season, when my (very) pregnant behind had no business on a stage, I sang both anthems all over the place. At each performance, I concluded with the same message: We are here. We are united. We are organizing. We are committed to change. And for me, that commitment started not in the halls of Congress or in some ivory tower, but with four old friends gathered over pizza while asking themselves a big question. That question birthed an idea. That idea birthed a song. That song became the anthem of a movement. And that movement, I hoped, would help dramatically reshape the world our children will inherit.

———

My husband has turned out to be our family's name-giver. Like he did with Egypt, he chose our second son's name. Weeks before my due date, we brainstormed all types of crazy names, most of them places. Harlem? Nope. Justice? Maybe. Brooklyn? Not quite.

"What about Genesis?" Swizz suggested.

"Huh?" I said. He'd recently had a dream about new beginnings, he explained, and the word *genesis* had been part of it. The more I thought about it, the more I loved it. We settled on Genesis, along with the middle name Ali—pronounced like the legendary boxer's name, yet also my nickname.

"Shouldn't there be an Alicia Junior in the world?" Swizz has been saying for years. *Um, not right now.* But there is our beloved Genesis Ali Dean.

Our son arrived on December 27, 2014—four days before his due date and five days ahead of the New Year. I like to think that my youngest son came early so he could get a head start on bringing our family joy. The second time around, the surging was easier and faster than it had been with Egypt, in part because I had a stronger awareness of my body and how it felt to give birth. When my doctor handed Genesis to me, I stared at his wrinkled, old-man face and his head covered in thick, black hair. His eyes were closed tight and he had the most serious expression. *Who is this?* I thought. I recognized no trace of me or Swizz in him, nor did he look like Egypt, who was born with very little hair.

"Look at the businessman," Swizz joked as the baby lay between us. "He's on a business call right now." Genesis was a full two months old before he started resembling any of us.

I had Genesis just a few weeks before my own birthday on January 25. Ever since my *Coming to America* surprise, Swizz had been saying, "You think you got me on that one. You killed it. But watch what I'm going to do for you." Frankly, the only thing I wanted Swizz to do for me this year, postdelivery, was hush and let me sleep.

"I don't want to leave the house," I told him. "I don't want to put on clothes. Honestly, I don't feel like it. I love you, babe, but please—no party. I just want to stay in my pajamas." When you've got milk dripping out of your nipples, you're in no mood to go out or even get dressed.

"I got you," he said with a sly grin. "That's cool."

My birthday rolled around. Not a peep from Swizz all morning. That afternoon, he came into our bedroom while I was nursing Genesis.

"Don't look out of any windows today," he said.

"What?" I said. He didn't answer; he just smiled and walked out. Have you ever tried to go hours without looking out of *any* window in your house? It's hard. So of course I peeked. I noticed all these trucks pulling up, as well as some people bustling around in the front yard. *What is Swizz doing?* Around six p.m., my mother and some of Swizz's family showed up, as if they were just stopping by to see me and the baby.

"Do you know what's happening?" my mother asked me. I shook my head. "Well, I feel like I need to tell you," she said.

"Ma, don't," I said, shushing her. "Just leave it."

A couple of hours later, Swizz stepped back into our bedroom. "I'm ready," he said, handing me a gift box. "Open this." I pulled back the flaps and lifted out a pair of colorful pajamas—the kind with feet. "Put this on, comb your hair, and meet me downstairs," he said, smiling. Minutes later, I appeared in my onesie. Swizz, who was waiting for me at the bottom of the staircase, had on a matching one. "This is for you," he said, putting one of his gold chains around my neck. I still had no idea what was happening.

Swizz led me through our back door and around the corner toward an indoor cabana where a hundred of our friends were gathered—all of them wearing pajamas! The scene was straight out of *House Party 2,* that 1991 comedy starring Kid 'n Play (Christopher Reid and Christopher Martin) and many others. In the movie, Kid, a college student, throws the "mutha of all house parties"—a "pajama jammy-jam." Swizz had set up a real-life jammy-jam: He'd covered our pool and transformed it into a dance floor. "You said you didn't want to get out of your pajamas," he said, "so I brought the party to you."

Some of the film's cast members were there: Tisha Campbell-Martin, Tichina Arnold, A.J. Johnson, and Full Force. Kid 'n Play took the stage to show off some of their famous dance moves from the film. Also on the dance floor: my girls Gayle King and Angie Martinez. And every person, from the DJs to the caterers, had on their version of pj's. Come to find out that Swizz wouldn't even let you in our gate if you didn't have on some kind of loungewear. La La Anthony killed it with her outfit: She rocked a bright, multicolored, airbrushed onesie, plus some kicks with hot-pink laces. It was crazy fun. And the best part? After the last guest had gone, I was already home and dressed for bed.

———

In spring 2015, I asked Oprah if I could meet with her. By this time, Genesis was mostly sleeping through the night. I'd returned to work on the album, which I'd set aside during my pregnancy along with the launch of We Are Here. And in the background of all of that, my management team was in transition. After Jeff's departure in 2010, I'd worked with a series of different managers. All of them brought major talent to the table. And yet none was exactly the right fit.

Partnering with me means understanding the many aspects of who I am—and that's a challenge because I don't fit into one category. There's my street side, that Timbs-wearing part of me honed in the alleyways of Harlem and Hell's Kitchen. There's my identity as a black woman. There's also the multicultural side of me, the biracial ancestry that allows me to connect with a wide spectrum of people. And then there's my spirit, that blend of glass-half-full optimism, introverted reflection, and outward-facing social activism. Every team I'd brought in had grasped a few of those sides, but never all. And I was left with a churning stomach and a lack of clarity about the path forward. That's when I called my sis, who welcomed me to her home for lunch.

At Oprah's dining room table over soup, I explained the process I'd gone through to find a great match. I'd had multiple interviews with many people, and from the start, I'd made it clear what I wanted in a partnership. But somehow, even after all that interviewing and then narrowing down the list, there still wasn't the right connection.

"With all the transitions you've had," I said to Oprah, "how have you found people who truly represent you and understand your vision?"

Oprah sat quietly for a moment before answering.

"For many years," she said, "I looked for someone outside of myself to dream up and create what only I could. I eventually realized that no one else can see your big picture. Only you know the journey you're on. Others can contribute, and you should definitely surround yourself with smart people who lift you higher and share in your vision. But the truth is, even with wise counsel, only you know what your next step should be. All my best decisions in life have come when I've tuned in to what felt like the best move for me."

I'd spent much of my life looking to others for answers, allowing their opinions to drown out my instincts. My default was to substitute others' desires for my own. In fact, I'd done that so much that it became a habit, one I'm still un-learning. I've needed a lot of practice at putting my own ideas and intuition at the forefront, and Oprah was encouraging me to again rehearse. As I sat there across from her, taking in her wisdom, I realized where my anxiety was coming from: I was expecting someone else to fill a space that only I could stand in.

I've read a lot about what it means to listen to your inner voice, that whisper in your gut that is always speaking. On paper, I understood the idea. But in reality, I was clearly still struggling. That afternoon, Oprah articulated the lesson to me in a way that turned on the lights.

"You know what a resounding yes feels like," she said. "It's undeniable. Nothing's going to stop you from doing it. You're excited. You don't have to convince yourself to move forward. You simply know this is the right thing—and that is what I live by."

I've made a lot of decisions from my head. I've chosen to go in this direction or that one based on finances. Or because something seems like a great opportunity. Or because I don't want to hurt people's feelings or disappoint them. Or because someone is pushing me toward an agenda that serves them. But when I've listened to my heart—when I've trusted what my spirit is telling me—that *yes* has always steered me right.

A resounding yes makes your heart rise up. It's the feeling that once led me to go with Clive to J Records. It's the inkling that carried me to Cairo to catch my breath. It's the excitement I felt when I first wrote "Girl on Fire." It's the passion that led me to get We Are Here off the ground. And it's the principle that's still guiding me toward full ownership of myself.

———

Even after Oprah introduced me to the resounding yes concept, I did not immediately implement it. I understood it in theory, but I still wasn't sure how to live in my own truth, how to breathe and exist in it to become fully self-referencing. It's not that I haven't always been aware of my instincts; it's that I haven't fully trusted them. That's why whenever a dilemma arose, I'd go on these excessive rounds of questioning, seeking everyone's input to either confirm or replace my own inkling. I left my lunch with Oprah thinking, *How do I come to a place where I really believe that I have my own best answers?* An experience soon after put me on that path.

Erika called me one afternoon with an idea. "Want to come with me on a meditation retreat in Los Angeles?" she asked. Erika, being the seeker that she is, has often tried various forms of spiritual practice. At the time, she'd connected with Guru Jagat, a teacher of *Kundalini* yoga and meditation, which is a sacred and ancient spiritual tradition. "This might be good for you," Erika went on. As someone who has known me since I was four, she'd witnessed the years-long struggle I'd had with trusting myself. "I think it'll resonate with you," she said.

The women's retreat would last four days. The idea sounded amazing, and yet the timing felt off. After Genesis's birth, I'd been thrust back into Baby Land: diapers, two a.m. feedings, and a feeling that I might never get my life back. That whole second-baby challenge is real. I'd figured out how to handle one, but how could I give all that I needed to *two* amazing souls? When Genesis was six months old, Swizz and I began sleep-training him. That was my first step back toward some sanity. By that fall, when Erika approached me with her idea, he was mostly sleeping through the night—but I didn't feel ready to be away from him for four full days. Adding to my reluctance was the fact that the last day of the retreat landed on my husband's birthday. We'd already agreed to take the chill, no-big-surprises route that year, but I definitely still wanted to be with him.

"I don't think it's going to work out this time," I told Erika, citing all the reasons reeling through my head. "Maybe we can plan to try it next year."

"I hear you," she said. She paused for a long moment and then asked, "Alicia, when was the last time you did something for yourself?"

Erika's question landed hard on me—and I didn't have a response. As I thought about it over the next few days, I could not recall when I'd last done anything just for me. Had I bought a nice outfit for myself or gone out for a great meal? Of course. But in regards to deepening and becoming more connected to myself, the answer was no.

I mentioned the retreat to Swizz. He was supportive as I described the gathering as best I could, given how little I knew then about *Kundalini* meditation. "And you'd have to miss my birthday?" he said, a flicker of disappointment in his eyes. I nodded yes. "Well, babe, if it's something you really want to do," he said, "then you should go." I booked my ticket to take part in the retreat's first three days. But the fourth day, I'd fly home early to be back for Genesis and spend at least some of Swizz's birthday with him.

Erika arrived in Los Angeles hours before me. Feeling reluctant about leaving my family, I flew out of JFK as late as I could. From LAX, a driver transported me a couple of hours away to the retreat center near Joshua Tree National Park. As we made our way up Highway 10 and finally turned off into the pitch-black woods of no-woman's-land, I began having second thoughts. *Where, exactly, is this place? And what have I gotten myself into?*

My first glimpse came moments later. When I walked into the main meeting room at around nine p.m., the final part of an intense, daylong group meditation was just getting started. About fifty women, all dressed in white turbans and clothing, were seated on the floor. Guru Jagat, a young woman with a beautiful aura, led the group in a chant. I, dressed in my New York City uniform of black, tiptoed toward the rear and took a seat on a mat near Erika. She and I exchanged glances. I'm sure she could read my face: *What is all of this?*

"*Ong Namo Guru Dev Namo,*" chanted the teacher in a mantra

she delivered as much like a melody as she did a rhythmic phrase. In unison, the women repeated her words. I'd later learn that her chant, known as the *ada mantra,* is a call to mediation, a way to "tune in" for the session to come; the opening chant means, "I bow to the Creative Wisdom, the Divine Teacher within." Following the mantra, the room crackled to life with a series of movements, each representing a mind state one is hoping to achieve. In some movements, the women stretched their arms heavenward or breathed deeply while drawing their navels in and out; in other movements, they rocked back and forth or twisted their torsos to the rhythm of the chants. I knew immediately what I'd eventually learn was true: *Kundalini* is not about sitting on a cushion with your hands resting in your lap. It is a super physical form of meditation meant to bring greater awareness to both your body and mind.

That all sounds cool, but seeing it in action stunned me a little at first. I'm not sure what I expected when I signed up for a *Kundalini* retreat, but it wasn't this. I settled nervously on my mat, trying my best to replicate the movements or at least repeat the *ada mantra* tune-in at the start of each segment. "Where *are* we?" I leaned in and whispered to Erika. "Just chill and relax," she said, smiling. Guru Jagat, probably noticing my nervousness, said to me, "Follow along as best you can." I glanced around as a jumble of questions crowded my head: *Shouldn't I be home with Egypt and Genesis? What kind of wife nearly misses her husband's birthday? Does everyone here know I've never done this before, and are they staring at me?*

They weren't. Because let me tell you, this was not the see-and-be-seen crowd. Every woman in there was too deeply involved in her breath, her singsong chants, and her movements to be paying even a little bit of attention to me. That gave me the space to just flow with it by flailing my arms back and forth, making a hot mess of the chants, and relaxing into the process. About a half hour in, I'd relaxed so much that I lay on my mat and passed out, dead asleep. That's how intense the experience felt. That's also how jet-lagged I was.

What happened next is what turned on the lights for me. An hour later when I awakened to the room filled with these amazing melodies, all of the chants were still foreign to me—but I could *feel* them. The aura in the room was so pure and beautiful, so palpable. I'm sure that same spirit was there when I'd first walked in. But it was only upon waking that I felt immersed in its presence. The words of the tune-in, sung in unison by this chorus of women, settled over me like a cool mist. "*Ong Namo Guru Dev Namo,*" chanted Guru Jagat. "*Ong Namo Guru Dev Namo,*" the room repeated. I knew something special was happening in this space. I knew it in the same way that I once knew "Girl on Fire" had its own powerful vibrational frequency. The evening's session concluded with a tune-out as soothing to me as the tune-in. Guru Jagat led us in repeating, three times, a phrase that means "I am truth": *Sat Nam. Sat Nam. Sat Nam.*

That ending was, for me, a beginning—a deep curiosity about a practice I hadn't even known existed. After the session, Erika introduced me to Guru Jagat, who greeted me with the same verve and warmth with which she'd led the meditation. She also shared more with me about the practice. She'd studied with Yogi Bhanjan, who became a Master of *Kundalini* when he was sixteen. In the late 1960s, he brought the sacred teachings from India and Pakistan to the West and trained scores of students. *Kundalini,* Guru Jagat explained, is primarily a yoga of awareness. It's a blend of physical and spiritual practice meant to activate the body's energy centers, increase vitality, and elevate consciousness. *Kundalini* is a Sanskrit word that means "coiled snake," and its earliest practitioners believed that divine energy was created at the base of the spine—so the practice is meant to uncoil and connect us to the divine energy within. Those who practice the meditation wear white, a color representing light, but it is by no means a requirement for practice, Guru Jagat told me.

"What time is our first session tomorrow?" I asked Erika as we turned in for the night. Without a hint of a joke in her tone, she answered, "Four thirty." "You mean four thirty *p.m.,* right?" I asked. "No," she said. "I mean four thirty in the morning." I stared blankly at her. Here I was thinking I was going to get a *break* from Baby Land, and yet I'd still have to be up in the middle of the night. As beautiful as my experience had been that evening, I'll keep it real: It wasn't pretty when my alarm went off at three forty-five.

Groggy eyed and yet somehow clear, I was up before sunlight for the daybreak meditation, called the *Sadhana*. What is true in the *Kundalini* tradition is true in many other spiritual practices: the hours between four thirty and six a.m. are believed to be the most potent time of the day. With the comforting, repetitive sound of the tune-in song, my sleepiness surprisingly faded. And by the middle of the hour-long session, the first of several during that second day, I began to feel the same strong presence I'd felt upon waking the evening before. The chants were gorgeous, a swirl of lyrics and music that just spoke to me. I have long known how music's power can reach into the souls of all who hear it. You don't have to understand what a French or Italian singer is singing to grasp the fervor behind every refrain; the singer's emotion and intention transcend his or her words. In that room, as Guru Jagat served as our conductor, guiding us toward a kind of musical journey back to our senses, I felt lifted by the power of the rhythm and repetition—and I felt something stirring in me.

As planned, I left the retreat early to get back for the tail end of Swizz's birthday. But even before I landed at JFK, I knew I'd found something I wanted to keep going with. "How can I start and what should I be working on?" I'd asked Guru Jagat. She gave me a small regimen of three *kriyas* (exercises involving posture, breathing, and chants) that I could practice for three minutes each, for a total of nine minutes. Once I got stronger in my practice, she told me, I could move onto four- and five-minute *kriyas*. Very doable. It still amazes me that, on the morning after Swizz's birthday, I was up before daybreak, singing my *kriyas*. In just a few days, the early rising had come to feel like a gift to myself.

That was in the fall of 2015. And since my return from the retreat, I have rarely missed a daily meditation. I'm now usually up at first light, with my eyes and heart wide open. I began seeing changes

in myself almost immediately. There was far less ruminating over decisions, far less seeking out everyone else's opinions. That's because,
in the silence of the mornings, I could hear myself. "You know what
a *yes* feels like," Oprah had told me. My *yesses* show up in the hush
before daybreak. That is when the world is at its most quiet. It's
when I once lay on my deck floating down the Nile, gazing up at the
boundless sky above. It's that time before the sights and sounds and
smells and distractions of our lives can intrude. It's that clear space
that allows you to tune in to your senses. You are a fresh slate that
the world has not yet written on. In that quiet, a *yes* indeed resounds.

# 16

## BARING SOUL

**KAT, ALICIA'S FRIEND**

Alicia and I grew up together in Manhattan Plaza. We went to different schools and had our own social circles, but we always came home to each other. Most days we'd get on the elevator, in our socks, and go visit each other's apartments. We're like sisters. And what I saw in my sister during childhood is what I see in her now: She has always had a nurturing spirit. It doesn't surprise me that she's a strong mother and parental guardian. Way back when she had her babysitters' club in our building, children gravitated toward her positive energy. She would sing to them and play the piano with them. Long before she became known around the world, she was first known in our building as a girl with an open heart.

#NoMakeup began as a private revelation—one I sat with on the shores of Turks and Caicos. In 2015, Swizz and I traveled there to celebrate our fifth anniversary. We took little Genesis with us. Egypt, who was four, was off living his best life on a cruise with my mom, his Mimi. One afternoon while the baby was asleep and my husband was out, I sat alone in our villa, soaking in the peacefulness, gazing from the window at the shimmering aqua waters. I took out my journal and began to write. What spilled out was a more personal version of everything I was sick of—like the constant judgment of women's appearances, which was high on my list.

The thought had been swirling for years, long before I scribbled it down on the list I'd made ahead of work on *HERE*. It had again resurfaced that spring. One afternoon, as I was preparing to pick up Egypt from school, I threw on some sweatpants and a baseball cap as an internal deliberation arose: *What if someone sees me like this and asks to take a photo? And what if that picture gets posted?* The dialogue wasn't new. For more than a decade, my first thought, upon getting out of the shower, was usually, *What can I wear that won't cause too much attention?* That was true whether I was planning to pick up my son or just going out to shop or work out. What was different, on this day, was that I caught myself in the middle of the neurosis, and it socked me right in the gut. I stopped, stared at myself in the bedroom mirror, and thought, *What is the matter with you? What is happening right now?* It was the first time I'd fully recognized how paralyzed I'd become. And it wasn't until I arrived in Turks, months later, that I got quiet enough to think through that realization, examine it, and try to make sense of how I'd grown so concerned with what others thought of me.

I've been hiding for most of my life, in many ways. The animalistic stares of men along the boulevards of Hell's Kitchen were what first drove me to cover up. I saw how they drooled at the women who pranced by in miniskirts and stilettos, how they undressed them with their gaze, hungrily eyeing their backsides. I noticed the raw desire in their eyes, their urge to lunge and grab what seemed theirs for the taking. It scared me. And in my baggy jeans and Timbs, I could escape notice. With my curls pressed down and tied away into a bun, there was no hint of flirtation, no provocation of fantasy. My loose-fitting sweatshirts became my uniform of survival, my safe place away from the prying eyes and whistles of strangers. There were no bright-red lips to draw stares my way, no formfitting dresses to display my curves and betray my vulnerability.

Fame brought a new form of hiding. The oversize jeans and tough accent got me labeled as hard. So again, I went underground, this time by easing out of who I'd always known myself to be and toward an apparently more digestible version. I traded the full head of chunky braids for cornrows in the front and hair down in the back. I changed how I spoke and eventually even found my way into some dresses. A lot of these changes were a natural evolution, just part of exploring and experimenting with different looks and growing into my full womanhood. But behind the shifting wardrobe, beyond the softening around the edges, there lurked a message: *You are not sufficient as you are.*

My industry reinforced that message. For every performance, every photo shoot and appearance, there's an expectation of female flawlessness. Ahead of each event comes hair and makeup—and I'm not talking about some light dust of powder. It's the works: heavy foundation, fake eyelashes and liner, three coats of mascara and lipstick. Creating this impenetrable armor of perfection is literally an hours-long production, and for my first fifteen years in music, I went through it nearly every day. The makeup would sit on my face for ten, twelve hours at a time, often under hot stage lights, always settling into every crevice of my face to clog my pores and lead to breakouts. My skin couldn't breathe. In time, nor could I. When I'd come home from whatever event I'd had, I'd scrub off all that foundation, rip off the eyelashes, pull out my fake ponytail extension, and stare at my bare skin. Without the makeup, I no longer even recognized myself.

My anxiety over appearance also invaded my private world. Any mother can tell you that after having a couple of babies, it takes frickin' *forever* for your body to recover; in some ways, it never fully does. For months after you give birth, you're like, *What happened? And how come I'm not bouncing back?* Add to that having others seemingly fixated on every ripple of my skin, every hint of cellulite. While on vacation, I'd play on the beach with Egypt as some long-lens camera swooped in to capture a close-up of my abs. I'd find myself holding in my stomach, praying the images wouldn't end up on some blog and go viral. They usually did. And though I know it's a fact of life in my industry, it still felt mean and intrusive. Nobody is supposed to snap a picture of someone's butt on the beach and then circulate that photo en masse. It's not natural. In fact, it's cruel. Meanwhile, because every model in every magazine spread is airbrushed to death, no one recalls what cellulite actually looks like. Women have loose flesh and stretch marks: that is the truth. And yet it's the lie—the unattainable standard—that is peddled in its place. We've been sold this lie so frequently that it has altered our very way of seeing.

That head trip is what led me to think twice about doing what mothers all over the world do every single day: leaving the house, without makeup and in sweats, to pick up my child from school. On those occasions when I did roll out with a bare face and a baseball cap, I often declined to take photos with those who asked. When I'd reluctantly agree, mostly because I didn't want to disappoint some-one with a sweet spirit, I'd freak out for hours afterward. *What if the picture gets put up on Instagram?*

There were only two options for breaking out of my prison: to always leave my house ready for a close-up, which every parent can testify is impossible, or to finally get comfortable with my true face, others' opinions be damned. On that Sunday in Turks when I sat scribbling my soul onto paper, I chose Door Two. My slow walk to freedom, which began as a flurry of painful and disjointed thoughts, eventually morphed into a published letter—one that inspired a viral moment.

———

The universe brought me yet another chance to uncover, this one in the context of family blending. My sons were born into a blessing, a loving tribe of siblings, all of whom have embraced their younger brothers. Swizz is the father of five: his eldest son, Nasir, a college stu-dent who's also an artist, writer, and producer; his daughter, Nicole, born in 2008 and living in London; Kasseem Jr., aka KJ, the son he and his first wife, Mashonda, welcomed in 2006; and, of course,

Egypt and Genesis. Swizz steps up for every one of his children. As a father, he is engaged and committed, beyond providing financially. He comes from a line of good men who, though human and flawed as we all are, still lovingly coached and guided him toward manhood. We are intent on building that same foundation for our five. Nicole spends time with us over summer breaks and holidays, and we stay in touch with her throughout the year. KJ, who lives close by, is with us consistently, and Nas is in New York for college.

Our family has become the definition of a successful blend. When you love someone, you love their journey—and that path leads you to the family dynamic you were meant to inherit and devote yourself to. Through my own childhood experience, I know how often we're taught what a family should look like. And if your family doesn't look like what we've been shown, we somehow feel incomplete. But really, families come in all versions, shapes, and sizes, and should be celebrated as part of our collective experience. That is what life has taught me.

Blending a family isn't always high fives and hugs. The process of coming together has involved unmasking ourselves, a peeling back of layers to reveal our deep personal truths. It has meant engaging in awkward conversations. It has involved spending the time to truly hear one another's viewpoints, and then finding a place to understand one another. That has had to happen with our entire family. That willingness to hear and empathize has been the starting point for creating a healthy environment. We're constantly working on getting it right.

One profound moment of this came the first time Mashonda and I connected over dinner. By this time, little KJ and I had already become close during his frequent visits to our home. Mashonda and I met in the private downstairs cellar at Philip Marie, a cozy Italian spot in downtown Manhattan. Once we got beyond a few pleasantries and toasted our meeting, silence set in. I could feel the guardedness in both of us. And yet, as much as there was to say, we didn't get too deep that evening. We had easy, fluid conversation. Toward the end, Mashonda made a comment that really struck me.

"One day," she said, "we're going to share grandchildren." She was right. Through the powerful connection of our shared son KJ, we'd be connected for life. One day, if KJ marries, she and I will be fussing over him and his partner, wanting every detail to be perfect. One day, Mashonda and I might both hold a small baby who is KJ's child. That baby will have three grandmothers, and I will be one of them. There is no writing each other off when love is involved. It's all about finding the way through. That first conversation was a start, a way for us to dip our toes into the waters of a real connection.

Not long after that first dinner, Swizz, Mashonda, and I also began meeting regularly, just the three of us. When you come together for the first time, trying to blend a family, it can be tough. There was a lot of talking over one another. I walked out of there thinking, *If we're going to make this work, we've gotta find a way to do it differently.*

We eventually did. One evening I said to Erika, "How do you get people to actually *hear* one another?" She mentioned the idea of active listening. Of having all parties agree, among other things, to hear one another without interrupting. You can't truly listen when you're constantly cutting someone off or already formulating a response in your head as he or she speaks. She'd seen the tool work for others, and it sounded like it could be of value in our process. So I brought it into our next roundtable.

I led us in an opening prayer. As we held hands, I asked that we reveal our highest selves and feel protected during the conversation.

"Let's create some ground rules," I suggested. Rule one: This was a safe space where anything could be expressed, but it had to be said with respect and love. Rule two: Absolutely no interrupting. Even if we heard something we totally disagreed with, we had to let the speaker complete his or her thought. If something came to mind while someone else spoke, we'd write it down and then wait to speak about it until it was our turn. Rule three: After one of us spoke, the others had to later repeat back to that person what they thought was said, as in "I heard you say *x*." That gave us the opportunity to be clear, to either say, "Yes, that is exactly what I meant," or "No, that's not it." We went around the table, one by one over several hours, and spoke our truths. Without all the interruptions, the vibe was calm. We didn't always like or agree with what each of us had to say, but for the first time, we fully took it in. It was the beginning of the openness we share to this day.

It was not until I became a mother that I truly understood the nature of selfless love, a care so profound that I'd do anything to protect our children. And because of my own upbringing, I know how important it is for all of our children to feel connected to their father. I know what it feels like not to have your dad around every day. It's one reason I work extra hard to bring us all together. It's why I'm often up at two a.m. arranging schedules and pick-ups, vacation times and family gatherings and joint parent-teacher conferences, or preparing to welcome Nicole and Nas in town for Thanksgiving or Christmas celebrations. It's why I'll help KJ with school projects and read with him before bed. It's why, even when I'm overwhelmed after a tour or have all the kids on my own while Swizz is traveling, I find joy in caring for our children. I know they are feeling consistently loved, and I'm a big part of why they feel that way.

When KJ was little he started referring to me as his stepmom, which didn't feel like the right vibe to me, especially when Egypt began mimicking KJ and also calling me stepmom. So Swizz and I came up with an alternative: KJ would call me *Umi* (pronounced OOH-me), a beautiful word that means mother in Arabic. Egypt and Genesis now also call me Umi, in addition to Mommy. Umi is one of my favorite words and identities. And being Umi to a wide age range of children also gives me parental foresight. By walking alongside a thirteen-year-old KJ, I get a peek at what may be ahead for nine-year-old Egypt. It's a real-life practice run. And Nas, who is navigating early adulthood, has his own unique relationship with me, given that I'm not his biological parent. There's a freedom and honesty in our connection, and I want to create that same safe space for my other children in the years ahead.

I'll always remember how KJ's eyes brightened when he first saw the video for "Blended Family," a song I'd begun work on even before I found out I was pregnant with Genesis. The video includes several modern families, all of whom have blended in some way. Our own beautiful blended family is featured; A$AP Rocky, the rapper and actor, also has a cameo. "He has a blended family *too*?!" KJ said. I nodded and smiled, thrilled that he'd grasped the message: Blending is not an exception, but a sweet commonality, one we share with the millions of families who've joined hands and linked hearts. What has happened in our home is proof that blending—and being willing to connect on a real level—can bring about a stronger family foundation.

Our family gatherings no longer have to be so structured or scheduled. We've eased into a rhythm that has us frequently in each other's homes and lives. For a recent weekend with KJ, for instance, I picked him up from school on a Thursday so he could be with us until Monday. Monday turned out to be a snow day (as in no school, much to the joy of our boys), so KJ spent that day with his brothers. That evening, while I was at the studio, Mashonda stopped by to pick up KJ. He, Egypt, and Genesis were in the middle of dinner, so she pulled up a chair and hung with them; she has her own relationship with our boys, independent of Swizz and me, and she sometimes even picks up Genesis from school, as well as brings the boys little gifts. None of this has to be planned. The blending, at this point, is fluid, relaxed, and second nature.

Blending is about more than bringing together families. You and I blend every time we have a conversation with someone who doesn't think like us, talk like us, look like us, or share our religious and political beliefs with respect. We blend when we initiate a compassionate dialogue with someone we've had a disagreement with. We blend when we set aside our own ego and agenda and consider an experience through another person's lens. We blend when we elevate a relationship with time and kind words. That is what it truly means to come together—not just to hear, but to listen with an open heart.

———

When Swizz and I returned from Turks, I began finalizing work on *HERE*. Most of the songs had been completed the year before; a few new ones were added. The promotional photo shoots were arranged ahead of the release of the first single, "In Common," and for that session, I arrived at the studio straight from the gym. My face was bare, without even a hint of ChapStick. I was dressed in a loose sweatshirt. My hair was still stuffed under a scarf and a baseball cap.

"I have to shoot you right now, like this!" said Paola, this incredible photographer I'd worked with before. I froze. *Now? Looking like this?* Paola and my then creative director, Earl Sebastian, had been brainstorming with me about how we could capture the rawness of me and my music, but I still needed a few minutes to wrap my head around this particular idea. They gave me a minute to let it settle in, and I finally agreed. Before long, Paola was clicking away.

I held my breath for the first full five minutes of that shoot; that's how nervous and insecure I felt about being photographed in my most plain state. Though for months I'd been thinking through and journaling about how frustrated I was with society's oppressive expectations for women, and how ready I felt to reveal my true face, that was all theoretical until the moment I was confronted with the lens of a camera. And, honestly, it frightened me. I'd told the universe I wanted authenticity, and the universe had answered in the way that it does: It sent me a test, a way to practice that visual honesty. And initially, I wasn't quite ready for that test. As Paola clicked away, a single thought raced through my brain: *Am I actually doing this?*

And then, as the session progressed, I started relaxing. Click by click, frame by frame against a plain white background, I dropped my shoulders and just leaned into the experience. Halfway through, I even started to enjoy it. I look now at the photos from that series, with my scarf tied into a topknot and my spirit as open as my expression, and you know what? I know who that girl is. That whole scene is totally my world, my vibe and energy. That's how I rock. And it flowed from a place that could not be more organic. It came from the freedom I've been reaching for all my life. It came from my willingness to, at last, show my unretouched, imperfect, and uncensored face.

That photo shoot, along with my journal entry in Turks, are what prompted me to write "Time to Uncover" as a piece for Lenny Letter—the feminist forum created by Lena Dunham and Jenni Konner. I'd been inspired and moved by some of the other Lenny Letters I'd read, so I gathered the raw pieces from my diary pages and turned that into a first draft. When I showed it to my husband, he said, "Really—you feel this way?" I did. And in May 2016 when the letter was published, a couple of the most honest lines I'd written made it into the piece:

"I don't want to cover up anymore," I wrote. "Not my face, not my mind, not my soul, not my dreams, not my struggles, not my emotional growth. Nothing." I still feel exactly that way.

The same month the letter was published, the barefaced images from the "In Common" photo series were released. The response to both the letter and the photos was unbelievable to me, even now. On social media, tens of thousands of people began posting images of their own faces with the hashtag #NoMakeup. It became a cultural lightbulb so strong that it outshined everything, including, at times, the music itself. The message resonated across socioeconomic and generational lines; even those I never would've expected to be following me were clearly paying attention. Many fathers came up to me and said, "Love that no-makeup thing you're doing! It's beautiful. I have daughters, and it's exactly what I want them to hear." Women and girls posted entries about how empowered they felt to go natural. On Snapchat, Gabrielle Union put up an image of herself, complete with her gorgeous freckles and a head scarf, and captioned it, "No makeup, head wrap . . . hey Alicia Keys, I see you!" And Kim

Kardashian rocked the no-makeup look at the Balenciaga fashion show in Paris.

In hindsight, there's one small thing I would've changed about my letter. Toward the end of the piece, I wrote, "I hope to God it's a revolution." If I had to do it over, I would've clarified that idea by inserting the word *personal* in front of the word *revolution*—because that's actually what I meant. The reaction to my letter was overwhelmingly positive, and yet there were those who interpreted it as a public campaign rather than as one woman's manifesto.

"Well if I looked like you," someone wrote, "I could choose not to wear makeup too." I responded at the time the way I do today: My deepest intention is that we all find a path to whatever freedom feels like for us—and that is unique to each person. I still wear makeup when I feel like it, though less of it, and I still enjoy experimenting with a new shade of lipstick or eye shadow. The point is that I, and everyone else, have a *choice*. And we should be able to freely make that choice, from one moment to the next, without society's "standard of beauty" hovering over us. I am my own standard-bearer. So are you.

The vast majority of people who read my letter embraced the spirit of it. A lot of us are over the fakeness. Much of what we see and consume in our world is so carefully constructed and polished, so highly curated. Like never before, we crave the authentic, not just when it comes to appearance, but also in our narratives. In our conversations. In our work and political spheres. In our friendships and intimate relationships. And as we uncover that truth, as we remove the masks and falsehoods and finally get clear on what's real, the work of our lives, as I see it, is to stand immovably in that truth.

# 17

# CROSSROADS

**AMERICA FERRERA, EMMY AWARD–WINNING ACTRESS
AND ACTIVIST**

Alicia and I met just as the Time's Up movement was coming together and women in entertainment were convening in an unprecedented way. She reached out to me to talk about how women in the music industry could be included in that conversation, in that community of artists. We really connected over a shared desire for sisterhood in our social justice work. What I love about Alicia is that she's a woman of her word. When we make plans to organize around an issue we care about—be it for a march in DC or a voter registration rally—Alicia shows up. There isn't a lot of hemming and hawing. It's action. Ahead of the Families Belong Together march in 2018, I'd just had a baby and was breastfeeding every couple of hours. "But I've gotta figure out how to be part of this solidarity," I told Alicia. "I'll be there with you," she said. And she was: She and her son Egypt were on a six a.m. train with me from New York City to Washington, DC. She shows up not only physically, but with her whole heart and soul. I've learned so much from her about the power of being a fully embodied and present woman.

Aside from my soul mate connection with Swizz and my infinite love for my children, I've had three mountaintop moments during my career as an artist—experiences so epic, so transcendent that they

raised the tiny hairs on my skin and kept them in salute. One was the Legends weekend with Oprah, that intersection of past and present and its sheer Spirit power. I left Oprah's house with my hand over my heart and a desire to walk taller and dream bigger. Another was the lunch my brother Bono and I shared with President Obama in the Oval Office. And the most monumental experience, at least up to now: taking over Times Square to perform live on John Lennon's birthday.

A year ahead of the November 2016 release of *HERE,* the seed for the idea was planted: Why not put on a live show in the city that gave me wings, a concert during a time when our culture is at a cross- roads? It was the perfect intersection of art and activism: I'd serve up a taste of fifteen songs—some old, some new, many love letters to my hometown—while standing for peace and nonviolent protest in celebration of a legend who embodied both.

From the beginning, my intention was to do more than deliver a concert. It was to use this platform—this unique moment in history, amid the most intense presidential campaign in decades—to shine a light. And what better place to lift a lantern than at the nation's epicenter, a concrete jungle that fifty million souls pass through an- nually and millions more are inspired by. That hub, the home of the brave and the birthplace of hip-hop, just so happened to include the five-block radius where I first learned my music lessons and dreamed my dreams, where the smells, the sea of yellow taxis, the yelling and the honking, the magic and the music made me who I am. We'd keep the free concert a "secret," revealing the details bit by bit on social media: first the date (Sunday, October 9), then the time (eight p.m.), and finally the exact location. That's how *HERE in Times Square* began—as a vision for the ultimate NYC block party.

The journey to my backyard was not without its challenges. With the album's release date already in cement, my team worked back- ward from that date when scheduling the concert. Such an enormous endeavor comes at a steep price, so we sought out major partnerships on multiple levels to help defray the expense. Trouble is, before we could lock down all of those alliances, up-front costs began mounting.

As the concert date inched closer, my organization had spent a couple hundred thousand dollars on hiring people to create footage and transfer that footage onto the fifteen or twenty jumbo electronic billboard screens we'd use during the event.

And yet the experience turned out to be so priceless, so worth every dime spent. On the morning of the concert, my team spread out over the fifty-seventh floor of the W Hotel at Forty-seventh and Broadway—close to the northern part of the Square where the stage was set, and near the famous TKTS booth. There was a sound check two hours beforehand. I walked from my hotel over to the stage entrance, balancing a coffee cup while gazing up at a sight that, in a zillion years, I never would have thought I'd witness: row after row of massive screens flashing "Alicia HERE in Times Square," with images of my various album covers alternating with beautiful messages like "Peace" and "Imagine." In the lead-up to the event, I'd seen the blueprints. I'd sat in on our meetings. I'd heard the details. I created the vision, I spoke of what I wanted, and we went through many incarnations of these ideas. And yet none of it came close to the amazement I felt as I stared up, taking in the moment. Near the iconic NASDAQ sign, thousands were already gathering along the sidewalks of my old 'hood for a "secret" that was now definitely out. NYPD officers closed off surrounding streets. Traffic was rerouted. One of the world's busiest intersections was slowing to a halt for me to perform my songs. I've dreamed a lot of big dreams over the years, but never in my wildest fantasies had I envisioned *this*.

My astonishment continued as I peered around the Square. On one corner was the little bodega where I used to get my fake IDs. On another was the city bus stop where I'd wait for rides in the biting cold. Around the corner stood the two mighty towers where my childhood played out, in a tiny living room divided by an upright. And down the street, near Forty-eighth and Ninth, was the performing arts school where I harmonized and improvised and studied the work of musical giants. Can you imagine returning to the neighborhood where you grew up and then having fifteen thousand people meet you outside on the corner? It felt so otherworldly to me that, during the sound check, I held back tears. There I stood, fifteen years after *Songs in A Minor* hit, ready to share music from six albums.

Later, just before I walked onto the stage for the concert, I prayed with my team, asking the Spirit to flow through all of us. Then, right as I went out to meet the crowd, I asked myself the question I ask before every performance: *Do you want to be good, or do you want to be* great? I answered by bringing my full self to that experience over the next hour and a half. From the opening note of "The Gospel" to the mix of "Holy War" with Lennon's "Imagine," I literally felt like I was floating, elevated by the crowd's energy, filled with thankfulness for the moment. My team purposely hadn't enclosed the stage: no roof to raise, no ceiling to break through. Out in the open air, I wanted to give those gathered a sense of limitlessness, of never-ending possibilities, of a 360-degree immersive experience that stretched beyond the skyscrapers and up toward heaven. I stood at the Yamaha piano, roaming freely between there and the front of the stage rather than sitting—my new way of performing so I'm not held back. And between the songs, I sprinkled in a few rousing encouragements.

"They know that our voice means change!" I shouted. "If you care about your life, where we are going, and your children, then vote for it—please."

Before the opening notes of "She Don't Really Care," I set the mood for a surprise.

"I think I need to call my brother really quick," I said into the mic. A dial tone came over the loudspeaker.

"Hello?" said Q-Tip. Moments later, my boy slid out onstage to perform alongside me. That was just the beginning: Nas joined me for "One Love." John Mayer rocked the show with a blend of his "Gravity" with my "If I Ain't Got You," while Questlove gifted us with his drumbeats. And with each selection, footage orchestrated to match the music flooded the screens. The crowd lost its mind when JAY-Z rolled out, seemingly from nowhere, to drop his rhymes on

"Empire." Meanwhile, I was on level one billion, my arms up, the wind having its way with my 'fro, my bare face covered in bliss, an electric current vibrating through my body. From the stage, I spotted my sons KJ, Egypt, and Genesis pointing up at the screens, surprised to see their Umi's name in neon lights as I sang "Blended Family."

"I love you with all my heart!" I said as the concert wrapped up. If I'd had my way, I would've stayed out there all night, but the NYPD had other plans. When I was fifteen minutes overtime, they began urging me off. I got in one last declaration before they were about to cut me off:

"Let's rise up and shine up!" Through that entire concert, I felt like I was about to faint, and when I made my way backstage, I nearly did. I have seldom been more dizzy with joy. "If this was my last day on earth, I'd be straight!" I said to my crew backstage. I mean, I'm not saying I *want* to die, but man—if it had happened that night, what a helluva way to go. As thousands dispersed, many heading toward the Forty-second Street train stop, the screens overhead proclaimed the world as I dream it: "Sexism is over." "AIDS is over." "Violence is over." "Refugees welcome." May it one day be so.

A month after that concert—and four days before Americans went to the polls—*HERE* hit the airwaves. I'd brainstormed a whole list of more complicated titles before choosing that one. *HERE* says exactly what I intended to say: Let's be present. Let's be right here in our experience, taking in every goose bump and gift. Let's live our lives more aware and awake to both ourselves and the surrounding world. Never before have we needed to be so tuned in to what's happening on the planet, or more clear about how we'll interact with the energy of our times.

I now live in woke mode. For me, every moment is a reawakening, a chance to meet myself exactly as I am. I'm finally allowing myself to just be. Be giddy. Be irritable. Be vulnerable. Be silly. Be exhilarated. Be whomever and *however* I am. That is my practice, my daily meditation. It's also my daily prayer for all of us—that we allow others the same freedom of expression that we are learning to grant to ourselves.

———

A few weeks before the presidential election, Swizz was away at Harvard for one of his three-week intensives. Between two of his early classes, he called me one morning.

"Babe, he's going to win," he said.

"What?" I said.

"Trump is going to be president."

"What are you talking about, Swizz?" I said. "Never say that. Hell no."

"For the first time," he said, "I see how it's possible." In class that day, his professor had asked for a show of hands: "Who's voting for Trump?" In a room filled with more than two hundred students from all over the world, 90 percent had lifted their arms. The question was obviously theoretical for the foreign students in the room. Even still, Swizz took note of the shocking number of hands in the air: some of them white, some of them black or brown, all of them representing various demographics. "There were hands raised that I never would've thought would go up," he said. "I'm telling you—he's going to win."

There is no denial more deep than the one I was in. *Surely, Americans will vote with some sense,* I thought. Surely, that *Access Hollywood* tape, which hit the headlines two days before my Times Square concert, would deliver a knockout blow to the Trump campaign. How could someone who joked about grabbing a woman by her genitals ever be considered fit for the highest office in the land? In my mind, there was *no way* he could win, and certainly not against a candidate who'd spent her life in public service. That July, two weeks after Bernie Sanders conceded, I had taken the stage at the Democratic National Convention in Philly and supported Hillary Clinton, doing all I could, through music, to heal the divided party.

We couldn't allow anger or apathy to keep us home. Seldom had there been someone with a stronger track record of service to run for the presidency. I trusted that Hillary would keep the issues I cared most about in the spotlight. I also trusted her finger on that nuclear button. But Trump? Compulsive. Unhinged. Dishonest. A man who'd spent years pouring gas on the birther conspiracy, questioning whether President Obama was even an American. A candidate who played to our nation's long-held racial fears, sending out dog whistles to stir animosity. That man? *No way on planet Earth.* And yet on November 8, the electoral college cleared its throat and answered otherwise. What a deafening wake-up call.

On that Wednesday morning, I was traumatized. My family and friends were also distraught. A lot of my social media fam joined me in that feeling: Thousands voiced anxiety about what this would mean for our nation and world, and many more were as stunned at the outcome as I was. As I moved through that day, the air literally felt different to me, as if the molecules had somehow been rearranged. It's like going to bed knowing the sky is blue and waking up to find it a permanent shade of piss yellow. It's disorienting—like, *Wait—what just happened?* Post-election, nothing seemed normal or felt right. And for me, the biggest travesty was that more than one hundred million of us Did. Not. Vote. Had even a small percentage of those people shown up at the polls, it might have changed the results.

The 24-7 news cycle, which was already moving at a headspinning speed, somehow got faster. When I look back on that time, it astounds me how much change has happened so quickly, how a ticker tape of events consumed us overnight: the forty-fifth president was sworn in that January, delivering a speech that set the tone for what was to come. The next day, more than three million protestors in cities across the US and thousands more around the world gathered for the Women's March, the largest single-day protest in US history. At the DC demonstration, I sang my heart out on behalf of girls on fire everywhere and delivered lines from Maya Angelou's poem "Still I Rise." And in a span of time that now feels more like a decade than a few years, the headlines just kept coming.

The culture quake shook more than the political landscape. The Harvey Weinstein story broke around the time of the election, with Ashley Judd taking on the then most influential man in Hollywood. Dozens of others caught the spirit of her bravery and admitted that they'd also been sexually assaulted. The aftershocks reverberated through Hollywood and well beyond as, one by one, women (and some men) raised their hands and said, "Me, too," using the phrase Tarana Burke coined in 2006. The steady stream of women, sixty in total, accusing Bill Cosby of sexual misconduct stepped forward. And on the heels of more heartbreaking killings of unarmed African Americans—including hundreds whose names never made the headlines—Black Lives Matter leaders shifted into sixth gear and stayed there.

In 2016, We Are Here met them on the front lines by releasing a video that still gives me chills even as it breaks my heart: *23 Ways You Could Be Killed If You Are Black in America*. Every other week, there seemed to be another black person's life unjustly snatched away, and so many of us were asking ourselves *What can we do?* This video was one small answer. I personally reached out to some of the individuals who appeared in the video; Leigh Blake—who'd first asked me to read all twenty-three ways myself, and then came up with the brilliant idea for us to expand the circle of those involved when I wasn't feeling that approach—called on several others she knew.

There was no glam, no expensive photo-shoot costs. Just raw and immediate footage, with each of us filming ourselves on a cell phone. One by one, we delivered the list of senseless ways that African Americans can be killed, which includes failing to signal a lane change (Sandra Bland); riding in a car with your girlfriend's child in the back seat (Philando Castile); wearing a hoodie (Trayvon Martin); and selling CDs outside of a supermarket (Alton Sterling). My husband, Swizz, as well as my friends Bono, Beyoncé, Janelle Monáe, Taraji P. Henson,

Queen Latifah, Chris Rock, Rihanna, Lenny Kravitz, Pharrell, and many others shared their voices alongside mine.

———

Music is one of the most potent forms of protest, the gateway to connection. Seldom has there been a more important time to raise consciousness and shift conversations by picking up a mic. A song, at its core, is a testimony. It's how we tell our stories, both individually and collectively. It's how we forget our troubles for a time, and how we remember who we are emotionally. It's how we rally and how we heal. A song, like no other art form, has the ability to curl up inside of our spirits and never move out. I may have become fluent in the language of social justice, but music will always be my mother tongue. My native language. My way of reaching a world that can never have too many songs in it.

It was in that spirit that I served as a coach on three seasons of *The Voice,* an NBC show giving new artists—potential trailblazers, in my view—a special platform to hone their craft. One of the coolest things about the show is its defining feature: blind auditions. A row of coaches (during my last season in 2018 that was Kelly Clarkson, Adam Levine, Blake Shelton, and me) sit with chairs turned away from the stage as a contestant launches into a song. During the performance, the second you hear something you vibe with—*boom*—you press your button and swivel around to see the artist. The singer and the coach then form a team. If more than one coach chooses a singer, that singer gets to decide which mentor to team up with. Teams of artists are guided behind the scenes by the coaches (my favorite part) and light up the stage with weekly performances (my *other* favorite part). And of course, America gets to vote for the singers who most inspire them. It all leads to a final round of performances and one triumphant singer hailed as "the voice" (shout out to my season-twelve winner, Chris Blue!).

During the blind auditions, I listen with my heart—because I can *feel* the intersection of natural talent and soulful expression. When

that happens, it sounds like a resounding yes. Even still, I'm sometimes surprised to discover, after I swivel around, that a sixteen-year-
old powerhouse sounds more like an old-school crooner . . . which
is exactly what many listeners thought when they first heard "Fallin'"
on the radio. It is a gift to watch artists blossom week by week, as
they work to implement your suggestions and feedback. As a coach,
you're not there to be a judge, a critic, or a commentator. You're there
to elevate emerging talent.

From the very start of the show back in 2011, I'd been invited
to be a coach. For a long time, I declined because it didn't feel like
quite my zone. But as I began stepping into my full self, living in a
more awakened space, I wanted to share some of that energy, that
consciousness—both with the contestants and the viewers. In order
to reach the people you most want to reach, you sometimes have to
go places you wouldn't normally go.

The whole reason to be on the show, for me, is to have a hand in
discovering and nurturing these musicians. It's also about widening
the spectrum of artistic expression by putting a variety of artists at
center stage. Christiana Danielle, one of my singers on season fourteen, is a perfect example. She is this stunning, dark-chocolate-brown
woman who oozes individuality. She wore her fashions and sang her
songs with flair, all on her own terms. She was bright and glittery
and vocally gifted. She was capable of shining under pressure, and
she was the type of unique artist that, in my view, America doesn't
see enough of. If the full range of our world's talent and beauty were
more often featured, we'd realize just how many choices and voices
and styles and sizes there are to celebrate. And maybe then we could
break out of these straitjackets, these boxes, these stereotypes, and
embrace our true identities.

I had more fun on *The Voice* than I ever expected to. Being on the
show gave me a chance to just play, to refuel myself in the middle of
all that was happening in the world. A couple of my castmates are
also my friends away from the set (Miley Cyrus and Gwen Stefani),
so coming to "work" during those seasons was like hanging with my

girls all evening. Even before I took the stage on the Los Angeles set, I was cracking up behind the scenes with the other coaches. The set itself just pulsates with energy. The joking between us is genuine; that kind of fondness (or, at times, biting humor) cannot be faked. Even when the cameras aren't rolling, we're often raggin' on each other. Adam, who (along with Blake Shelton) had been on the show the longest, is like the granddaddy of coaches. He's playful, but don't get it twisted: He's also super competitive, as we all are.

One of the funniest off-set moments came in 2017. While preparing for that night's show, Adam Levine noticed me putting on makeup.

"I thought you didn't wear makeup," he teased. I stared at him, half-grinning but completely serious when I replied: "I do what the fuck I want." Adam just walked away, smiling and shaking his head. And I kept right on rocking things my way. Onstage. Offstage. In life.

———

After the election shook the country to its core, I got numb—and then I got busy. What's true about a personal crisis applies to a national one: It rattles you awake. So after a week of grieving, I pushed past my despair and laced up my work boots. The momentum was strong: Millions who were as dumbfounded as I'd been by the results were suddenly passionate about organizing. What we'd always regarded as important now felt downright urgent. It was time to regroup and join forces, across all corners of society, during this abrupt shift in our times. The suddenness of the change is why, at the start of 2017, I began a transition away from my work on We Are Here. During three years, the organization had raised both awareness and millions, and those efforts continue through the nonprofits we put in the spotlight. Yet the strong political headwinds thrust me toward a pressing desire: creating sustainable change as part of a nationwide community of leaders. I recognized that we can get the most done when we strive in unison.

That's what first led me to reach out to America Ferrera—aka firecracker number one—toward the end of 2017. In the throes of the Weinstein uproar, she and dozens of women in Hollywood as part of the Time's Up movement were gathering for closed-door conversations about restoring women's power in the workplace and beyond. My girl, Janelle Monáe, and I showed up to a meeting in Los Angeles, with the intent of trading ideas and then working to bring change to the music industry. While there's some overlap between the Grammy and Oscar worlds, the two industries are vastly different. What works to bring about change in the film and stage businesses doesn't necessarily translate to the music world. But it was an inspiring starting point, and once back home in New York, I began brainstorming with Ann about how we could bring more women to the table in our studio.

That conversation eventually turned into She Is the Music, a nonprofit I cofounded in 2018. I and three other industry leaders (Ann Mincieli, sound engineer and founder of Jungle City Studios; Jody Gerson, CEO and chairperson of Universal Music Publishing Group; and Samantha Kirby Yoh, WME partner and head of the East Coast Music Department) were the crew of original visionaries, but we've now brought together about one hundred women leaders across our industry. That number is still growing, which is the point. Together, we are creating opportunities for women to break in at every level of the music world—from choreographers and lighting designers to engineers, lawyers, stage hands, and producers. There's also mentorship, including an all-female writing camp. It's our way of erasing pay and power disparities by lifting women into key decision-making roles. When you're in the position to hire people, as Ann and I are, you have a responsibility to hire and promote those intent on elevating women. That notion is part of what sparked the idea for She Is the Music.

In summer 2018, after I had a powerful phone call with Rosario Dawson about how we could all band together for change, America and I linked up again—this time, to stand on behalf of immigrant families under attack at our borders following the president's "zero-tolerance" policy. More than three thousand children were forcibly wrenched from their parents' arms. Even now, scores of those children have not been reunited with parents who are locked away in US immigration detention centers. I took one look into the eyes of my own precious children and made a call to America.

"What can we do about this?" I asked her. At six a.m. on the day of the Families Belong Together rally, she and I (along with Egypt and my brother, Cole) boarded an Acela train from New York Penn Station to the nation's capital. In more than seven hundred cities across the nation, tens of thousands of demonstrators joined voices in a plea for the administration to end its cruel policy.

"My seven-year-old son is here with me today," I told the crowd. "His name is Egypt. I couldn't even imagine not being able to find him. I couldn't even imagine being separated from him or scared about how he is being treated. . . . Our democracy is at stake. Our humanity is at stake. We are out here to save the soul of our nation. We need all the children reunited with their parents. We demand to end the zero-humanity policy."

There is power in sisterhood. Our voices are strongest as part of a chorus. And there are many ways we can come together around issues we care about. These days, I'm dreaming of a fellowship of crusaders, a community of like-minded influencers who stay in constant dialogue and action. *Action*—that's the key word. Marching has its place, and we should continue to flood the streets and the National Mall. Yet I'm also looking for ways to turn our protests into meaningful policy change. Time's up for just talking. Game on for flipping the script.

# 18

## HOMELAND

### SWIZZ

Alicia's first trip to Egypt was a retreat—a way to slow down, catch her breath, and reevaluate some things. The second trip was a real pilgrimage. Sometimes you have to be at a certain point in life to truly see a place. I know people who've been around the world but never fully experienced it or learned anything about the culture. This trip was all about learning. Months before we left, Alicia did a lot of homework, a lot of research and studying. We both wanted to go there for the uncut knowledge, the authentic vibes.

Since Alicia and I have been together, she has always been on a spiritual journey. She is open-minded. She has wondered about many different religions—Christianity, Buddhism, Islam, and others. She respects all these beliefs and sees wisdom in them. I think our trip brought her closer to her own relationship with the Most High, outside of any one religion. I see her looking inside of herself for answers. I see her listening to her own spirit. And more and more, I see her moving closer to the truth of who she really is.

The first time I traveled to Egypt, I went in search of solitude. Twelve years later when I returned with my family, I found a part of my identity I hadn't known was missing.

My journey back to the motherland began a whole year before

the flight was booked—and in a way, it began a lot earlier than that. Since becoming a mother, I've been intent on teaching my children about the heroes that built our country. I want them to know about Frederick Douglass, the prominent abolitionist who used the power of the pen to tell his own story. I want them to celebrate the brilliance of scholar W. E. B. Du Bois, and the bravery of Sojourner Truth, the freedom fighter who once asked "Ain't I a Woman?" I want them to know the courage it took for Harriet Tubman to lead families through swamps and darkness toward freedom's fresh air. But before I can tell those stories—before I can explain what enslavement is—I first want to teach them their African ancestry, the extraordinary kingdoms they come from. One afternoon in 2017 when my son asked me a question, it became clear I needed to step up my lesson plans.

"Mom," Egypt said as I drove him to school. "What's the N-word?"

I swallowed hard and tried to keep a straight face. I'd known this question was coming at *some* point; I just hadn't expected that point to be age seven.

"How did you hear that word, babe?" I asked.

"My friend said it," he told me.

"Oh yeah?" I said. "Which friend?"

He didn't answer. "You can tell me," I said, sensing his hesitation. "It's cool." He explained that a girl in his class had said it that day. She hadn't directed it at him, he said, nor had she used the actual word.

"So what does it mean?" he asked again.

"It's a word we don't use," I told him. "And it's a mean word that has been used about people of color. That's why we don't use it."

After that conversation, I got focused. For years, I've been frustrated with how history is taught—and *isn't* taught—in American schools. The introduction of black people is presented in the context of *enslavement,* the word I use in place of the dehumanizing term *slave.* I don't believe in the word *slave* because no one chooses to be owned by someone; an enslaved person is a human being whose freedom has been stolen. As I've raised my own consciousness through reading and studying, I've become intentional about properly framing our story for my children. More than anything, I want them to understand their true identity: who our people were before four hundred years of bondage. I want them to know the strength of our ancestors' spirits. And I want them to hear that story in a way that makes them feel empowered rather than victimized.

My brain went into overdrive after Egypt's question. *How do I talk to him about enslavement in a way that doesn't emasculate him?* After some thought, I landed on an approach: I'd share with him the many moments in history when people of various backgrounds have suffered unimaginable cruelty and death at the hands of others, like the Holocaust. Sadly, the list is long.

I first shared with Egypt the many amazing innovations of the ancient Nile River Valley civilizations—from creating a complex planetary system that became the basis for current-day astronomy to inventing an ingenious farming and agriculture practice that allowed them to grow large crops.

"That's *me*, Mommy?" he'd say, connecting his name with the greatness I told him about.

"Yes, that's you," I said. Then, in one conversation at a time over the next several weeks, I slowly introduced him to the ideas of war and genocide. I began by focusing on the abuse of refugees and indigenous groups before moving on to the Holocaust. Finally one afternoon, just after Egypt had excitedly returned home with a bucket of minnows he'd caught at a little brook nearby, I sat down with him for the last talk in the series.

"You remember how you asked me that question about the N-word?" I said. He looked at me, nodded, and then returned his attention to the fish swirling around in his bucket.

"Look, Mommy!" he said, pointing at the minnows.

I pulled him close to me. "Babe, I need you to pay attention right now so we can have a big-boy conversation," I said. "And I think you're ready for this talk because you're thoughtful and responsible.

Do you think you can handle it?" His eyes widened. "Yes," he said. His expression turned serious.

In the most gentle voice I could muster, I reminded him again of our ancestors' amazing legacy. I then explained, in simple terms, that there had been many wars throughout history. I told him that mothers and fathers and children were sometimes captured and separated from one another. Some were even sold to other people.

"That is called enslavement," I said slowly, "and it's terrible and it's wrong. No person owns another person." I gave him a few examples of the cruelty we'd talked about in our earlier conversations, and I wasn't sure he was grasping the idea. But his eyes lit up when I said this: "Sometimes, the people who were captured weren't allowed to read or write." He gasped.

"*Really?*" he said. That clicked. As the book lover my son is, he couldn't imagine that anyone wouldn't be allowed to do something he does every day: read.

"The conditions were very unfair," I said. I was going to leave the conversation at that. But then he said, "Mommy, you didn't answer the question. What's the N-word?"

I paused. "You know how you've been learning the word for *black* in Spanish?" I said. One of his sitters, Ms. Kiki, who speaks Spanish, had been teaching him the language.

"Yes," he said. "It's *negro.*"

"Well, in Latin, it's *niger,*" I told him. "And from those two languages, the N-word became a hate word."

He stared at me. "How do you spell the N-word?" he said.

I spoke each letter slowly. "So that was the unkind word used against our ancestors," I said. "And, unfortunately, you're going to hear that word a lot as you grow up. That's why I want you to understand the reason we don't use it."

At one point in my life, I did use the word—starting when I was around sixteen up until I was twenty. One of my first songs ever released was "Girlfriend" which samples Ol' Dirty Bastard's "Brooklyn Zoo." Near the end, I sang the word I now detest: "It's enough to make a n— go crazy." At the time, in the privacy of a studio when I was creating that song—and long before I was sure anyone would hear any of my music—I thought it sounded so fresh because it was such a memorable part of the original record. But years later, when the record came out and I realized the entire *world* heard me saying that word, it shook me in a way it never had. Before then, I hadn't thought about the fact that millions would hear me use and endorse it. It was at that point that I decided, *I'm never using that word again.*

I'm well aware of the debate surrounding the term. I've heard the logic: "We've reclaimed the word." I definitely understand that there's more than one way to see the issue, and I respect other perspectives. And yet I'm clear on how I see it: Words have tremendous power, and that word has a painful, horrifying legacy attached to it. In my view, it can never be reclaimed as a term of endearment because it is steeped in poisonous energy. If you're talking to your brother, why not say, "Hey, brother?" Swizz and I have come up with an honoring term: *king.* When my husband is rolling with his closest friends or spending time with our sons, it's now, "Hey, king. Come on, king. See you later, king." My son might one day decide he's comfortable using a word soaked in a hurtful history. I hope not, but in adulthood, that will be his choice. All I can do is give him the information he needs to know who he truly is. And I can insist that the word will never be spoken in our home. My husband and I see the issue a little differently, but he supports my position and knows that it's for the good of our children. In the name of the countless black people who were once lynched, their bodies hanging lifelessly from a noose as angry mobs spat that word at them, I will never again use the term.

After my conversation with my son, I began planning a trip to the nation that shares his name. Egypt—along with the countries now known as Uganda, Ethiopia, Sudan, and Burundi—are all part of the Nile River Valley civilization that served as the cultural center of the ancient world. What better way to introduce Egypt to one of the world's oldest regions—the place where kings and queens built pyramids with the kind of mathematical precision that still confounds architects? What better way to help him embrace his rich heritage? In August 2018, I set out again for Cairo with a single intention: to show my family the full spectrum of our incredible ancestry. What I didn't know is just how deeply it would impact all of us.

————

Two Christmases before our trip, my father-in-law (Swizz's stepdad, Adrian, whom we call Poppi) referred me to a powerful video. On it, the late Dr. Yosef Ben-Jochannan, a kemetologist—one who studies ancient Nile Valley civilizations from a non-western perspective— gave a fascinating talk. Dr. Ben, who passed away in 2015, spent his life uncovering historical truths about the contributions of the ancient Nile River Valley civilizations. The three-hour video lecture, during which Dr. Ben presented evidence of Africans' advanced systems, took me a couple of weeks to get through; like every busy mom can testify, uninterrupted time is hard to come by.

But the more I watched, the more riveted I became. Dr. Ben's assertions were in line with what I'd already begun discovering through my own reading: So much of the "history" we've been taught is told through a single lens—usually not an African one. Some of the narratives that have been handed down through generations are filled with half-truths and unquestioned assumptions, and Dr. Ben's work challenged many of those story lines. Dr. Ben referred to Egypt by its ancient name—Kemet (pronounced KIM-et), which means "land of the black people." At the time, I was drawn in, but not enough yet to plan a trip. Fast-forward to a year later, when Egypt and I had that challenging conversation over a bucket of minnows, and I began contemplating an expedition. I recalled what I'd learned from Dr. Ben and set out looking for a kemetologist—someone who, in contrast to an Egyptologist, could guide us through the untold story of our ancestral homeland.

My research led me to Ashra and Merira Kwesi, a Dallas-based couple who lead organized tours through Kemet. Ashra, who has completed more than three decades of field research in the Nile Valley, was an apprentice to Dr. Ben for fourteen years. Merira has studied the fashion, culture, and spirituality of Kemet, and she and Ashra have lectured extensively around the world. My assistant reached out to them about arranging a private tour for my family. They didn't initially respond because, as I'd later learn, they thought my assistant's email was a joke. After a round of acrobatics, including tracking them down at an event they participated in at the National Black Theatre in Harlem, we finally connected. They agreed to lead us on a fifteen-day excursion through Cairo, Luxor, Aswan, and cities along the Nile. The trip would have to take place while the kids were out of school, as well as when Swizz and I could carve out time in our schedules. That's why I chose August for the adventure.

"Babe, I love you," Swizz said, "and I know this is a trip of a lifetime for us. But do you know it's, like, one hundred and ten degrees in Cairo during August?" His friends who live in that region had told him it was the absolute *worst* time to visit, weather-wise.

"We are going to Egypt," I said, laughing. Around the time of that conversation, we were in Arizona on a hot day. "This is what one hundred and ten feels like," I told him. "Feel that? It's how Egypt's going to feel. Get ready for this heat."

My husband got on board and we booked our flights. As the trip got closer, it looked as if Swizz, who was working on the *Poison* album, might not be able to get away for the entire fifteen days.

"Of course I want you to come on the whole trip," I told him, "but if you need to arrive a few days late, that's cool. I support whatever you decide"—and I truly meant that. But his assistant, Monique, wasn't having it. Mo is like family to us, and she'd helped me coordinate the trip months earlier.

"You're going," she playfully said to Swizz. "Alicia and I have been planning this for way too long." It turned out that my husband was able to shift some dates and, voilà, he was in again.

We rolled out deep. Joining us on the journey: our kids Nas, Egypt, Genesis, Nicole, and KJ; Granny Sandra, Swizz's grandmother and our family matriarch; my mother; my brother, Cole; my god-daughter and her mother; our friends Naki and Nyheike, and their son, Nien; and, of course, Poppi, who'd gifted me with the Dr. Ben video, as well as Swizz's mother, Kim, whom our kids call Nana. What a contrast to my 2006 solo journey. On this trip, we were a mighty tribe of seventeen, ready for a cross between an exploration and a vacation. I love relaxing on a beach with a margarita as much as anyone. But as I kept telling everyone before we departed, this was not that trip. This was an adventure of a lifetime—a classroom on the road.

Cairo was the furnace we'd expected it to be: over one hundred degrees when we arrived. The country was celebrating *Eid al-Adha*, a four-day Islamic festival marking the end of the Hajj, the annual pilgrimage to Mecca. That meant school was out, and by night, the city was in party mode. Starting in the late afternoons, families and friends gathered around scrumptious meals of tahini and couscous and bright curries, singing and celebrating into the early hours of the next morning. Then from sunrise until after lunch, it was crickets in a city of twelve million—until the revelers again emerged, blurry-eyed and blissful and ready to do it all again. The morning vibe stood in contrast to the chaos I'd witnessed when I'd arrived more than a decade previously: no traffic signals or lanes, cars weaving in wher-ever they could, whole families crammed into vans and standing up without seat belts, donkey carts alongside taxis.

To beat the heat, we began each day at sunrise. First, at seven a.m. sharp, we set out on the drive for that day's excursion. Then a two-hour visit, followed by a return to the hotel for lunch and a swim-ming break for the kids. Next came a round of gems from Ashra and Merira in the evening, in preparation for the next day's site visit. Swizz is no early bird, which is why it's crazy that he was up and dressed by six a.m. That's how invested he was. I was the most en-thusiastic, and you can imagine how excited Poppi was. The kids sat in on the talks for at least thirty minutes, which is as long as you can expect any young child to sit still before dashing off to play in the sands of time. Evenings were my favorite: relaxing beneath a blood-orange moon while savoring thoughtful conversations about all that we were learning.

On my first trip, I'd visited Karnak, a majestic temple complex that is the largest ever to be constructed. This time around, I got an astonishing reintroduction to the temple from a kemetic perspective. The walls of Karnak—or what the Kemites called Ipet Isut, a "divine house"—are covered in elaborate hieroglyphics. These "books in stone," as Ashra referred to them, are a kind of unerasable ancient newspaper—a permanent account by the Kemites of their own legacy. Over centuries, conquering kingdoms sought to desecrate the temple; bullet holes still riddle some of the fire-blackened walls. But conquests by the Greeks, Persians, and a long line of others hadn't been able to demolish what the ruins reveal: evidence that the Kemites first referenced many of the doctrines found in our world's major religions. In fact, during ancient times, Ipet Isut was recognized as an epicenter of world culture. And yet scholars believe there was an attempt by early Egyptologists to deny that the ancient Nile River Valley civilizations were sophisticated—the region where my ancestors reigned as kings and queens (*nesu* and *nesa*) for thousands of years.

The ancient Greeks apparently made themselves right at home in Kemet. It's well documented that classic Greek and Roman thinkers often spent years there, at the temple universities of both Ipet Isut and Aset (aka Isis). Socrates, Aristotle, Hippocrates, Plato, Pythagoras, Homer—each studied the Kemetic Mystery System, a vast body of knowledge, developed over 4,500 years, that incorporates advanced principles in mathematics, physical science, and the supernatural. Hippocrates is the Greek name for Imhotep, the astrologer and architect who designed the pyramids of Saqqara. The true founders of medical science were the Kemites—they established diagnostic methods thousands of years before the Greeks. Homer's epic poems, *The Odyssey* and *The Iliad,* have their origins in Kemet. And the Roman numerals are strikingly similar to the original numeric system created by the Kemites.

One site visit and lecture at a time, Ashra opened my eyes to just how many kemetic innovations became the basis for our modern world: architectural methods, irrigation systems, calculus and geometry, astrophysics, medicine, religion, and government. It is truly magnificent. Some Greco-Roman thinkers acknowledged Kemet as the educational capital of the ancient world. In *Metaphysics,* Aristotle wrote that Egypt is the "cradle of mathematics—that is, the country of origin for Greek mathematics." Some historians believe that when European societies eventually began enslaving Africans, they also started downplaying the major contributions of both the ancient Nile River Valley civilizations and the kemetic culture, as well as concealing its African lineage. I'm no scholar on the subject, nor do I claim to understand all of the intricacies and nuances of global history. But during my trip, I definitely heard and saw enough to make me question what many of us have been taught.

I was also intrigued by kemetic spirituality—a metaphysical system of beliefs that, among other things, celebrates the interconnection of male and female energies. There is no masculine without the feminine, and all creation has elements of both. The Kemites understood this. When a god was created, so was a goddess, and they were equal in what they represented. Kemites also believed in continual transformation, a rebirth experienced during every breath from womb to grave. That rings true to me. In fact, I feel a connection to many of the principles of the kemetic belief system: All living things have a vibrational frequency (which I call a vibe). There's a rhythm and flow to life. Every cause has an effect—and you cannot participate in one without taking part in the other.

During just two weeks, my little Genesis, then three, grew up before my eyes. At the pyramid of Khufu in Giza, he climbed the steep stairs one tiny foot at a time, making it all the way to the top and never whining for me to pick him up. He may not have comprehended all of the history lessons, but he stepped into a greater independence. And Egypt and KJ were enthralled by what they learned and understood the enormity of what we'd been taught.

We all received a replica of a cartouche—also called a *shenu*, which is a two-sided nameplate pendant the Kemites attached to the coffins of kings and queens.

"What name do you want to put on your *shenu*?" I asked Egypt. "I want one side to say Egypt," he said proudly, "and the other side to say Kemet." He'd made the connection.

Later, after we left Heru-em-Akhet (aka the Sphinx), Genesis spotted some figurines of Nefertiti and Tutankhamun.

"Mommy, those are my ancestors!" he said, pointing. I smiled and nodded. We all left Kemet with a newfound sense of pride in our astounding history. Even Granny Sandra, who's in her mid-seventies, said at the end of our trip, "I needed this." It validated some part of her she hadn't known was lacking affirmation. In a world overrun with images and stories that portray black people as victims rather than victors, as perpetrators rather than innovators, as a people once granted only three-fifths of our humanity under the Constitution, we stand taller when we hear our story in its glorious entirety. We dream bigger when we know that brilliance is our birthright and royalty is in our DNA. And we understand the importance of defining ourselves, rather than allowing others to ever do that for us.

Pride in one's heritage isn't about separation. It's about connection. Every one of us is part of the same energy flow, the same rhythm of life the Kemites believed in so strongly. We all stare up at the same sky. We each have value, and our commonalities make us more similar than different. And yet celebrating the greatness we've come from allows us to bring that value to every conversation and every community we're part of. It's how we show up as our entire selves, with all of our wondrous history, and give the world our best. Because only when we know our true worth can we stand, shoulder to shoulder and heads up, with all others who share our planet. I returned home from Kemet wishing that every person in the world could travel there, as a way to understand just how connected we all are.

I also returned home carrying the spirit of the ancient homeland.

To feel as free as I do means that I'm moving closer to the center of myself. I'm not pretending to be someone I'm not; I'm stepping into the fullness of who I am. And who I am is the descendent of Hatshepsut, the powerful female pharaoh. I am the daughter of a civilization shrouded in history and mystery, intelligence and spirituality. I am intuitive and curious. I am a child of the Most High and a woman connected to the Source of all creation. And with every word and every intention, I am creating the masterpiece that is my life.

# 19

## FULL WATTAGE

### MICHELLE OBAMA

I first saw the truth about Alicia when my daughters and I visited her recording studio in New York. At the time, we were in the heat of Barack's reelection campaign, and the invitation came in like a blast of cool air. By then, I'd met Alicia a few times. She'd played events with us, including Barack's first inauguration, and she'd promoted a mentoring effort with me at the White House. But visiting the studio, I wasn't sure what to expect, other than hopefully hearing some good songs.

I got that (the album she was working on, *Girl on Fire*, would quickly become one of my all-time favorites), but I also got to immerse myself in another melody—the sounds and reverberations of Alicia's spirit. Her son, Egypt, was toddling around, happy as could be. Her mother, Terri, was there, too, making easy conversation with me and the girls. Alicia plinked away at the varying notes of her life—mother, daughter, friend, performer—with natural grace. There was none of the pretense, none of the thirst that often accompanies celebrity. There was simply Alicia— light and sweetness, creativity and power, peace and hope. I saw then that it was real, all of it.

Over the years, we've grown closer, and I've seen Alicia continue to shine in a way that only she can. Her family has grown larger now, and she's got even more awards. Yet what continues to impress me is her choice to grapple with the big questions. What is my purpose? What can I do for others? How can I use this fame for good? Somewhere in there is, if not an answer, at least a glimmer of the truth that I think we're all seeking. And by sharing her music and her soul, Alicia's bringing us closer to it than even she may realize.

Remember that time I hosted the Grammys?" is not a sentence I'd ever thought I'd say. But in February 2019, at the start of the sixty-first annual awards show, I stood arm-in-arm with a row of my sisters: Jada Pinkett Smith. Lady Gaga. Jennifer Lopez. And Forever First Lady Michelle Obama. The real story isn't that we were standing there. It's what it took to get us onto music's grandest stage.

Our beautiful moment of sisterhood began the fall before with a question from Ann: "Would you ever want to host the show?" she asked me. In addition to serving as a music partner to me, Ann sits on the board of the Grammys.

"Hell yeah!" I said. "That would be crazy fun."

"Well good," she said, "because they're looking for a host. I'll pitch the idea to them." James Corden, who'd hosted the previous two years, wasn't planning to take the stage again. Other names were being tossed around, Ann said. Why not throw my name out there, particularly during a year when so many amazing female artists were nominated? *Done.*

I mentioned it to one of my two managers.

"Listen, what do you think about this whole Grammys thing?" I said. "It could be sick." He agreed and began talking up the idea to CBS. The network came back with an idea: What if I hosted *with* someone? That didn't feel right. This juncture of my journey is all about stepping into the fullness of who I am and owning my light. So I sent back word that I'd do the show if I could host by myself.

In December, that same manager called me.

"They're offering you the chance to be the solo host," he said. *Boom.* And yet by the time I heard this news, I'd started cooling off on the whole idea. I'd run it by some trusted members on my team, and not all of them were feeling it.

"I don't like the hosting gig," said my other manager. "It moves you away from your main space as a musician." Even Swizz wasn't so sure at first.

I understood where they were coming from. Hosting is not an easy layup; in fact, it can be pretty unforgiving. You're balancing what the network wants with the vibe you want to put out there. I felt I could create the right energy. But after the input from my crew, I was torn. That's when I got on the phone with DJ Walton, my longtime friend and the president of my company.

"To me, it's a no-brainer," he said. "You're going to smash it. You've been saying you want to listen to your resounding yes. You can't keep doing this thing where you feel the *yes* and then don't honor it." He was so right. The moment I first heard the idea, it resonated. The doubt only came when I began talking it over with others—when I got all mental and started looking at it from every angle.

I decided to meditate on it. "I'll give you my answer tomorrow," I told my team in early December. So I sat in silence and asked the Spirit for clarity on whether this was the right move for me. Outside input is great, even necessary. It's smart to receive feedback. But once you've heard all the opinions, there comes a point when you have to make your own choice. And in the quiet of my bedroom at sunrise, my heart said yes.

"We're doing it," I told the team. That sentence set in motion a flurry of creativity. *What could we do to make this special? How could we elevate it from "just another awards show" to an evening viewers would never forget?* Me and my crew got to work on creating an overall concept for the show. The Grammys' producers also threw out ideas. I hired my own scriptwriters to create dialogue that would set the right tone. Meanwhile, my fashion team began pulling my looks together. In January, Swizz stopped by our brainstorming room and noticed a list of possible show ideas written up on a whiteboard.

"Some of them are cool," he later told me. "But I need you to have a hell-yes moment. I need the trophy to already be in the locker room before the game begins. I need you to go out there and win."

"And how do I do that?" I asked him.

"You call Michelle Obama."

"*What?!?*" I squealed. "Now is the time," he said. "You need to get her on the phone and explain why you want her to stand with you as a representation of strong sisterhood."

That is Swizz through and through: the king of all dreamers. There's no one in my life who blows the roof off a house like he does. As I stood there dumbfounded, he was like, "I'm serious, babe. With all the craziness and conflict in our world right now, imagine if you were able to bring together some phenomenal women and celebrate what we all have in common. It could be huge."

I'd seen Mrs. Obama not long before. While on tour for her best-selling memoir, *Becoming,* she'd asked me to appear with her onstage at the Barclays Center in Brooklyn. I was happy to do it, and while she was in town, we reconnected over lunch. The energy was positive and supportive, and yet somehow, it felt like the strangest thing on the planet for me to reach out to her about the Grammys. While away on vacation in Tulum, Mexico—Swizz surprised me with a short trip for my birthday—I worked up the courage to text my friend. She responded right away and said I could call her the next day.

The cell phone service in Tulum was terrible. Normally, I'd love that in my constant quest for quiet. But can you imagine getting on the phone with Mrs. Obama and possibly having the line go dead? *Ugh.* With my fingers and toes crossed, I dialed her from our hotel room.

"Now, why are you calling me on your birthday?" she said, laughing.

"Come on," I told her. "This is the best gift *ever!*" Trying to disguise my shaky voice, I painted the picture. "This is obviously an amazing time for women," I said. "We have to make it known that there's no holding us back. And, well, uh . . . I'm hosting the Grammys. I want to make the opening the most viral moment of the night. I want to send a message of sisterhood, and how we're all connected through music." I then asked her if she'd come stand with me and a few other friends at the top of the show.

"I love it!" she said with no hesitation. "I think I'll be on the West Coast on February 10. Let me check with my team and get back with you."

"She's in!" I told Swizz as I jumped up and down. No, she hadn't yet given me the final word, but she sounded super positive. There was none of that backpedaling people do when you can tell they don't really want to be part of something. That was on a Friday. On Monday, I received the best news: Mrs. Obama would be there. Sunday was her day off from her book tour, and she'd be willing to fly to Los Angeles from Seattle. *Whoa*—followed by another major hula dance.

I'd been thinking about some other awesome women who could join me onstage: Serena Williams, Misty Copeland, and Ellen De-Generes. But the producers wanted to keep the spotlight mostly on musicians. Made sense. Jada was the first to come to mind. She and I have been cool for years.

"I love the energy you're bringing!" she said. "Of course I'll support you." I then hit up Gaga, who said, "Wow, Alicia. The intention behind that moment is so powerful. I'm honored to be a part of it." When I called J. Lo, I loved how dialed in she was to the political moment.

"Did you see how all the women in Congress wore white during the State of the Union speech?" she said. "Maybe we should do something like that." We didn't end up going that route, but her idea aligned so beautifully with my purpose in bringing us together. And with the crew who'd agreed to stand with me, I was ecstatic.

The week leading up to the Sunday show was intense. I handle stress pretty well; unless I'm performing a classical piece, I'm not the type to get all flustered and freak out. But this was a level up. For the first time, I'd be doing a live, three-hour-plus broadcast from start to finish. There are so many moving parts, so many things that can go wrong, and good timing is critical. Then there are the fittings, the promotions, the slew of choreographed moments that had to be perfected. I wouldn't have called myself stressed, but our bodies tell us things that our mouths have yet to speak. On that Monday, I got a major cramp in my neck and my right shoulder blade was on fire. I tried my usual remedies: getting massages, drinking gallons of water, doing yoga and Pilates. Nothing helped. Then my face broke out like I was sixteen.

Just as I was obsessing over a blackhead, Mrs. Obama's team checked in with us. A former First Lady can't just roll up to an event and walk out in front of a large crowd. Getting her anyplace involves multiple security clearances—backstage, onstage, and well beyond—to ensure her safety. Even transporting her from her book-tour stop in Seattle to the STAPLES Center would be a major operation. Out of concern for me, Mrs. Obama didn't want to make things complicated, said her team. She thought it was best for her to step aside and free me from all the layers of meticulous preparation. When I got the message, my heart fell from its place up in the sky to the ground below. I knew I had to call her again. Swizz reminded me to keep the energy high.

I reached out to Mrs. Obama and we scheduled a convo for the next day, a couple of hours before I boarded a flight to LA for the pre-Grammy rehearsals. My mother and my assistant, Ana, were both in the car with me as I was making the call.

"You're gonna hear me grovel like you ain't *never* heard me grovel," I said, laughing. "But I need to remind her how important this moment is." We said a little prayer together and my mom went into an *om* as I dialed the number. In retrospect, that whole scene feels comical to me. But in that moment, I can assure you it was no joke.

"Hello, sis," Mrs. Obama answered. Right away, she explained how something so important to her—showing up for a friend—had become so complex. Aside from the Secret Service security sweeps, there was her rapid-speed book-tour schedule, as well as the many hands involved in steering her ship.

"It seems like everyone is trying to figure out how to make me comfortable—but this is *your* moment," she said. "And that's not fair to you." I told her how much I appreciated her concern. I then shifted into beg mode. "I want to maintain my dignity," I said, "but I'm going to implore you to change your mind." I reiterated my vision for a strong display of sisterhood at a time in our country when unity is so lacking. "I can't represent sisterhood by myself," I told her. "I know you're trying to set me free to fly, but if you're not there, the opposite will happen—I will fall. I don't have a Plan B, and I can't come up with one this close to the event. So please . . . if we can find a way to do this, I will be forever grateful." Mrs. Obama sighed.

"I'm so sorry about all of this, Alicia," she said. "Let me connect with my team and call you back." Within hours of my plea, a miracle happened: We were on again—and I was back over the moon. A day later, when she texted to ask me what colors and styles I had in mind for outfits, it felt even more real. This was actually happening.

From the very top of the show when my sisters stepped out on stage, I was determined to wow the world. The crew threw out some ideas for the big reveal. I wasn't feeling any of them.

"How about if we have all of the women darkened in silhouette, so that you can only see their faces once they walk forward?" I suggested. The team tried to make that work, but we ended up with a wack variation that involved the audience members immediately being able to see the women's faces, while only the television and streaming viewers would enjoy the surprise. When the producers insisted this was all they could do, I insisted otherwise.

"This can't just be good enough," I said. "It has to be *great*." I was a bit of a maniac, yes, but it was for a good cause. My opening moment, with four phenomenal women, had to be nothing short of extraordinary. After I pushed, we at last found a way to pull off my idea.

In addition to hosting, I'd also be performing.

"How are you going to make it spectacular?" Swizz asked me while we were in Tulum. "I'm going to play two pianos, just like Hazel Scott did," I told him. I'd been an admirer of Hazel since the day, years earlier, when I'd watched her simultaneously play two baby grands in the 1943 movie *The Heat's On*. The Trinidadian-born classical and jazz pianist broke ground. She and Lena Horne were the first to refuse to play roles that stereotyped black people, and in 1950, she became the host of *The Hazel Scott Show*—making her the first African American to have her own television program. Not only was her two-piano feat the coolest thing ever, but adding her to the program would bring the spirit of a trailblazer to the Grammy stage. In tribute to Hazel, I'd play Scott Joplin's "The Entertainer" on two pianos.

Every single place I went that week—from LA to New York and back—I had two keyboards set up so I could practice. It took me all of that Monday to adjust: How do you play the treble clef with your right hand and the bass clef with your left, all while keeping your feet on both pedals? I had new respect for Hazel as I attempted it. By Tuesday, I'd found my groove. But what would be the theme? I thought about choosing hits that had won the Song of the Year since the very first Grammy show in 1959. That's how I landed on "Unforgettable," the Nat King Cole classic. The duet of Nat's version, sung with his daughter, Natalie, won multiple Grammys in 1991. I moved on from that idea and began thinking about honoring some of the female artists who'd inspired me—like Nina Simone and Patrice Rushen. That was cool, but I wanted to be more inclusive. I eventually settled on a concept that brought both those ideas together: choosing songs I wished I'd written. I'd weave together musical snippets from artists including Nat King Cole, Roberta Flack, Lauryn Hill, Juice WRLD, Drake, and Ella Mai. I'd close out the medley with the chorus from "Empire."

That all sounded fantastic in my head. But it sounded *crazy* when I first played it. And no matter how much I practiced on that Tuesday and Wednesday ahead of my Thursday soundcheck, it Would.

Not. Come. Together. I started with the Hazel Scott number at the two pianos, but after that, I couldn't figure out how to smoothly alternate between both for the remaining songs. And what was the point of having two pianos up there if I wasn't going to play them *throughout* the performance? Aside from that, I'd been given only five minutes to complete my medley. With so little time, it was difficult to set up my whole "Club Keyz" dialogue at the beginning, and then still squeeze in all of these songs. It felt rushed. When I played it for Swizz, he confirmed my fear.

"That's not it," he said.

"You know what?" I told my music director, Adam Blackstone, just before midnight. "If I run this medley tomorrow and it's still not working, I'm going to pull it."

I arrived on set to rehearse early Thursday morning and cut out some songs, as well as to practice moving between the pianos throughout the medley. It still wasn't 100 percent, but the streamlined version got me closer to my original vision. Ken Ehrlich, the show's producer (and someone I've known since my first day in the business), was there for my run-through of the medley.

"This is going to be special," he said. He then began throwing out ideas: What about this? Or have you thought of that? After incorporating a few of his suggestions, I played it again—and he didn't say a word when it ran six minutes rather than five. Clearly he was in. Certain parts were still wobbly, but I knew I had two days to lift it from great to extraordinary. Between Friday and Saturday night, my fingertips hardly left those ivories as the crook in my neck at last disappeared.

Show day arrived. I began the morning as I always do, with my meditation practice. I even had a potent one-on-one session with Guru Jagat. *The world deserves this energy,* I repeated. *And I am worthy of standing in this moment.* And stand I did. That evening, soon after I came out onstage to the sound of "Superwoman" and the screen parted to reveal my four sisters in silhouette, my eyes filled with water. My vision had come true. There, in living color, was the full representation of exactly what I'd imagined, only it felt far more magical in real life than it had in my dreams. *You are not going to cry at the top of this show,* I kept telling myself. *You are going to keep it together.* Reveling in the crowd's deafening applause and holding back a flood, I linked arms with my friends and beamed at their center.

Every moment of the next three hours was pure girl power: the heartwarming tributes to Dolly Parton and Aretha Franklin. Diana Ross, regal in red, gracing us with her heartfelt performance. Janelle Monáe electrifying viewers with her dope guitar and moonwalk. Lady Gaga rocking the stage in her glittering bodysuit. Chloe x Halle's musical shout-out to Donny Hathaway with their smooth rendition of "Where Is the Love." A stream of female artists, clutching their trophies and making her-story. And I, seated at dual pianos, paying homage to music's incomparable power—and paying tribute to the city that taught me the notes.

Hosting the Grammys was an honor. Long after I've eventually passed the mic to the next host, the lessons of the experience will live on. The lead-up to the celebration was, for me, a leap forward in growth. When my resounding *yes* arose, I at last had the courage to follow it. I believed that I alone could hold my space on a stage before millions, and when I stood firmly in that truth, others joined me in it. I refused to settle for mediocre and instead required greatness. I even got on the daggone cell with one of the most sensational women on the planet and made a bold request. For years, my daily prayer has been the same: that I become the very best version of myself. That I shine more brightly by the day. That I operate not at half-dim, but at full wattage. This time when the universe tested me on that prayer, I aced it.

––––––

The path to self-discovery is not a straight line. It's a zigzag. We move in and out of awareness: one step forward, three steps to the left, a baby step back, another leap forward. A lightbulb moment might shine brightly one day, but then flicker the next. It takes work to hold tightly to a certain consciousness, to live in its wisdom. Every day, I have to intentionally maintain an awareness of my value. I know I'm worthy. But you don't cross over into the Land of Self-Worth and just become a permanent resident. You have to keep your passport current. You have to work to preserve your status.

I still catch myself hiding my light. Not that long ago, I had a breakthrough about that. At home, I was sitting in a cozy room decorated in shades of brown: brown walls, brown rug, brown couch, a soothing vibe for me. My brother, Cole, and I were reconnecting after we hadn't seen each other in a while. It's crazy how we don't always take the time to sit down with the people we really love. Like, *How the hell are you anyway? What are you enjoying these days? What's annoying you?* So we were having a nice catch-up. At some point during our conversation—and I can't recall exactly what we were talking about that prompted this thought—it dawned on me how often I'd suppressed myself over the years. How I'd dimmed my light so it wouldn't blind others or make them uncomfortable around me.

I was super young when my career took off. Everything in my life changed literally overnight, and I desperately wanted to hold on to old friendships. I ached for the familiar, for something to ground me as the Earth moved me off-center. Mom and Kerry were of course very supportive. So was Erika, who shared in my joy. But no one, not even those closest to me, could truly understand how vastly different my new world was. And with so much changing so fast, I wanted one thing I cherished to stand still: my connections with those I'd grown up with around the neighborhood, in school, and in my buildings. Without even recognizing that I was doing it, I began shifting myself so I could keep the dynamic in my friendships in balance.

It was subtle. "Oh, man, I know stuff must be *crazy* for you, Alicia!" a friend would tell me. "You're on a whole other level." I constantly played it down:

"Oh, it's not all that great," I'd say. "I'm real tired a lot. I'm working all the time. I'm always on the road." That was my MO: *What I'm experiencing is no big deal.* And yet I was traveling overseas, meeting

legends I'd spent my lifetime admiring, and sitting at boardroom tables where multimillion-dollar deals were being negotiated. In those
years, none of my friends or the other aspiring musicians I'd grown
up with were in these kinds of rooms. Nobody was signing with
Clive or getting the chance to perform live on Oprah's show. The
opportunities coming my way were unheard of.

But rather than basking in the glow of those miracles, I shrank.
At certain moments, I even dumbed myself down or chose not to
talk about the many blessings I'd received. I feared that if I shared
my experience in its entirety, if I took the lid off my joy, it would
push others away or make them feel small. As my career progressed,
that tendency took another form in my interactions around the
industry. *I don't need much. Nothing has to be too grand. I'm cool
with my little piano, my bench, and a cup of water.* In a sense, that
was true. I've never been an over-the-top kind of girl. But what's
also true is this: Some part of my spirit was always signing up for
less because that is what I believed I deserved. For many years, I
thought I was just being modest. I never wanted to come across as
self-absorbed, or as someone with a big head. It's how we women are
brought up: Don't ask for more. Don't take credit. Don't outshine
others. But there on the couch, it hit me that my alleged modesty
was just a disguise—a mask for a lack of self-worth. It was a huge
revelation.

For me, that seed of worthlessness was planted in childhood. As
well intentioned as Craig was, and as much as he was dealing with in
his own life, his absence impacted me in ways I'm still uncovering.
It left a hole in me. When a child's parent is not there, even if the
reasons are completely legitimate, that child interprets the absence
exactly as I did: *I don't matter enough for you to show up for me. I'm not
important.* And in those early years when I was forming my identity,
I took on a belief parallel to that interpretation: *If you don't value me,
then I must not be valuable.* A big part of my journey has been about
changing that view, as well as getting clear on the other beliefs passed
on to me by my parents.

"There are only two people you ever have to deal with," a life coach recently told me. "Your mother and father." As I deal with the man who gave me life, and as we work to create a new story, what I've discovered is this: Neither Craig nor my beloved mom is responsible for where I go from here. I am. The price of admission for self-ownership is total responsibility. And I can move forward only if I'm willing to keep asking myself the hard questions and examining my beliefs.

In life, we don't get what we ask for. We get what we *believe*. And what we believe about ourselves shows up in our energy. It's how we walk into a room. It's how we communicate, through body language, *I don't deserve to be here*. It's whether we sit up straight or hide out in the back of a meeting. At times, my own energy has been saying, "I'm cool with the bare minimum. Don't give me more." Without knowing it, I stunted my growth because I was scared to be magnificent and doubtful that I was. If you'd asked me, at age twenty-two, whether I thought I was worthy, I would have answered loud and proud: *yes*. But it's possible to declare "A Woman's Worth" and yet not fully know your own. It's possible to say you want a grand life but then continue to play small.

In many ways, I have played big. I've embraced experiences I never dreamed I'd have, and I've risen to some enormous moments. But there's still more I can do, other ways for me to grow. And as I keep relearning, it's okay to own a desire for more. In fact, it's how we honor those who've paved the way for our place at the table.

"You don't want modesty," Maya Angelou once said. "You want humility. Humility comes from inside out. It says someone was here before me and I'm here because I've been paid for. I have something to do, and I will do that, because I'm paying for someone else who has yet to come." When we dim our light, we don't do anyone a favor. It's a disservice. Because when you're in the presence of someone who knows his or her worth, like the extraordinary Maya did, you want to shine brighter. Self-honoring energy is contagious.

At the start of my career, I thought I was such a novice. But at nineteen, I knew the one thing that is most important to know: I understood who I was at my center. I was closer then to my truth than I'd become during my twenties. It's not that I wasn't authentic, to some degree, at every stage. It's just that, out of a desire to please others or to squeeze into a mold, I made the outside world my point of reference: *Will they like me if I dress or speak or walk or talk this way?* Finally, in my early thirties, as I stepped into my "Girl on Fire" energy, I moved back toward my essence.

On the cover of the *HERE* album, I recognize myself in all my hippie 'hood glory: that untamable Afro. That bare and radiant face. That divinely inspired set of songs that said exactly what I wanted to say. That is who I am. It's who I've always been, really, and yet I had to take the journey to rediscover what my spirit had already told me. I don't have to fit in. None of us does. Our uniqueness isn't a scar, but a beauty mark. What makes us different is also what makes us wildly, boldly, and marvelously who we were born to be.

# LAST WORD

To be nobody but yourself in a world which is doing its best, day and night, to make you like everybody else means to fight the hardest battle which any human being can fight . . . It takes courage to grow up and become who you really are.

—e. e. cummings, poet and playwright

My husband recently blurted out a sentence that still makes me laugh. "You never tell anyone you're Italian," he said seemingly out of nowhere.

I set aside the book I'd been reading and stared at him. "What?" I said.

"Never once have I heard you tell anyone that you're part Italian," he said.

"That's not true," I said, wracking my brain to recall the last time my ethnicity had even been a topic of discussion. "And anyway," I said, "everybody knows that I'm half Italian. Why would I need to mention it?" Whenever I'd visited my mother's homeland, the Italians seemed super clear on my heritage and had always embraced me.

"But I've never heard you actually say it," he went on.

"And what's your point?" I asked with a smile.

"I think you should be acknowledging all sides of yourself," he said. "That's all."

I don't know what prompted Swizz's assessment that afternoon. But it planted a seed that put me back on the beautiful path called identity. Who are we, really? What are all the various pieces that form us? Which parts of ourselves do we embrace or dismiss, and what does that mean or not mean? Most of us are comfortable with expressing certain aspects of ourselves, while other sides might get left in the shade by default. For me, the latter was apparently happening on an unconscious level. Without realizing it, I'd been omitting little pieces of myself by seldom speaking about them. These ideas and questions are what live at the heart of my seventh album, *ALICIA*.

*ALICIA* is a musical exploration of identity—both my own and ours collectively. For so long, I've been cautious about showing all of who I am. I've been much more likely to reveal the Zen, calm, rational Alicia than to ever show the crazy, freaked-out, seeing red, yelling and screaming Alicia—the one who doesn't have it all together. I am strong and fierce and brave, no doubt. Yet I'm also someone who has found myself on the bathroom floor, boo-hooing and feeling vulnerable. I'm also the woman who doesn't always know how to rise to my feet and take the next step. This album—this life—is about accepting all of those parts of myself, those dichotomies.

Every song on *ALICIA*, every lyric and refrain, in some way represents the pieces of who I am. My identity can be glimpsed in "So Done," a song I wrote with Khaled and Childish Gambino's producer Ludwig Göransson. On this album, the three of us collaborated for the first time. What emerged from our sessions was a fresh, soulful energy that wraps you up in its powerful rallying cry: "I'm living the way that I want." That line captures where I am in my life right now. I'm working to set aside others' expectations and judgments, their ideas about who I should be. One breath at a time, I'm choosing to be over the old me and making room for the newest one. More of my truth comes through in the sonic and timbre of

"Show Me Love," which has a "Diary" feel to it. It's a head nod to what I believe we want most: to be loved, seen, and accepted for all of who we are.

While at work on the album, I played many of the songs for friends who came by the studio. Over and over, I heard some version of the same feedback: "You sound like yourself—but it's you like I've never heard you." For an artist, there is no comment more gratifying. Because while making this album, my intention was to be true to my DNA even as I push myself creatively. It's why I gave the album my name: I'm finally able to actually be my full self. This music bears every swirl and crevice of my unique handprint.

In addition to Khaled and Ludwig, I collaborated with many others. During my earliest days as an artist, I just wanted to be left alone in a room to create in isolation. That instinct was mostly about fear. Fear of having my own voice silenced. Fear of being misunderstood or squeezed into an artistic box I was never meant to fit in. Fear of being emotionally naked in front of another person. In seven albums, I've come full circle. These days, the fear has been replaced with a sense of freedom. I am more secure in my identity, both as an artist and as a woman. I actually crave building and connecting and exchanging ideas with others because it makes the music so much richer.

While I was in the thick of my creative process on this album, I brought in Johnny McDaid, the awesome singer-songwriter who's a member of the band Snow Patrol. He's penned songs with artists like P!nk and Ed Sheeran. But for me, what makes him most special is that he is a world-class listener—and powerful listening is at the root of all the best creation. Johnny also happens to be Irish, and I've always been drawn to Irish people. They remind me of Black Southerners. There's a deep soulfulness in them, heard in the lyrics and rhythms of the Celtic traditional folk music. It sounds like the blues: honest, unvarnished, potent, and poetic.

One evening as the sun kissed the Hudson, Johnny and I sat out on my studio's terrace, just sharing some of our own experiences as

New Yorkers scurried past on the sidewalks below us. The conversation turned toward all the varieties of people in the world. Givers and takers. Builders and breakers. Dreamers and bystanders. I tend to want every person to embody the best of humanity—for all of us to be givers and builders and dreamers. That's not reality. At different seasons in life, we each fall into various categories. Even still, every one of us also has a strong behavioral tendency, and that is okay. I'm coming to terms with the fact that so-called perfection—this idea that everything should be beautiful and in order at all times—is just not going to happen. My conversation with Johnny that evening is what led us to write "Authors of Forever," a song that captures that theme. The lyrics say it best: "We are lost and lonely people and we're looking for a reason and it's all right / So let's celebrate the dreamers, we embrace the space between us, and it's all right / We're all in this boat together and we're sailing toward the future and it's all right / We can make the whole thing better, we're the authors of forever— and it's all right."

*ALICIA* is a reflection of my evolution, a snapshot of where I am at this moment in my journey. For as long as I am alive, I will be growing and improving, wielding my pen as the author of my own forever. But even as I lift my life to the next level, I hope to always recognize my reflection. I want to know who I am and accept every part of that identity. I am frightened and I am fearless. I am weak and a warrior. I am uncertain and I am confident. And by learning to embrace the paradox in all of it, I am more myself.

# ACKNOWLEDGMENTS

The journey to creating this book has filled me with as much gratitude as I feel for the evolution I share on these pages. Above all, I honor The Most High for always holding me, keeping me safe, and showing me the light, truth, and magic of life. I'm thankful to be your light warrior.

I am the person I am because of the love of my magnificent mother, Terri Augello. Mommy, thank you for never giving up on me. Thank you for all the hard times and sacrifices, and for all the late nights you spent wondering if everything was going to be all right. Thank you for your wisdom and knowledge, and for showing me what a woman looks like.

To my husband, Swizz—my living, breathing romance novel. Our divine connection is unreal. Thank you for showing me how to be more free, more connected to the present, to dream bigger and become greater than what I ever thought was possible. Thank you for expanding my imagination.

One of my greatest joys in this life is being a mother. To Egypt, Genesis, Kassy, Nas, and Nicole, thank you for loving me so deeply, for teaching me and making me wise. Thank you for showing me the purity and simplicity of wonder and possibility. Thank you for being the most beautiful, boundless North Stars.

To the whole AK Worldwide team and the Oven Studios team that sustain me every day. Thank you for all the hours, the hustle, the dedication, the brilliance, and for living and breathing the details—late evenings, early mornings, and sleepless nights for the bigger purpose. This work would not be possible without you. I adore you.

Ms. O, I'm so blessed to have you as a guiding light. Thank you for always having the best words for me at just the right moments, and for encouraging me to share mine. The love is real.

Michelle Burford, thank you for being so patient, caring, steadfast, reliable, and trustworthy, and the most important therapist I've ever had. Thank you for your hours and hours of listening and deep understanding. I've had some of my greatest aha moments during this writing process with you. Thank you is not enough. You are beyond special to me.

To my team at William Morris Endeavor, and especially to Jennifer Rudolph Walsh and Andy McNicol: You see me and always want the best and greatest for me. Thank you for being such beautiful and brilliant partners. Your strong leadership inspires me. May we continue to soar.

I'm grateful to the Flatiron team, headed by the amazing Bob Miller. Thank you for your vision, as well as for seeing mine. Our partnership feels like the beginning of something tremendous! Also, thanks to my editor, Sarah Murphy, for her sharp eye and editorial insights. I'm thankful as well to the many people, both on the front lines and behind the scenes, who've helped me bring my story to the world.

I'm deeply grateful to all of the special friends and family members who took the time to share your stories, perspectives, and beautiful memories on these pages. I honor you!

To my Roc Nation team, here's to an unbounded and incredible future.

And I am forever grateful to my AK fam. Words don't suffice in expressing my sincere appreciation. You are so intricately a part of this journey . . . my story is truly *our* story. Here's to many more amazing memories and ways to grow as we become more of who we really are.

## ABOUT THE AUTHORS

*Alicia Keys* is a modern-day Renaissance woman—a fifteen-time Grammy Award–winning artist/songwriter/musician/producer; an accomplished actress; a *New York Times* best-selling author; a film, television, and Broadway producer; an entrepreneur; and a powerful force in the world of activism. Since the release of her monumental 2001 debut album, *Songs in A Minor,* Keys has sold more than forty million records and built an unparalleled repertoire of hits and accomplishments. Keys resides in the New York City area with her husband, super-producer/visionary and entrepreneur Swizz Beatz, and their children.

Visit her website at AliciaKeys.com.

**Michelle Burford** is a #1 *New York Times* bestselling collaborative writer and a founding editor of *O, The Oprah Magazine.* A native of Phoenix, she now resides in New York City.

Visit her website at www.MichelleBurford.com.